D1596782

This book examines the ways in which Pascal posed and solved intellectual problems in three very different areas of his work: mathematics and mathematical physics, religious experience and theology, communication and controversy. Hugh Davidson shows how three of the classical 'liberal arts', rhetoric, dialectic, and geometry, pervade Pascal's method as liberating and guiding influences in his search for truth. They appear throughout his production, and are used and adapted with great skill both in his attacks on tradition in mathematics and physics, and in his defences of tradition in the sphere of religion and morality. Professor Davidson throws new light on both the diversity and the unity of Pascal's thought, and places it in the context of other seventeenth-century innovations in the use of traditional disciplines.

Cambridge Studies in French 46

PASCAL AND THE ARTS OF THE MIND

Cambridge Studies in French

GENERAL EDITOR
Malcolm Bowie (*All Souls College, Oxford*)

EDITORIAL BOARD
R. Howard Bloch (*University of California, Berkeley*),
Ross Chambers (*University of Michigan*), Antoine Compagnon
(*Columbia University*), Peter France (*University of Edinburgh*),
Toril Moi (*Duke University*), Naomi Schor (*Duke University*)

Recent titles in this series include

A complete list of books in the series is given at the end of the volume.

PASCAL AND THE ARTS
OF THE MIND

HUGH M. DAVIDSON

Department of French Language and
Literature, University of Virginia

CAMBRIDGE
UNIVERSITY PRESS

Published by the Press Syndicate of the University of Cambridge
The Pitt Building, Trumpington Street, Cambridge CB2 1RP
40 West 20th Street, New York, NY 10011-4211, USA
10 Stamford Road, Oakleigh, Melbourne 3166, Australia

© Cambridge University Press

First published 1993

Printed in Great Britain at the University Press, Cambridge

A catalogue record for this book is available from the British Library

Library of Congress cataloguing in publication data applied for

ISBN 0 521 33193 5 hardback

TAG

To L. and A.

La méthode de ne point errer est recherchée de tout le monde. Les logiciens font profession d'y conduire, les géomètres seuls y arrivent, et, hors de leur science et de ce qui l'imite, il n'y a point de véritables démonstrations.

L'art de persuader a un rapport nécessaire à la manière dont les hommes consentent à ce qu'on leur propose, et aux conditions des choses qu'on veut faire croire.

Pour moi je n'ai pu y prendre d'attache et, considérant combien il y a plus d'apparence qu'il y a autre chose que ce que je vois, j'ai recherché si ce Dieu n'aurait point laissé quelque marque de soi.

Contents

Preface and acknowledgments

The history and nature of the liberal or intellectual arts has interested me for several years; and in the course of my acquaintance with the works of Pascal I have come to see many traces, even explicit developments, testifying to the presence of these arts in his intellectual universe. And so I have undertaken in this exploratory essay to study in some detail the relation of certain ones of those basic arts to Pascal's thought and works.

My intention has been less to interpret his achievement in some novel way than to watch him at work, to describe his practice, and to see to what extent that working could be related to the more general topic with which I began. As a starting point, it has seemed to me that Pascal recurrently finds himself in or puts himself in situations where the problems, paradoxes, mysteries that he needs to treat arise under three main headings, having to do with (1) things and quantities, (2) creatures and their Creator, and (3) polemical or dialogic communications.

However, one sees not only recurrent problems but also reappearing lines of attack on them, tendencies that bespeak something conscious and deliberate. From that observation it is easy to reach the idea of intellectual habits, of arts of the mind. I say arts, and not sciences, because the tendencies in question, although they abound in theoretical implications, are in essence practical and productive. As a result of their presence and functioning they make a large contribution to the fact that certain realities with determinate characteristics – the works of Pascal – have come into existence. I believe that to be a true statement, and offer it as pointing to active components in the line of necessary causality; I have no illusions regarding the answer to the question of whether my argument provides anything like a sufficient explanation.

How to think about such arts? They are elusive: to do justice to them requires us to respect their ambiguity, while at the same time noting their movement, in particular contexts, toward fixity, toward a kind of crystallization. The same point may be made conversely: it is advisable to define them with some subject-matter in mind, with some intention regarding their application, in order to escape the risk of making them so abstract that they seem out of contact with reality. Moreover, in any particular case one must pay constant attention to the danger of conceiving and applying the notion of art itself in a reductive way. It is easy to let it become rigid and serve to inspire a set of rules or intellectual tropes, which then have little connection with the free judgments and spontaneous activities of a mind like that of Pascal. Finally, in a project such as this, one is tempted to simplify what is happening in works notable for their shifting combinations and balances of elements, and, as a result, to pass over without adequate comment the complexities into which the texts tend steadily to draw us.

Without claiming to have succeeded in overcoming those difficulties, I should like at least to state some principles that have guided me. These arts have a triple derivation. (1) They come out of the personal experience of Pascal; (2) they come out of the intellectual tradition as its possibilities were actively confronted in the first decades of the seventeenth century in France; and (3) they come out of what might be called a "heuristic matrix," a procedural framework consisting of a set of variable factors, all of them interrelated, and subject as a group to different kinds and degrees of determination.

In connection with the first of these conditions, I would say that what Pascal had to do, starting from his personal experiences, was to generalize, so as to get above the particularity of those experiences and to extract from them the materials of scientific, moral, and religious truth. In the second place, he was called upon to innovate against a background, to find new ways of conceiving and using three traditional disciplines. In the third perspective – and I wish to emphasize that this is the one that has interested me most and has influenced most what I have done here – Pascal had to specify, to be clear about his assumptions and their consequences for inquiry and communication. He had to make his way from general themes concerning interpretation, discovery, arrangement, and synthesis to more and more definite formulations, so that he might deal effectively with the characteristics of the objects before him for study.

In showing how Pascal may be approached in terms drawn from the matrix just mentioned, I have decided to use rhetoric, dialectic, and geometric as the names of the three principal arts to be analyzed, the last being my way of generalizing the sense of the term "geometry," which seemed less suitable because of its more limited and more strictly mathematical connotations. I realize that all three have had complicated histories, and that they have ties to particular – and often opposed – thinkers and theories. My way of using the various authorities has been quite free – *à mes risques et périls*. I believe that the various borrowings have come together into something like a coherent ensemble. In any case, what is said in the following pages will illustrate the powers of geometric, dialectic, and rhetoric, and give, I hope, some plausibility to my hypothesis concerning the way in which Pascal understood and appropriated them for use in realizing his projects.

Readers familiar with the writings of the late Richard P. McKeon, for many years Distinguished Service Professor of Philosophy and Greek at the University of Chicago, will recognize my indebtedness to him and in particular to his publications regarding the liberal arts. I do not mean to suggest that he has been in any way responsible for my investigation or its conclusions. In fact, I have developed and applied a number of notions in ways that diverge markedly from lines of thought suggested by his analyses. However, it is a pleasure for me, in making this acknowledgment, to recall his intellectual generosity and his keen interest in the extensions and sometimes surprising transformations that ideas and methods undergo as they pass from mind to mind.

The substance of this book is closely related to work done and conclusions reached in seminars offered in two Spring terms (in 1980 and in 1989) at the Folger Institute in Washington, D. C. I wish to express my thanks to that unique institution for the opportunity to have a part in its research programs. I have also gained much from conversations with colleagues: Professor John Lyons, Professor Mary McKinley, and Professor David Rubin, all of the University of Virginia; Professor Buford Norman, of the University of South Carolina; Professor David Wetsel, of Arizona State University; and Professor Jean Mesnard of the Sorbonne. I owe a great debt to recent scholarship on Pascal; I list gratefully the principal items in the bibliography.

And, especially, I wish to acknowledge the help of Doctor Katharina Brett, of the Cambridge University Press. I consider it a great stroke of good fortune to have had her patient and friendly assistance over a period of many months.

Editorial note. In the body of my text I give the locations of passages quoted in three editions: (1) that of the *Oeuvres complètes* of Pascal in one volume by Louis Lafuma (Paris: Editions du Seuil, 1963, in the collection "L'Intégrale"); (2) that of the *Oeuvres complètes* in the monumental series being published by Jean Mesnard (Bruges: Desclée de Brouwer, 1964 *et seq.*), the fourth volume of which appeared in 1992; and (3) that of the *Pensées* published by Philippe Sellier (Paris: Mercure de France, 1976).

Each reference includes an item showing the page in the Lafuma edition; after the page number – preceded by "L" – I use the letters a, b, c, and d to show the quadrant of the page in which the passage is to be found. Where the text is also available in the Mesnard edition, I give a second page indication, preceded by "M" and I, II, III, or IV, according to the volume number. Passages cited from the *Pensées* have always two notations, the first referring to the Lafuma edition and the second, preceded by an "S", to that of Sellier. For added convenience where the *Pensées* are concerned, I include after the page indication the letter "f" followed by the fragment number. Examples: (L65c; MIII329) or (L550a, f417; S40, f36).

CHAPTER I

Nature and the world

As an introduction to the questions of how and in what specific ways Pascal goes about solving his problems, let us in a rapid survey try to gain a sense of certain distinctions and choices regarding *what* he wishes to consider and investigate. I take it as a valid assumption that he, like the rest of us, has more things to think about than he has ways of thinking about them. It seems worthwhile, therefore, to recall in a preliminary fashion the range of his curiosity and the scope of his inquiries. I realize that, although *what* he thought about and *how* he thought about it may be distinguished, the two cannot be finally separated. Nevertheless, in this introductory chapter, I should like, first, to attempt a survey of the former and then, against that background, to propose concerning the latter a group of intellectual arts that Pascal used in defining and exploring the subject-matters of interest to him. The topics set by those arts will be given detailed developments in the remaining chapters of this book.

Pascal is basically a realist; he constantly stresses being and things; he may refer at significant points to what he calls *le néant*, nothingness, but he poses against that everything else to which he intends to give sustained attention. Because of his gift and appreciation for mathematical thinking he does not escape completely the appeal of idealism, of clear and distinct ideas that tend to replace reality. However, he does not start from thought – as did Descartes, who got to things indirectly, by a complicated line of reasoning that took off from self-awareness and the contents of consciousness. Nor does he begin with action: Pascal is not a pragmatist, though what people do and the possible or actual consequences of their behavior interest him eventually very much. Nor does he expect to find his ultimate ground in language, in the linguistic medium and its omnipresent influence. I do not mean to say that he neglects thought, action, and expression; Pascal has, in fact, complex and carefully thought-out roles for each of those factors as complements to his overriding concern with things; I simply want to give at once an indication of what – in my judgment – is fundamental for him and what will be found to be in some sense derived.

Along with this first commitment to a basic realism, Pascal has also, where any inquiry is concerned, a commitment to truth. It is precisely here that the three arts of the mind – geometric, dialectic, and rhetoric, as I analyze them in the following pages – emerge as the chief means to that end. For Pascal they are habitual ways of finding, setting forth, and defending the truth. They are applied to a wide range of problems: making distinctions, defining terms, establishing principles, carrying out interpretative, inventive, sequential, integrative operations, assembling the results into typically diverse accounts of subject-matters. Each of the three arts, considered in itself, would be enough for a lengthy study, especially if historical precedents were brought forward and comparisons made; but of course Pascal is not interested in them for themselves. He brings them to different degrees of explicitness and completion according to his needs. In turn, I have sought to use the outlines and elaborations visible in his works as the basis for my essay.

The best way to begin, I think (and as I have suggested), is to look briefly at the series of subject-matters with which Pascal is concerned, and then, with that tableau in mind, to follow him as he moves over it, drawing freely on his methodological insights and habits for assistance in his search for the truth.

Since his deepest interests are obviously religious, we must from the first take God into our considerations. The things or beings to which Pascal turns his attention quickly become more definite, as   God on the one hand and as the whole of his creation on the other. There is little risk of error in saying that

this division between God and creation is the supreme distinction in the universe of Pascal's thought; and according as his
emphasis falls on one or the other of those two terms he works in
one or the other of two broad contexts or frameworks. Actually,
the same realities are present in both, but they are described and
weighted differently.

In the first framework Pascal examines the created universe,
as a totality having its order and way of working – in short, as
Nature. It is endowed with a certain degree of independence,
though of course it can never escape – nor should it – from its
original subordination to God. Within this created order Pascal
distinguishes between man and Nature, which emerges here
primarily as an object of knowledge. It may be known in a
collective sense, when one looks at it as a whole comprising all
things; or it may be known and explored in its parts, in which
case the manifold of existent things (with their separate natures;
note the plural and the small *n*) comes into view. Man has a
place in this creation, both as a body and as a mind; however,
in the perspective I am now sketching he appears especially as
the latter, and as a spectator. Looking outside himself, he seeks
to grasp Nature and natures in their own terms, with only
occasional excursions into broader reflections on his situation in
the universe.

In the second framework, the climate in which Pascal thinks
changes radically. God appears still as creator but rather more
as sustainer and as last end. Although the order of Nature is still
there, the former emphasis on the universe as a great whole –
with its operations, causes, and effects – gives way to stress on all
of that as directly related to God: what he has made is conceived
regularly in terms of its dependence on him. Here as before
Pascal distinguishes between Nature and man; but now, in an
essential contrast, Nature is conceived primarily as offering
objects of desire and distraction – in short, as being the secular
world. The human creature, instead of being included in
physical Nature, appears as distinct from it in some important
ways. Instead of directing his mind to what surrounds him as an
enveloping order to be grasped or as a multiplicity to be
investigated, he turns within to engage in a reflexive inquiry, so

as to know and understand himself, to see how the World relates to him, and to say how both stand with reference to God.

THE FIRST FRAMEWORK: DIMENSIONS OF NATURE

In an exposition such as this it is fair to say that Pascal begins with Scripture and revelation, for as he recalls in *De l'esprit géométrique* (L351d; Miii401): "Deus fecit omnia in pondere, in numero, et mensura" (from the book of Wisdom, xi, 21). This verse supplies one of Pascal's truly basic principles. It presents the whole of Nature to him in a way that properly recognizes God as creator and, at the same time, allows his inquiring mind to make an assimilation of great heuristic value. This little sentence shows the universe as a product arrived at through God's use of particular means and criteria; and the fact that everything came thus into being inevitably suggests to Pascal a discipline with which he is familiar – geometry.

Taking up what the verse says, he rounds it out, regularizes it, gives it a smooth and consistent interpretation. The statement contains three terms: God acted *in pondere, in numero, et in mensura*, but Pascal converts them by implication into four, the four aspects of physical reality that he calls *temps, mouvement, nombre*, and *espace*. What God did may be understood, Pascal thinks, in terms that happen to state exactly the four subject-matters of geometry. (It should be noted that in the context of *De l'esprit géométrique*, Pascal gives occasionally to "géométrie" a generic and comprehensive sense such that it includes the whole of mathematical and natural science.)

As a first consequence of the insight gained from Scripture, Pascal directs his and our attention away from concern with the qualities of things and into the realm of the quantitative. Magnitudes will appear in his discourse but not data of the senses, such as sounds, colors, smells, tastes, or textures. And is there not another moment in the development of the insight: the moment of extension, when Pascal and we become aware of the unifying power inherent in the biblical *dictum*? Nature *in toto*, Nature as *omnia* lies before him as a vast ensemble, its four underlying aspects revealed and attested by God. As stated, I am basing this description and analysis on what he writes in *De l'esprit géométrique*. Something similar is clearly going on in the fragment entitled "Disproportion de l'homme" (L525d, f199; S125, f230) in the *Pensées*, except that there Pascal begins not by going back to Scripture; he starts instead with something immediately accessible, with an experience open to anyone who steps outside on a clear night and raises his eyes to the stars.

But, to return to the fourfold aspects of Nature: Pascal establishes a close relationship among them by a series of immediate inferences, starting with motion and bodies. We cannot imagine movement, he says, without presupposing *something* that moves, so that by an immediate inference movement calls up a real object; and then, by a second such leap, he assures us that this thing in motion, since it is one, leads us to the notion of unity, that is to say, to the origin of all numbers. We have gone, therefore, from movement to things in motion, and from things in motion to the subject-matter of arithmetic. The next step is easily made: space, he says, is presupposed for movement. Such is, to pick up his phrase, the necessary connection ("la liaison réciproque et nécessaire") that holds together the three fundamental aspects of the universe. However, he has not finished this series of immediate inferences. Motion presupposes not only space; it necessarily calls for time. The bit of Scripture did not mention time explicitly, nor did Pascal mention it earlier on the page when he recalled the three subject-matters of mechanics, arithmetic, and geometry. He now sees that he must make a place for a fourth object or reality that enters, in its turn, into the mutual relation that binds the others together.

LEVELS OF DEFINITION

The specification of subject-matters takes place on more than one level. One may note, in fact, three stages of differentiation in what Pascal sets before his mind, the first resulting in the comprehensive view just outlined. It sets forth distinctions indispensable for the start of all his technical inquiries. The

second or intermediate stage brings into sight particular sciences
and their characteristic concerns. The third stage, which one
might call final or local, takes us down into the contexts of
particular treatises and introduces their problems in detail.

On the intermediate level several points may be made. (1)
For one thing, Pascal chooses, it seems, to work especially with
two of the basic aspects of reality, space and number. They are,
respectively, the continuous and discrete magnitudes that form
the general subject-matters of geometry and arithmetic. (2)
Whereas Descartes seeks a fusion or at least an exact correspondence between the analyses of continuous and discrete
quantities, Pascal tends to keep them separate, though it is true
that from time to time he does suggest *rapprochements* and
convergences. Nature loves unity, he says, and he takes
advantage of occasional opportunities to draw the two kinds of
quantity together. (3) The customary distinction between
plane and solid geometry throws some light on Pascal's interests,
for the problems that he attacks fall now in one, now in the
other, or in both. Often solutions found and objects studied in
one of the two lead directly to comparable objects and solutions
in the other, the usual direction of movement in Pascal's
reasoning being from the properties of plane to those of solid
figures. (4) He is quite aware of the division between pure and
applied geometry. Investigation of the former sort is what he
comes back to most often, but like Bacon and Descartes he is
disposed to put into practice what he discovers in theory; the
ideal realities that appear in treatises may assume the status of
models and then be embodied in physical things.

FIGURES AND NUMBERS

When we take up one of the particular treatises in the field of
geometry, we arrive at the level where what is to be investigated
is specified to the greatest degree. The pages on the generation
of conic sections are of particular interest, inasmuch as they set
forth the genesis of a subject-matter and its arrival onto the
plane of conscious attention. As it happens, we never get beyond
this stage. All of *Generatio conisectionum* is missing with the

exception of this beginning chapter. We know something of
what the other chapters included from a description given by
Leibniz, who saw all the documents in question. In the pages
that do remain Pascal tells us how a cone is generated and how,
when it is brought into contact with a plane, six figures result,
since the intersection of the two can take place in six different
ways. The products of these imagined encounters between the
cone and the plane are: a point, a line, a right angle, an ellipse,
a parabola, and a hyperbola. Every one of these entities has its
own identity or nature; and, in turn, this nature functions as a
source from which properties flow. Pascal's approach to the
roulette or cycloid curve is similar. As before, he wants us to know
how the object to be investigated comes into being: the cycloid
curve is the figure described by a nail turning on the
circumference of a wheel as it moves over a flat surface. As with
the conic sections, each of the cycloids or related curvilinear
figures has its essential character, and this underlying principle
is the ground of properties to be discovered, defined, and
measured.

In arithmetic we turn from continuous quantity to discrete
quantity – or, to be quite specific, quantities that are by nature
numerical. As we look more closely at what Pascal investigates
here, we see that these discrete quantities tend to be simple
elements, the mission of which is to enter into complexes of some
kind. As a result, there are always two or more levels of
consideration according to changes in the degrees of complexity.
Already present in the geometrical figures and treatises discussed above, this strategy, this work of composition strikes us
particularly as we observe his work with numbers.

He may select as the object of consideration a particular
number and then study it as a sum or a product and therefore
analyzable into its factors. Or he may have before him a
complex term – binomial or polynomial – that serves as the
point of departure for his investigation. Or, along still another
line of thought, he may assemble numbers into series that then
enter into series of series. Or, again, he may decide to create a
physical arrangement of numbers, as when he inserts them in a
triangular figure or into the so-called "magical" square (where

the inscribed integers, when added up and down or across or along diagonals, give equal sums). Such arrangements show us Pascal bringing about a *rapprochement* of arithmetic and geometry: by putting the numbers in a spatial figure he creates for analysis and discussion a mixed quantitative entity that is a locus of specific properties and possibilities. Or, finally, as in the papers on the *règle des partis*, he may put numbers together into an ensemble of factors that are taken by turns in various combinations, the aim being to establish a scale of probable outcomes in a gaming situation.

MECHANICAL APPROACHES TO MOTION

When Pascal turns from abstract figures and numbers and begins to inquire into the behavior of things having mass and weight – and therefore involving *mouvement* – he enters the sphere of mechanics. He has little or no interest in continuous or circular motion; nor in any precise sense is speed or acceleration a concern for him. Leaving aside the field of falling or orbiting bodies, crucial objects of study for Galileo, Kepler, and Newton, Pascal concentrates on movement as it may be seen on its way to rest. *A fortiori*, he does not treat questions concerning light, heat, or magnetism, areas in which assumptions regarding the motions of bodies as particles were to be applied extensively in the seventeenth century and later.

Taking his inspiration mainly from Archimedes, it would seem, Pascal looks for new and diverse applications of the principle of equilibrium, of the balance of weights or pressures. In the *Nouvelles expériences sur le vide* and in the *Traité de l'équilibre des liqueurs* we find him working with such things as mercury, water, wine, oil, air, copper, wood, and wool. It looks like a diverse group of materials, and in a sense rightly so; however, all of the substances mentioned lose their obvious or "secondary" characteristics and appear to Pascal as quantities. The quantities have, however, aspects that determine and specify them: they have weight and shape. Without weight, Pascal would have no motion and no mechanics in his natural or physical universe; and without concern for shape, he could not frame his inquiries in terms of what solids and liquids do. In short, he conducts experiments on a collection of solid and liquid quantities having weight, pairing them off in many different ways that exemplify the principle of equilibrium to which he is committed.

It seems to me that the production of the *machine d'arithmétique* is primarily an exercise in applied mechanics, although Pascal mentions in connection with it physics and geometry as well as mechanics. Here he works on a problem more complex in nature than before, one that does not resolve itself finally into the relation between two weights. The machine is composed of many small parts, so shaped and assembled that when they are activated (not by natural force, as in the cases of the equilibria, but by a human intervention), they produce a specific effect, a configuration having a symbolic aspect and giving the result of a calculation.

Indeed, one might say that the invention of the machine requires that we notice a fundamental distinction and two basic though opposed subject-matters that follow from it. Pascal achieves something like an instance of psycho-physical parallelism, since he is obliged to analyze and recombine simultaneously not only bodies – the parts of the machine – but also mental operations that involve numbers and the rules of arithmetic. His device sets in motion a train of physical events that gives a product corresponding to that achieved by the other train of motions located in and proper to the mind.

A NOTE ON TIME

In the context of experimental science and mechanics, Pascal seems to have found less to say about time than about number, space, and bodies. The relationship between time and movement is not precisely specified, though Pascal sees the connection as "necessary." His occasional use of the word "durée" suggests the idea of interval or duration as being helpful in fixing the sense of "temps" for him. A greater or smaller, a longer or shorter instance of duration is always possible, Pascal says; and it would seem that he intends, in the document on *l'esprit géométrique*, on the geometrical turn or habit of mind, to align time with motion and to conceive of it as the means by which motion is measured.

I should like, however, to point out that we find in the scientific works another conception. In the papers dealing with the *règle des partis* Pascal uses implicitly – without it the probabilistic reasoning would not make sense – the idea of time as divided into past, present, and future. Then it becomes the background of dramas involving human beings. Situated in the present with a particular sequence of events behind them, they face an uncertain future. In calculations of probability they are not measuring quantity of movement but attempting to minimize risk. After studying the structure of a present situation having more than one possible outcome, Pascal makes a translation of the antecedents and the possible consequents into the language of arithmetic and its rules, and then he can arrive at a reasoned answer. Each of the possible events can be arranged according to its likelihood on a scale of fairness or attractiveness.

THE ZERO DEGREE OF SUBJECT-MATTER

In Pascal's mind and imagination it seems, therefore, that the four fundamental and interrelated aspects of the natural order provide four sets of objects to observe, analyze, judge, and present in scientific statement. All four assert themselves: they are. But each aspect may be considered in relation to its absence. Although this fact is not treated at length in *De l'esprit géométrique*, it does receive attention, for it has an important logical place in the set of distinctions guiding Pascal in his thinking. Absence occurs at four distinct vanishing points – one for each of the four subject-matters.

(1) Take away all movement and you have rest, *repos*;
(2) take away all number and you reach zero – Pascal here uses both *zéro* and *néant*;
(3) diminish and remove all space and you have nothing or nothingness, *le néant*;

(4) do the same for durations and you arrive at a pure negation of time-intervals, "un pur néant de durée."

(L352a; MIII402)

We must be careful to note the hypothetical status of those four propositions. Rest, zero, nothingness, and instant bear witness in Pascal's universe to a radical discontinuity. God created Nature, and Nature presents the four visages of quantity; they are real, as I have just said; and as long as we are attending to the real, no matter how small we make the portion of reality that is under consideration, we can never arrive at something that is indivisible, that opens out on the absence, pure and simple, of magnitude. Pascal postulates outside of Nature and creation four absences – or should I say, simply, absence? – lying beneath and beyond every one of the series. It is hard to use such terms without reifying their meanings. They represent for Pascal approachable but unattainable stages in the search for ultimate principles of real quantities. His tactic is apophatic; it consists in defining the negatives from the standpoint of the positives.

Considered in themselves and as natures rather than in contrast to an external zero degree, the four physical realities of motion, number, space, and time have what Pascal calls *propriétés communes*, the knowledge of which, he says, opens the mind to the greatest marvels of Nature. The *double infini* is the particularly impressive, indeed, the principal common property attached to these four basic aspects of Nature. Each of them, though it appears to be simple and single, has in fact a property that divides into two; and so it lends itself to description in paradoxical terms, since it can be extended without limit in the two directions of greater or smaller size. Pascal occasionally lays out logical surprises of this sort in connection with matters of detail in geometry and arithmetic, but he makes a great deal of them when he comes to take a broad view of Nature.

THE SECOND FRAMEWORK: INFINITES
AND HUMAN NATURE

In fact, an important transition takes place when Pascal turns decisively to a consideration of Nature as a whole, as a surrounding and enveloping order, rather than as locus of particular problems to be dealt with in corresponding treatises. What I mean is that man enters explicitly into the scene presented by Nature. Thus far in my account he has been present implicitly no doubt, but always in the role of scientific observer. Now Pascal brings him into his reflection not as an implied knower but as an element in the composite picture: a body among all the other bodies in Nature and thus subject to the essential quantitative characteristics of the whole.

Starting from things hinted at in *De l'esprit géométrique*, he works out with great power in an extended fragment of the *Pensées* (L525d, f199; S125, f230) the view of human nature and the lesson in humility indicated in his title for this text: "Disproportion de l'homme." First he invites his reader to go out into the open and to contemplate Nature in its vastness, considering at first visible and then imaginable things and distances. At a second moment, the reader is asked to extend his vision in the opposite direction, mainly this time by the use of the imagination, so as to grasp the scale of worlds and beings stretching away toward infinite smallness. The spatial framework, as Pascal evokes it here, makes it possible for us to bring together sweeping and nearly simultaneous glances – one upward and the other downward – so as to achieve a maximum of concentration; and the question "Qu'est-ce que l'homme dans l'infini?" can have its stunning effect.

Pascal now has before him what will henceforth be his principal subject-matter – human nature, and more exactly still, the human self. For he has composed in the "Disproportion" an exercise in self-knowledge. He establishes our human situation and its worth in two ways: first, by referring us to Nature and, second, by turning – with what has been seen and learned – to a survey of what is within us. (1) In the first moment: when we observe the heavens, we are humbled as to size, *masse*; but we become giants as we study the miniature worlds lying below us in magnitude. That relativization is a preparation for what Pascal invites us to inspect as we cross the metaphysical line that separates bodies from minds. (2) In the second moment: as he shifts to our inner human nature and situation, Pascal shows us a play of unreconciled and opposed qualities. He makes his point in the broadest possible terms: "Bornés en tout genre, cet état qui tient le milieu entre deux extrêmes se trouve en toutes nos puissances" (L527a, f199; S130, f230). In this encounter between Nature and the self Pascal engages himself (and us along with him) in a complex act of observing, imagining, and feeling, that is turned outward in its first phase but later reversed so as to become introspective; and each phase ends on a note of bafflement and recognition of human limits.

SOME CHANGES IN VOCABULARY

Geometrical treatises have, along with their much appreciated precision in statement and certainty in conclusions, one precondition that is now in some ways unfortunate. All such inquiries require us to turn our attention away from the things that surround us. I think this is one of the most important lessons of the distinction Pascal makes between the *esprit de géométrie* and the *esprit de finesse*. The subject-matter of the former is isolated, decanted, so as to give our knowing faculties a particularly favorable milieu in which to work; the subject-matter of the latter is everyday reality with all its movement and confusion. And so, although Pascal certainly understands and makes use of what the sciences see when they focus on man – a paradoxical machine set between the two *infinis* – his most characteristic reflections regarding human nature may be associated roughly, at least, not with *géométrie* but with *finesse*.

In the *Pensées* and in the *Ecrits sur la grâce*, therefore, we encounter some specific complications in the vocabulary he uses. Superimposed on ordinary language comes a mixture of technical terms from other sources – philosophy, theology, and religious practice. First, we become aware of terms like *mémoire*, *sensation*, *imagination*, *raison*, *volonté*, that come out of the classical tradition in philosophy and psychology. The realities these terms designate and define are distinct powers or faculties of the soul. Second, although Pascal could not, it is plain, operate without those vestiges of philosophical psychology, nor do without their moral and metaphysical overtones, he subordinates them to still another group of terms coming out of the Bible and out of the theory and practice of religion. To these he gives priority; I am thinking, for example, of *corps*, *âme*, *esprit*, and *cœur*.

Conceiving human nature as having a basis in faculty psychology to which an essential biblical overlay has been added, Pascal comes in his observations to distinguish, on the side of the soul, two great tendencies, *esprit* and *coeur*, one assigned to knowing and the other to desiring (but one must always be prepared for synonyms, analogies, and contextual variations): *esprit* and *coeur*, mind and heart. I am particularly interested in this tendential aspect of the soul, because it points to something quite characteristic in Pascal's way of conceiving his human subject-matter. Rather than think about it in substantial terms as an underlying structure in which an ensemble of powers is rooted – even though he uses constantly items from that vocabulary and their cognates – he treats human nature mainly as tendencies, as dynamic and impelling forces working along two lines.

THE STATES OF HUMAN NATURE

This distinction of tendencies brings Pascal to an even deeper level of consideration. What he wants us to understand is a particular and corrupt *state* in which the object – human nature and its two aspirations – finds itself: the powers of knowing and willing are in disorder. This step leads to several others, as the implications of the notion of *state* are filled in. He asserts that, as a consequence of this disorder in our powers, it is not possible to understand the corrupt state – indeed, even to recognize it as such – without referring it to its original Edenic state.

The picture – it reminds us of a triptych – is now about to be completed. That look backward to the first panel of the picture has its counterpart in the conception of a prospective third state, in which the disorder has been put right: the régime of grace, of that *grâce efficace* for which Pascal is the untiring champion. Actually, this third state, when and if it is attained in this life, is subject to change; the soul may fall back into its old and wrong orientation, where self came before God. The *Ecrits sur la grâce* are emphatic on this point; on the authority of the Bible and St. Augustine fear and trembling form thus a dark but appropriate background to the working of this efficacious grace. And finally, Pascal refers at important points in the *Pensées* and in the *Ecrits* to what we may imagine as a fourth panel, placed above the other three. It evokes the condition that may be attained at death: definitive redemption, life in the presence of God, with aspirations to the True and the Good ending in fulfillment and possession.

What a contrast with the subject-matters of geometrical and physical science! There Nature as quantity opens out into four parallel and simultaneous aspects for study; I say "aspects" and not "states," for mass, number, space, movement are not involved in any sort of narrative or hierarchical scheme. Nature as created stands, of course, in ontological dependence on God; and the two infinites of greatness and smallness unite in him and in him alone, as Pascal says in the "Disproportion." But God is relatively remote; we certainly do not find him at or near the center of attention as Pascal treats problems in arithmetic or geometry.

On every one of those points a different situation holds as Pascal inspects human nature, that odd union of quantitative mass and immaterial soul, of mechanism and thought, which is involved in the drama of its various states. For one thing, those four states – Edenic, fallen, redeemed, present *dans la gloire* – are not simultaneous. They correspond to great and crucial episodes in the history of the human race; they take their places in a chronological sequence ordained by God; and by analogy they define, on a shorter chronological scale, the itinerary of each individual in his lifetime. If the double infinity of Nature is contrasted with and logically absorbed in the mind of God, the states of human nature lead to something quite different – to the union of finite persons with the truth and goodness of an infinite person. Whereas one can investigate the subject-matters of the quantitative sciences with only occasional references to God and none to history, that is quite impossible in a study of human nature. From start to finish, in order that its attributes and inclinations may be grasped correctly, its dependence on God and its movement toward eternity is never out of Pascal's sight. He may in the *Pensées* decide to show man in the first part of his apology as he is in observable fact, and to make his case "par la nature" rather than "par l'Ecriture." But always in this descriptive mode he has ready his explanatory principle, his *idée de derrière la tête*; it is just a question of deciding on rhetorical grounds when he will make it explicit.

Two remarks may be added. In reality Pascal assumes on good authority a fifth state, emerging after death and belonging to the order of divine justice rather than to that of beatitude. Without this possibility, the well-known wager on the existence of God would have no force; and for *chercheurs* who happen not to be gamblers in a literal sense, the concept of a terminal state of punishment and of separation from God must, nonetheless, have its role to play in their spiritual lives. Second, although Pascal's natural and human subject-matters turn out to have strikingly different characteristics, there is an interesting similarity on the point of movement. Movement in the physical world is something that Pascal treats as being oriented toward rest, to be attained when bodies are related to a point of balance or center of gravity. Perhaps one could call motion and rest the two "states" of Nature. Do we not see a similar theme in the sphere of human morality, where the mobility of opinions and desires causes a great deal of agitation, and where Pascal's inquiry locates at last an end to movement – in God, grasped provisionally in this life, definitively in the next?

COMING TO CONCLUSIONS ABOUT SUBJECT-MATTER

In the preceding pages I have presented Pascal as exploring two
great problem areas in his search for truths and truth. The first
is scientific, and includes mathematics and physics. In those
domains, as a matter of principle, he decides to focus on
quantity, both continuous and discontinuous – and of course,
since the disciplines in question are arithmetic and geometry,
quantity as abstract and apart from things or bodies. Then he
moves out into the physical world, still studying quantity, but
now in the measurable aspects of weight and extension as they
may be observed in certain isolated bodies – paired or otherwise
assembled – and made subject to experimentation or manipu-
lation. Finally, he rises to a panoramic view of the natural order,
conceiving it as having four dimensions, distinct but closely
related, in fact implying one another. They have the common
property of being doubly infinite; and this striking property
inspires at the last reflections on the situation of man in the
physical universe, reflections that furnish an easy and logical
transition to the other large problem area of interest to him.

That is, of course, the area of morality, and for Pascal it
embraces the realities of Nature, man, and God, all to be
studied eventually in the light furnished by religion. A new
selection of objects comes into play: nature as mathematical
and mechanical reality merges with the reality of social existence
and becomes *le monde*, the world; and the world functions as an
external source of satisfactions and distractions for mankind,
because Pascal refers it constantly to the vital tendencies and
varying states of human nature. Finally, those states reflect the
changing relations of the human creature and person *vis-à-vis*
another person, its divine author, preserver, and end.

To review in this way the two sets of distinctions and subject-
matters that emerge in Pascal's field of vision gives some sense of
the diversity and depth of his problematic; and it gives also a
hint of the sequence and the interrelation of parts that make up
a systematic whole. If that is true, we must go on to ask, it seems
to me, this question: what are the assumptions, aims, and
procedures implied in such a plausible and comprehensive way

of schematizing realities? Pascal seeks truths and the truth about those realities: the outline and the distinctions that I have presented are in a real sense *points de départ*; and the eventual body of understandings and doctrine that he reaches concerning them may be seen as the *point d'arrivée*. Between those points of departure in subject-matters and the conclusions that make up Pascal's eventual position – and works – there stands, like a bridge, an elaborate structure of principles and discursive justifications.

The study of this bridge and these presuppositions is what I want to attempt here. It lies in the interval between what Pascal looks at and what he finally says about what he has seen. It is the place where the inventive energies of his mind are actualized. It is the place where a coherent ensemble of intellectual instruments does its work, for otherwise the Pascalian texts would not leave us, as they do, with a powerful impression of consistency in spite of their often unfinished state. This organon has the status of something recurrent, sustained, habitual, and effective: and that is why, when it is analyzed, one may apply to its components the term of *arts*. They are productive habits of mind that make constant contact with the various subject-matters, and they do so for the purpose of bringing into existence and justifying the tissue of assertions and negations that is the final product of Pascal's efforts.

Such is my hypothesis: that it is possible to achieve, by an examination of his works and by reflection on what he has done, some understanding of Pascal's characteristics as an intellectual artist and, in particular, some grasp of the diverse arts that guided his energies as he went from his points of departure to his conclusions.

A SUGGESTIVE COMPARISON

In formulating the problem that I have in mind and in indicating the questions I shall attempt to answer, one can hardly avoid recalling the traditional, chiefly medieval, notion of the basic arts as consisting of a quadrivium and a trivium –

respectively, a fourfold way including arithmetic, geometry, music, and astronomy, and a threefold way including grammar, rhetoric, and logic. And it is enlightening to compare their typical problem areas with Pascal's intellectual landscape. Where arithmetic and geometry are concerned, Pascal is obviously quite at home; there he did truly creative work and made numerous discoveries. In a fundamental sense music, as one of the original liberal arts, took as its province the mathematical analysis of one class of natural phenomena; and Pascal, like many of his contemporaries, extends this approach to all such phenomena, adding experimentation to the tools of measurement and inquiry furnished by mathematics. As for astronomy, although Pascal seems not to have been interested in the details of that science, he was surely aware of the infinite area open for investigation in the stellar universe and in interstellar space, a fact that is attested by more than one important fragment of the *Pensées*.

Pascal exercises his talents, therefore, on things and questions commonly associated with the four arts of the quadrivium. Let us reverse the usual order in thinking of the trivium. In "De l'esprit géométrique" Pascal intended to set down the outlines at least of an *art de penser*, a logic of demonstrative thinking based on the procedures of geometry; then in the correspondence with Fr. Noël, in the *Préface* to the treatise on the *vide*, and in the accounts of his experiments he adds to that general logic a very serious concern for the rules of empirical investigation. In the seventeenth century and ever since Pascal's readers have recognized in him a master of rhetoric – of "la véritable rhétorique," as the Port-Royalists said of him; moreover, he has set down in the document just mentioned the principles of what he calls explicitly an "art de persuader." That leaves grammar: if we understand that art in the narrow sense of a discipline focused on expression, on correctness in the choice and arrangement of words, we can find fragments in the *Pensées* and passages elsewhere that bear witness to such a grammatical line of thought – not to mention what is implied in Pascal's practice as he expresses himself! But if we take grammar in the wider sense of an art concerned not only with expression but also with interpretation, we see that a great deal of Pascal's energy has gone into grammatical activities of that sort; he is clearly proud of his skill as an exegete, whether he is expounding the sense of texts from the Jesuit casuists, from the theologians of the Council of Trent, from St. Augustine, or last, though certainly not least, from the Bible. In short, Pascal was concerned with the subject-matter and often the theory of each of the traditional arts of the mind.

ANOTHER WAY TO PROCEED

As suggestive as those analogies are, I have decided to take a different route in treating Pascal's procedures. The intellectual arts in any given period are dependent on certain logical possibilities; they are, in fact, ways of elaborating and realizing those possibilities, in the light of prevailing cultural needs and circumstances. We may thus think of them as having been invented by the Greeks for philosophic purposes, made encyclopedic and turned into a practical curriculum by the Romans, then further codified and put to new uses in medieval culture – this is true especially of the trivium – for the solution of problems in canon law and theology, only to be redefined and reordered once more in the Renaissance with reference to the requirements of fine arts and *belles lettres*.

Such cultural adaptations, noted as collective phenomena, testify to the extraordinary vitality and usefulness of these basic techniques, but they are not where I want to start in connection with my hypothesis. More important here is the kind of personal appropriation of the arts that takes place in the mind of a great thinker and writer. What I should like to do for Pascal is to study his particular way of reinventing and using the perennial possibilities that lie behind even the variations that are shared in a collectivity at a given time. For that reason I have chosen to step back, so to speak, to return to a vantage point behind and beyond the formulation of the seven liberal arts, and to take as the basis of my study four fundamental intellectual operations, each of which I take to be supported by a guiding and perfecting art. I am quite aware of the ambiguities attached to the terms

I am using at this point, but the operations in question seem to me to be inevitable. Consequently, my approach has been to look for evidence of their presence and functioning in Pascal's works; and then, whenever he has recourse to them in relatively unambiguous ways, I have attempted to recover the specific forms of the arts involved by studying the contexts in which the operations appear – or which they engender – and by identifying the particular devices of inquiry and statement chosen by Pascal to go along with them.

The first operation that I have in mind is recovery or interpretation. The characteristic question that it seeks to answer is, what is to be done if one wishes to find out what is already known about a problem being discussed or treated?

The second operation is discovery or invention. Since there is usually some inadequacy in what is already known, the typical question here is, how can difficulties and incoherences in present knowledge and understanding be remedied?

The third operation is presentation or arrangement. Looking back at the two preceding activities, it asks, what discursive structures or sequences are necessary in order to justify the terms and statements used in recovering what is known and in discovering needed additions to that knowledge?

And finally, the fourth operation is integration or systematization. It asks, in what way can one draw unity out of the multiplicity appearing in the solutions that have been found to problems posed in the three preceding enterprises?

To designate the arts that tend to emerge as ways of supplying the means for perfecting these operations, I propose to use traditional names that have at least some connection, though it may not be strict, with the activities and questions I have just listed: respectively, grammar, rhetoric, logic, and dialectic.

The sequence in which I have introduced them is intended to indicate a coordinate and mutually supporting relation that holds among these arts. I have distinguished them in a rather abrupt way, but in practice, of course, things do not stay neatly in place: intrusions rather than exclusions are frequent. One must expect frequent exchanges and borrowings that allow every one of them to benefit from the others. The questions and answers, the maneuvers and tactics that are prevalent in one often find a secondary use in one of the others.

It would have been possible, while somehow taking into account these examples of cross-fertilization, to compose four chapters in which I discussed one after the other grammar, rhetoric, logic, and dialectic as derived and specified by Pascal. That way of proceeding would have made for simplicity in exposition. However, I have decided against it: it would lead not only to a distortion of what *can* happen in the interrelations of the arts, but also, and as a consequence, to an inadequate grasp of what *does* happen in the writings of Pascal.

As I have just said, there may be influences back and forth within a general framework that coordinates the arts, that gives them more or less equal rank and importance. Another possibility may be realized, however, in which one of the arts takes on a role so prominent as to be controlling, with the result that a recasting of the basic techniques occurs within the perspective of the art that has thus become architectonic. Indeed, there is reason to believe that more often than not that is what happens: a researcher becomes so fascinated by what one of these arts can do, by the way in which it corresponds to the needs of the time or of his program of research, that the other disciplines fade in importance. As a result, they lose their autonomy; their fundamental operations are transformed; redesigned, they must support the undertaking of the art that has been granted overall jurisdiction.

It seems to me that this second case, in which coordination gives way to subordination, often holds in the works of Pascal that I shall be discussing. Although overlappings and borrowings are frequent as he constructs his arguments, sorts out his thoughts, and examines things, it will be important to note the changes in status and the recastings that take place in his methods as he shifts from one terrain to another. This phenomenon is, in its way, a symptom of the virtuoso-like freedom with which he defines problems and selects devices that he thinks will lead to solutions. Paralleling what he wrote in another connection, he might have said: "La vraie méthode se moque de la méthode."

But at this point I should like to be quite specific. In Chapter 2, which is given over to a study of geometric in certain works of Pascal, it has seemed fair to me to assume – on the basis of evidence to be presented – that in certain problem areas geometric has in fact taken on for him the role of a controlling or comprehensive art. And so my treatment is divided into four main sections, one for each of the original four arts, but now reoriented and defined in the light of the needs that go with the mode of thought that is characteristic of geometric. Chapter 3, on dialectic, is organized in a similar fashion. Since, in certain areas, Pascal attributes universal scope and application to this mode of thought and the consequent art, and since he then becomes involved in the task of tailoring the four original arts and their operations in ways that promote the objectives of dialectic, I have divided my treatment once more into four sections. In other words, geometric and dialectic, when universalized, become complex ensembles. In Chapter 4, on rhetoric, my remarks are presented under a different set of headings, as will be seen, because of the peculiar status of rhetoric in Pascal's practice.

CHAPTER 2

Elements, complexes, and geometric

INTERPRETATION

What happens when Pascal assigns to the geometrical mode of thinking the status of a dominant or controlling art? What activities and habits of mind appear as he does his work within the bounds of that discipline? It seems to me that each of the four arts that I have taken to be fundamental undergoes, under the *présidence* of geometric, interesting modifications. The operations basic to them – statement, invention, connection, systematization – are all transformed in various ways that adapt them to the requirements typical of an attitude in which Pascal puts a premium, in the search for truth, on making explicit (1) the least parts or factors in every situation and (2) the conditions under which those elements may be recombined into a complex that will be satisfactory in theory or effective in practice. In the present section, I should like to offer some remarks on the consequences for the art of statement and interpretation when it finds itself in the régime of geometric.

MANY DIFFERENT STATEMENTS

Let us approach the subject genetically, as though we were watching Pascal's strategy of composition coming into being. To treat the question thus has its dangers; as I go along, I shall try to make clear the part of hypothesis and to show that it is a way of covering and explaining the main facts.

It seems fair to say, first of all, that as an intellectual artist in this mode Pascal must direct his attention regularly to state-

24

ments: statements of facts, of truths, of judgments. He cannot avoid making and interpreting them, whether the emphasis lies on the words involved, on the concepts that have been assembled and proposed, on what is designated by the words and grasped by the concepts, on the value of what is said. The first habit or way of working that we need to consider in studying the place and role of geometric has, therefore, such statements in all their variety as its subject-matter.

As to the broad fields or frameworks where statements are to be made in the light of geometric, it is obvious that Pascal favors mathematics and physics – we saw that in the preceding chapter. He intends to investigate and understand certain mathematical objects, but also to take serious notice of things, as they are given in Nature, and especially as they offer themselves for measurement. Here, however, I do not wish to leave out the notion of made objects, resulting from inventive activity on Pascal's part. For a list of things referred to in Pascal's statements, perhaps something like the following will serve, as we go on a scale from mental to real entities:

(1) mathematical beings, which are purely imaginary and rational, though they may be exemplified in the real world;
(2) machines, as the *machine d'arithmétique*, where what is denoted in statement has physical reality but only as the result of the creative imagination and reason of the inventor, who has determined its existence and nature;
(3) corporeal beings given in Nature, occurring as solids and liquids, which have weight and have or assume shapes (thereby occupying space) – they do not depend on us for their being, and our ideas about them are hypotheses that have no definite status or value until verified.

Some qualifications will help us to grasp precisely what Pascal is doing. It will have been noted that matters connected with *morale* or *éloquence* do not appear in our list. As will be seen later, those are fields for which Pascal has chosen to make use of another intellectual mode and other arts. Furthermore, within the areas of mathematics and physics, his facts are not historical or particular in reference, except incidentally, as they may appear in narrative accounts of problems, solutions, and experiments. What Pascal turns to by preference and as a matter of method is the universal manner of statement, which allows him to assert not what is or was the case but *what must be the case*, given the figures he is writing about in geometry (triangles, squares, curves, straight lines, spheres, and the like) or the physical objects he is working with in the experiments (mercury, water, wine, oil, air, tubes, syringes, bellows, and the like). And, as I have suggested above, one should add to this list the calculating machines with their wood and metal parts (straight pieces, curved pieces, gears, chains, wheels). These geometrical, manufactured, or naturally given physical bodies, along with their properties and motions, furnish the starting points for Pascal's definitions and statements; they are what he is trying to capture in general or universal terms.

Here we must make one other important addition, in connection with Pascal's work on *la règle des partis*. The probabilistic statements emerging from those calculations are the result of his effort to reduce happenings at the gaming table to something that is not entirely irregular; turned toward future events, it is a statement of what will probably be the case. But even in this instance the enunciation is pulled, so to speak, in the direction of necessary truth, for there is a kind of demonstration that underlies it: did not Pascal proudly call his technique of analysis a science of chance, an *aleae geometria*?

A COMPLEX INSIGHT

Familiarity with a large number of facts and statements of a mathematical sort – or of a sort that fits into a science of physics – is only a beginning in the genesis of the intellectual technique in question here. No art can come into being unless there is a measure of insight, of penetration into causes or decisive factors at work in the problem areas that interest the researcher. Here we become conjectural, but we must make the effort to say, on the basis of Pascal's practice, what he appears to have seen in the statements and facts and propositions that fill the mathematical and physical treatises. My proposal is that he saw them, first and positively, as being bearers of truth, answers to questions, formulations that, when understood, compel assent; and then, second, as having a negative force or implication, in that they exclude all interference from disturbing factors such as desires and feelings, imaginations and opinions.

Solide is an adjective that Pascal likes to apply to the word *connaissance*. I think that says something important for us: the statements with which he wishes to concern himself will be notable for their stable and unbreakable qualities. It is also very appropriate to recall the distinction he made in his letter to Père Noël, according to which a judgment is true under two conditions: either it is an *évidence* or it may be deduced from an *évidence*. (Incidentally, it seems to me that this is the key to Pascal's way of using the two terms "maxime" and "conséquence.") In any case, either a statement stands alone, and has by itself the power to cause assent or, by following as the consequence of a statement that stands alone, it takes on the force of the primary statement by a kind of borrowing or transfer.

But I think that the creative insight occurring here, at the origin of this intellectual habit, has a further aspect. Such true statements, with their charge of *évidence*, proper or borrowed, appear within the bounds of a coherent inquiry; and it is with reference to this framework that the statement takes on its final sense and rightness. Pascal is quite aware of the structure into which he intends to fit particular statements; for example, he knows what a geometrical inquiry looks like and includes; he knows the sort of stated fact that it gives rise to. Thus, in addition to its degree of self-evidence, I would say that a statement in the geometrical mode carries an implied coefficient to the effect that it belongs in a technical treatise, in which it will eventually take its place as required. Notice that Pascal has not really invented anything here. He has come to understand and appreciate the characteristics of a discipline already in existence for a long time: he presupposes the validity and style of

geometry in its essentially Euclidean form; and within the
conditions of that intellectual genre, he undertakes to make
appropriate statements about mathematical or physical (or, *à la
rigueur*, all) subject-matters.

FROM STATEMENTS TO OPERATIONS

Familiarity with statements in three different but related realms
(mathematics, mechanics, and physics) and insight into causal
and contextual factors that affect those statements lead Pascal,
it seems to me, to a third step in the genesis of his art of
statement. It concerns the operations that are associated with
such experience and insight – and that are indeed, derived from
them. If, for example, Pascal studies two or more propositions or
statements, he wants to do whatever is required to find the
answers to certain questions. How can he determine whether
the assertions are equivalent, though the words used are not the
same? Are they different and equivocal, in spite of similarities of
expression? Are they opposed and paradoxical, laying down a
challenge to the mind? Does the second propound an objection
to the first? Is it part of a demonstrative sequence? Is it best
understood as a corollary, or as a remark that has its proper
place in a scholium?   Everything that happens regularly
between the posing of such questions and the arrival at the
answers defines the mental operations required for the possession and exercise of the art I am attempting to identify and,
in some degree, to define.

SYNONYMIES

Pascal attaches great importance to these scrutinies and
manipulations of statements. At the end of the *Traité sur les ordres
numériques* he offers a little development on the subject of saying
the same thing in different ways. After expressing a theorem in
his own way, he goes on to say: "Les manières de tourner une
même chose sont infinies"; and then he presents an "illustre
exemple." It turns out that he and Fermat had once the same
idea at the same time, though they were separated in space,

Fermat being in Toulouse and Pascal in Paris. But they found different ways of stating that same idea. Returning to the matter immediately at hand, Pascal concludes:

Voilà comment on peut varier les énonciations. Ce que je montre en cette proposition s'entendant de toutes les autres, je ne m'arrêterai plus à cette manière accommodante de traiter les choses, laissant à chacun d'exercer son génie en ces recherches où doit consister toute l'étude des géomètres: car si on ne sait pas tourner les propositions à tous sens, et qu'on ne se serve que du premier biais qu'on a envisagé, on n'ira jamais bien loin: ce sont ces diverses routes qui ouvrent les conséquences nouvelles, et qui, par des énonciations assorties au sujet, lient des propositions qui semblaient n'avoir aucun rapport dans les termes où elles étaient conçues d'abord. (L65c; MIII329)

In this rich and stimulating passage, Pascal shares with his reader one of the secrets of his own intellectual strength: a habit – or as I am also calling it here an art – of looking at a proposition from more than one angle, stating it differently, comparing it with many others, linking it with apparently unrelated propositions; and he surely knows that one can develop the habit by systematic exercise, preparing thus the way for "going far" and making progress in the discipline of geometry.

He has the same capacity as regards physical things. In the "Avis," composed to explain the use of the arithmetical machine, he answers at one point a hypothetical objector who might wonder why the pieces of the machine were not less complicated or arranged in a different way. He imagines this person rather uncharitably as a "savant imparfait" and takes pains to assure him that he could show him several other models, including one much less complicated, less "composée." And the rest of what he says shows that he saw quite clearly the possibility of more than one design; in making his final choice he considered not only degree of simplicity or complexity but also criteria such as durability and solidity and convenience of use. What concerns us here is that Pascal could and did imagine many machines that would be, rather like so many propositions, synonymous or equivalent, and capable of producing the same consequences or results in spite of differences in design and execution. In fact, in the "Privilège" obtained in 1649 for the manufacture and sale of the machines it is stated that "le Sr Pascal" had made more than fifty different models of the machine – "tous differens"; and furthermore, that he is working "continuellement" to produce a simpler and less expensive version that will carry out the same operations: "un mouvement plus simple et qui opère néanmoins le mesme effet…" (L192b; MII713).

Similarly, he finds something naturally prolific in facts and statements of facts. Often, as we go from one treatise to another, he assures us that many more propositions of the same sort follow from what has been said; or, that there is an abundance of further examples of this kind, but he will leave them for the reader to develop; or, that what has just been found and said can be generalized, and so, from the higher plane thus reached, he and we include in our vision still more facts. In a typical case he looks at the *triangle arithmétique*, works out some theorems, moves on to applications (and other statements), and then declares it to be surprising how fertile "en propriétés" the triangle is. Whether engaged in mathematics, physics, or mechanics, Pascal's mind seems to work in the middle of a sea of possible and actual statements (already known to be true or, if not that, present for testing). On the side of consequences and applications the scientific disciplines are, for him, entirely open-ended.

STATEMENTS AND THEIR COMPONENTS

Pascal's art of statement, as it is implied and applied in geometry, arithmetic, and physics, must from time to time focus on topics below the level of the proposition: on terms, their meanings, and their references. Definitions and denotations must be brought out into the open; and they must be compared and contrasted with formulations proposed by other *savants*. The correspondence with Père Noël furnishes a good illustration: Pascal distinguishes carefully between his way of using words like *néant*, *espace*, and *corps* from that of his opponent, who starts with metaphysics rather than from geometry. Thanks to acts of discernment such as these, Pascal can make a rational choice; he can isolate methodically the subject-matter of a problem or a treatise, giving it at the same time form and status that make investigation possible.

He seems to have achieved an early mastery of this process of clarifying and defining terms. But that is not all, for at this level of analysis he encounters once again the problem of truth. He is not content to look at propositions from a neutral point of view, to tabulate the relations among them, and to analyze them into their respective elements. The analytical operations are subject to the overriding condition that they bring into a satisfactory relationship words, meanings, and references; and by that I mean, of course, a true relationship. Everyday language and commonly understood usages are not acceptable: words must be defined univocally and the assigned meaning must remain unchanged throughout the discourse; they must be applied to properly identified objects; and they must be combined discursively in a way that brings all three dimensions of statement – terms, meanings, and objects designated – into agreement and congruence.

ELEMENTS, QUESTIONS, AND CONTEXTS

There is, in my view, another pair of operations that must be appealed to; I have in fact already mentioned them above. Statements and vocabulary must be seen as relevant (or irrelevant) to two factors, the first being the particular impulse or question to which the statement or assertion is the response. An effective art will not see the statement in mathematics or physics as something fixed or frozen or independent, but as something whose meaning, bearing, and value are functions of its particular place in a line of thought along which the mind is moving. Then, in the second place, there will be the question of another kind of relevance and appropriateness based on a broader context, that of the disciplinary framework within which assertions are being put forward. This is something more ample than the immediate impulse to discover a local truth; it requires comparing a statement with what has been said and with what will be said in an ensemble of demonstrations, and then finding its place – if it has one – in the total sequence of an inquiry.

In short, as a consequence of his fundamental insight into the nature of the kind of assertion that he wants to make, Pascal assembles a set of productive operations, with their characteristic devices, that would include something like the following:

(1) comparative examination of propositions;
(2) analysis of propositions into their constituent elements, which may then be inspected critically;
(3) determining truth values on a graduated scale (such as: compelling, probable, undecidable, false, illusory);
(4) considering the relevance of terms and propositions both to the immediate question being answered and to the whole investigation being realized by the activity of the *chercheur*.

Such operations, adjusted to their proper ends and carried out repeatedly, tend to generate rules. When learned, operations and rules form a productive habit or art; and knowledge of the rules both simplifies and aids the learning process. In these scientific works of Pascal, the desire to arrive at general statements, to define methods, to give practical advice appears often as he comes to the end of a demonstration or sums up his solution of a particular problem. And there can be no doubt that he thinks of these principles as guides and as part of the mental equipment that one should acquire. In his own case, the process of habituation took place in an extremely favorable set of personal circumstances, one that provided instruction and encouraged discovery – both at home and in the remarkable circle of his father's scientific friends. By means of these valedictory passages put at the end of his treatises Pascal wishes, it would seem, to communicate to his reader something of the principles underlying the art that he has the good fortune already to possess.

INTERPRETATION AND GRAMMAR

If one were looking for a single term to cover the aims, activities, rules, and dispositions I have just treated, perhaps it would be grammar, understood not only as an art of statement and expression but also and equally as an art that deals with problems of interpretation. It has the complex task of fixing or elucidating the characteristics and values of words, thoughts, and things as they appear in a geometrical or quasi-geometrical mode of thought. Let us take note, however, of an ambiguity. The art in question is exercised in two situations: (1) when Pascal is expressing his own ideas, making statements *de son propre chef*; and (2) when he is reading a text written by someone else, making sense out of it, and offering his version of what it says. He must work with similar semantic factors in the two cases, but the operations involved will be ordered differently, according as he produces a text or learns from a text.

More often than not, I believe, one may distinguish the two exercises but not really keep them apart; and so a third situation applies: (3) when Pascal is engaging simultaneously in (1) and (2), in both expression and interpretation, in a comprehensive grammar that regulates both saying and reading. This complex state of affairs becomes particularly noticeable when we turn to Pascal's work as an innovator in mathematics and physics, and study there some essential aspects of his art of invention. In that new problematic context we shall want to see precisely how he goes about placing himself with regard to past thinkers and with regard to his contemporaries, as he undertakes to make his own contributions to the scientific culture of the seventeenth century.

INVENTION

EXPERIENCE WITH PROBLEMS

Pascal develops and uses a second art in the geometrical mode. After the art of statement or interpretation, which starts characteristically most often from familiarity with what is already known, he moves onto the terrain of a complementary art, focused on discovery; it is based on an attitude and a habit of mind that go beyond the current state of knowledge, with the aim of making an orderly approach to what is, as yet, unknown. Like every art, the art of discovery has at its origin a fund of experience; and that experience serves to throw light on a class of things, on a subject-matter, and opens the way to a decisive insight.

From early childhood Pascal was fascinated by problems of geometry, arithmetic, and physics. At home his father encouraged him, at first reluctantly and then enthusiastically, to develop his interests and activities, which gave striking signs of an investigative turn of mind. Later his father introduced him to the circle of physicists and mathematicians organized by Marin Mersenne. From that time Pascal played an active part in one of the great centers of scientific discussion and achievement in the seventeenth century. At the meetings he and the others were regularly engaged in studying and judging scientific or mathematical projects and results – and not merely those presented by the members of the circle. Mersenne and his friends corresponded with other investigators in several European countries. It was easy for Pascal to learn about a wide variety of current activities in the mathematical and physical disciplines; beyond that, through the analysis of the *inventions* – as they were called – of others, he could see how and why investigations succeeded or failed.

He clearly absorbed the competitive spirit so noticeable in seventeenth-century science. He was well placed for learning of problems being worked on, but not yet solved, and of differing opinions regarding them. Contradictions and uncertainty in such cases stimulated him to think for himself about ways of approach that seemed promising. Here, for example, is a particular question: in gambling, how should one divide the stakes if the game is interrupted? That was the stimulus that led Pascal to work, in thinly disguised competition with Fermat, on ways of calculating and stating mathematical probabilities. Or, in plane geometry, what of the curve called the *roulette*? According to Pascal, it was known to the ancients; some of his contemporaries – Mersenne and Roberval – had discussed it or worked on it; but no one had studied its properties adequately or found appropriate ways of measuring it. Or, for the most striking example of all: the controversy over the vacuum. Pascal certainly knew what was being said by others on the subject; he had performed numerous experiments in coming to his own grasp of the facts and to plausible hypotheses that might explain them. Here, too, the element of competition had a part, for the person who settled the argument over Nature's *horror vacui* would obviously be celebrated in every scientific center of Europe. My point is that, in several important areas of mathematics and physics, and by the time he was twenty years old, Pascal had gone far beyond a merely receptive attitude in several important mathematical and physical areas; he approached them and their unsolved problems in a spirit that was informed, confident, and primed for a contest.

INNOVATION AND INSIGHT

At the start of an inquiry the investigator finds himself in a state of serious doubt regarding the principles of explanation that are commonly applied to a problem. Innovation begins with the attempt to see things differently. Pascal enacts in a particularly clear way this aspect of the process in the disagreement he had with Père Noël, after the publication in 1647 of the *Nouvelles expériences sur le vide*. Noël expresses his opposition to Pascal in language centering on the notion of *plein*, and its application to nature, which he – Noël – takes as being always and everywhere full. As a result, he explains the behavior of the mercury in the inverted tube as an instance of substitution: when the mercury falls, a *corps subtil* fills the space left behind. Pascal states his view in language centering on the notion of a *vide*, of an actual vacuum; and he sees no reason to think in terms of a substitution and to invoke, consequently, the principle of Nature's horror, since there is nothing present to be explained. Why not, he proposes, judge the space in the glass tube to be in fact empty, as sense and reason would seem to attest? But in any case, if there is to be any hope of progress in solving the problem, this conflict of statements and arguments requires an effort to clarify vocabulary and, above all, to select appropriate concepts.

Pascal sees or thinks he sees what must be done. Since the question is ultimately one of truth, firm and certain, he proposes to his correspondent that they both agree on something that, in Pascal's view, regulates the entire discussion. We have already noted the principle above in connection with statements: it is the notion of *évidence*, of what is self-evident. He sets forth what he asserts to be a universal rule, one that all must observe if undoubted knowledge and true explanations are what we seek. He points to two instances in which we know that we have a grip on the truth: (1) when we have before us a principle – in the strong and axiomatic sense of the word, in the sense of an affirmation to which we cannot not assent or a negation with which we cannot not agree; and (2) when we have before us a statement or judgment that follows undeniably from the kind of principle recognized in (1). After laying down this basis, Pascal adds:

Tout ce qui a une de ces deux conditions est certain et véritable, et tout ce qui n'en a aucune passe pour douteux et incertain. Et nous portons un jugement décisif des choses de la première sorte et laissons les autres dans l'indécision, si bien que nous les appelons, suivant leur mérite, tantôt *vision*, tantôt *caprice*, parfois *fantaisie*, quelquefois *idée*, et tout au plus *belle pensée*, et parce qu'on ne peut les affirmer sans témérité, nous penchons plutôt vers la négative: prêts néanmoins de revenir à l'autre, si une démonstration évidente en fait voir la vérité. (L201b; MII519)

The lines repeat for emphasis the main point and then give a good indication of what the wrong or doubtful principles might be called. Pascal is cautious, however: he makes it clear, as he continues, that one would lean in practice toward a negative judgment of statements proposed as capable of compelling assent, though always reserving the right to change one's opinion if later evidence showed that the affirmation in question fell under (1) or (2) above.

With varied and relevant experience behind him, with a grasp of the problematic situation, and with a fundamental insight regarding the *évidence* that motivates true judgments, Pascal is well on the way to acquiring and exercising an art of innovation or discovery. But let us generalize somewhat the two-pronged insight. If we think of it as an opposition of antecedent to consequent, of something prior from which the posterior is derived, we have before us, in my opinion, a topic that plays a fundamental role in all of Pascal's explanatory efforts. He often writes in terms of "principles" and "propositions," and then our attention tends to fix on matters of language and expression. What I want to do, however, is to set aside the linguistic connotations for the moment – or at least not to emphasize them. Let us think instead simply of two *terms* or *factors*, whatever the context may be – linguistic, mental, or real. One is an undeniable antecedent and the other is an undeniable consequent. Considered together they form a single explanatory commonplace, a fertile intuition that Pascal intends, of course, to bring to bear on the controversy with Père Noël, but its usefulness does not end there: he has in hand a criterion for acts of discernment and construction in many other contexts.

SOME MENTAL OPERATIONS

After – or below, if one visualizes the process in spatial rather than in temporal images – self-evident principles, the inquirer moves onto the terrain of operations directly connected with the art of discovery. There he goes to work on a subject-matter, about which has arisen an intellectual situation involving contradictory views and posing, therefore, a challenge. One thing that Pascal may feel impelled to do immediately, as in the exchange with Père Noël, is to show that the opponent has not obeyed the universal rule concerning antecedents and consequents. That belongs to the negative or discriminative phase of the argument. On the positive side, the question that must be answered is this: how can the fundamental insight be applied or adjusted so as to meet the demands of particular investigative contexts? It must undergo, it seems to me, a series of specifying operations, each of which makes it pertinent to a distinct set of problems. Some examples drawn from Pascal's practice will clarify the point.

The broad rule of the two possibilities for truth, one involving what is self-evident and the second what is derivable from the self-evident, generates, when Pascal turns to mathematics, a

distinction between axiomatic principles and conclusions refer-
rable to them. At this first degree of specification, the terms
place us in a context of mental and verbal realities, of notions
and propositions. However, in mathematical work Pascal does
not remain on that level; although he knows that a particular
kind – a deductive kind – of thought and language must be
attained if he is to reach the truth in mathematics, he seeks to
achieve a second and more concrete degree of specification.

When he fixes his attention on what he is making statements
about, namely, abstract quantity (in arithmetic and geometry),
he finds another way of conceiving the pair antecedent–
consequent. Again and again, apropos of numbers and figures,
he uses two terms, *nature* and *propriétés*, that surprise us
somewhat, given Pascal's preferences as to vocabulary: this pair
would be more at home in a metaphysical discussion. Nevertheless, he speaks readily of the "nature" and "properties" of
the arithmetical triangle; similarly, he attributes to the *roulette*
as a kind of curve a special nature and properties. The "nature"
of a mathematical object points to something given, assumed,
stable; and the "properties" follow with necessity from that
"nature." The basic principle that governs the process of
discovery and innovation, by which I mean the interrelated
pair of antecedent-consequent, does not change, therefore,
though its particular embodiment does vary at different levels of
the process.

FROM MATHEMATICS TO PHYSICS

When Pascal turns to the behavior of liquids and to various
questions in the domain of physics, he applies another version of
the same explanatory device. He obviously adopts a basically
mechanical view of Nature and of the phenomena that may be
observed in it. His dyadic rule of analysis undergoes another
redefinition so that it will serve in a problem area usually
characterized by observable motion or change rather than by
logical inference. It seems clear that Pascal conceives of change
as occurring in Nature when a movement, taken as prior and
causal, brings about a subsequent movement, which then

becomes intelligible as an effect. In the physical world the regulating concepts for explanation may be reduced to those two, I think: an action on the part of something that provokes a reaction on the part of something else, a push from some source that causes something else to be displaced. The notion of change being used by Pascal is entirely consistent with a common habit of thought among seventeenth-century physicists: it tends to be essentially local movement, change of place, with little concern for notions like generation or corruption, or change of quality, or passage from power to act, as might be the case in scholastic theories formulated under the more or less distant inspiration of Aristotle.

The *machine d'arithmétique* offers a particularly good case in point. It illustrates clearly the *leitmotiv* of action–reaction. Pascal saw the problem of designing such a machine as fundamentally that of contriving and combining frames, wheels, gears, rods, and assorted other pieces in such a way that an orderly series of movements in one part of the machine would lead to just that, another orderly series of movements, elsewhere in the machine. When one piece is moved at the beginning of the train, all the others move through a predetermined sequence, according to the arithmetical operation to be performed. Events occur in pairs, and the first event, which functions as a given, self-evident antecedent, causes the second event, which is the necessary consequent; and it becomes, in turn, the first member of another pair and the source of movement in the second member of that pair.

The phenomena studied in connection with the vacuum and the equilibrium of liquids exemplify in still another way the working of the dyadic rule. The difference consists in the fact that, in the course of the experiment, the push exerted by the weight of one column of liquid is equalled finally by the push coming from the weight of the other and opposed column. The sequence of events ends in a balance and a cessation of movement. Perhaps one should say then that there are two antecedents and no consequents; or that each of the two is simultaneously an antecedent and a consequent, so that, caught up in a special relation, each acts on the other.

Let us summarize for a moment. The operations connected with discovery, taken in their intellectual aspect, begin with an act of discrimination. Pascal must analyze and evaluate an inadequate set of terms that some other person has applied to a problem. But in addition, he must do some specifying, some particularizing, so as to adapt the inclusive terms of his own and presumably correct insight to the changing circumstances of inquiries. This he does by redefining his two basic factors, antecedent and consequent, one of which is independent or axiomatic and the other derived or dependent. From the abstract pair we descend, in the discourse of mathematics, to principles and conclusions, and then, in connection with the entities or quantities actually studied in mathematics, to natures and properties. This last distinction turns up occasionally in Pascal's physical treatises, but the more typical pair in physics is something else, I think: action and reaction, traced in a context of local motions or changes.

If we reflect on the implications of the foregoing, it is apparent that selecting, defining, relating, and ultimately applying the two terms (along with their synonyms, antonyms and other associated words) underlie and guide the work of investigating or problem-solving that takes place. But those activities still have something of a general and final aspect: as ends that define an inquiry they leave us suspended in the air at one or more removes from actual contact with subject-matters. They call for further refinement until they provide relevant means or devices of inquiry in particular circumstances. And this leads us – and Pascal, as I see it – to still another degree of specification. It emerges with special clarity as Pascal under-takes innovation in his mathematical and scientific works; it is the conceptual level nearest to the first steps of actual inquiry, to the moment when he comes to grips with the data of the problem.

In treating conic sections, Pascal has recourse with great success to the hexagon as a heuristic device: that figure, when inscribed in the conic section, sets in motion the process of discovery and the deductive sequence. Or again, in the matter of the *roulette*, where he wants to define the nature and properties of the curve described by a point on the circumference of a turning wheel: there the wheel or circle, considered as generative, as entailing one or more consequences, serves as the conceptual device that sets him on the path to successful measurements and demonstrations. In physics and the investigation of the vacuum, one sees something quite comparable: as I suggested above but in less concrete terms, the entering wedge in the inquiry is the notion of a balance or an equilibrium; with that as a stimulus Pascal moves from his hypotheses to that series of experiments concerning the equilibria of liquids that caused, eventually, an intellectual revolution.

I suspect that something of the sort holds for the case of the *machine d'arithmétique*. What could it be? Since the idea of a calculating machine involves joint innovation on two quite different planes – the mental plane of mathematical operations and the physical plane of moving parts in the machine, the thematic means might be something like the notion of "equivalent" or perhaps, "parallel." The problem for Pascal is to find a way of making a set of physical movements in the machine parallel or translate the series of mental operations that would take place in the mind of the calculator. He himself alludes to the difficulty in terms of a reduction of the mental to the physical: " ... mon dessein n'ayant jamais visé qu'à réduire en mouvement réglé toutes les opérations de l'arithmétique" (L189c; MII336).

STATEMENTS AND FRAMEWORKS

In preparing for an inquiry and in carrying it out, Pascal proceeds from topics to concepts (a matter of specifying commonplaces to particular meanings) and thence to judgments or statements (a matter of combining the conceptual elements just found). The process that I have described – the step by step specification of the notion of antecedent–consequent and the invention of the heuristic terms based on it – serves to create in Pascal's mind a new vocabulary, a new system of mental and verbal associations for use in statement.

However, the elements (technical words, terms, concepts)

from which statements are formed – and, indeed, the statements themselves – are dependent and relative in an interesting way, since they function within the disciplinary context or framework adopted by Pascal for a particular investigation. As new terms and new truths are discovered and stated, the role and status of that framework come to the fore in two ways. (1) On the one hand, the new findings may be integrated into the body of what is already known. Thus, Pascal's treatises on numbers complement one another, so as to form a coherent ensemble; and, moreover, they do not depart in a radical way from his understanding of what the mathematical community that he knows might propose and accept. He builds on his own discoveries, and he builds on current theory. For another example, in connection with the vacuum: it is obvious to the reader (and Pascal says so himself) that his experiments arise out of work done by others and, especially, by Torricelli; he is participating in a common and widespread investigative effort.

But there is, of course, another possibility. (2) The work of discovery may *not* have simply the character of an extension of what is already known within the accepted framework, since progress may depend precisely on making changes in it. Present difficulties and incoherences may be such as to require another kind of mental activity, one that great discoverers have characteristically the ability and the courage to perform. They are willing to modify the intellectual structure with which they begin; it has for them only the status of a supposition, something that may have to be revised later. And they are not daunted by the prospect of having to replace it more or less completely in order to find and state the solutions to their problems.

In the experiments on the vacuum one sees both of the possibilities indicated under (2) above: moderate revision and fundamental reformulation. At first, rather than discard completely the notion of the *horror vacui*, Pascal defines narrowly the limits within which Nature seems to experience this revulsion. But finally, when he is convinced of the correctness of the conclusions derived from the *grande expérience* of the Puy-de-Dôme he abandons the whole framework derived from the notion of Nature as a *plenum* and adopts a perspective that asserts the reality in Nature of empty space, within which bodies exist, move, and move one another. Denying the world of Noël and the pseudo-physics – more accurately the bumbling meta-physics – that sought to explain it, Pascal proposes a Nature that is mechanical and, to account for it, a science that bases its explanations on observable and measurable motions: in short, a physics recast along mathematical lines.

Pascal's art or technique of recovery and interpretation, as we saw in the preceding section, tends to be conservative in matters of terminology, vocabulary, reference; it seeks to determine or to fix the meaning of factual statements already made; and it tends also to take for granted the disciplinary background against which elements and statements are being located. His approach to the art of discovery, however, introduces us to a more complicated situation. It starts from the preceding, but takes a free attitude toward it; what is presumed to be known cannot be simply taken for granted; contradictions or implausi-bilities found in it may mean that the process of interpretation, with its ensemble of terms, statements, and structures, has to be reviewed. At any time elements of that ensemble may be examined for comparison with what might be the case if partial changes were to be made, or indeed, if a wholly new structure (with its implications for terms and statements) were substituted for the old. This work of comparing, contrasting, formulating on all three levels – of concepts, statements, and frameworks – is the characteristic process that reveals and shapes the art of discovery in the geometric mode. As Pascal practices it, we see a clear awareness of the commonly accepted structures into which terms and statements are to be fitted, whether the field is arithmetic, geometry, or physics. He is by no means averse to completing what is already known; but he does not shrink, at critical moments, from proposing and justifying either revisions in the traditional discipline or a broadly conceived alternative to it.

ON RULES AND METHOD

The suggestions I have just made may help us to understand
how certain operations come to be formulated into rules and
then combined into a method or art. For rules emerge into view
as the technical operations are carried out; they are, in fact,
generalizations based on those activities as judged according to
their effectiveness. In the mathematical writings Pascal misses
few opportunities to regularize and methodize. As a result his
general art of discovery gives rise to a little family of subordinate
arts. Direct and striking evidence on this point may be found in
the presentation he made in 1654 to the academy of Mersenne,
in which he reviewed the "fruits mûrs," of his, or as he expresses
it, "our" geometry.

The list includes thirteen items, all of which report briefly his
results, but four of the entries contain explicit references to
method or art, and two others imply such references, I think.
Actually, he uses the list to accomplish several things. At first he
alludes to the problem treated and the solution found; and then,
at or near the end of the item, he mentions method. In almost
every case there is an adjective or some other qualification
pointing out the advantages and innovative aspects of his way of
posing and solving the problem in question. And, finally, he
defines at some point the relation between his work and that of
his predecessors, indicating the progress he has made.

Two treatises, he says, have already been published, both of
them dealing with problems in number theory. In the second of
these, concerning numbers that are multiples of other numbers,
he tells us that he has found a method for discovering quickly
those other numbers (or factors); and it calls for nothing more
than the simple addition of integers. In this little description, he
manages to refer to a method, to characterize the principle
around which it is built, and then to say, by implication, that it
is easy to apply.

All of the remaining treatises are to appear in published form
later, "s'il plaît à Dieu"; in any case Pascal assures us that they
are complete. The next item on the list, having to do with
numbers that are "magiquement magiques," contains, again, a

mention of the fact that Pascal is ready to present a new method for this technique of inscribing numbers in squares so that they have, when added, certain prescribed characteristics (such as the property of giving always the same sum when the columns or ranks composing the squares are added). He has not only, he says, furnished a way of solving the problem on a level that is relatively easy (as when the square is left whole); he has also found a way to deal with such magic numbers in situations that are much more difficult (as when one removes one by one the outer bands of numbers, thus reducing systematically the size of the square in which the numbers are inscribed). Once again, his habit of thought about his accomplishments comes to the fore. He wants us to know that he has located a method for solving the problems in question, and that his method has advantages; or specifically, here, that it not only does relatively easy things – it can solve problems that are much more difficult. Incidentally, this kind of problem, which posits a framework wherein elements are to be placed so as to satisfy a particular condition, reminds us graphically of the investigative situation analyzed above, where statements are to be assembled in a disciplinary context; and, on occasion, the context itself will be modified, as here the original boundaries of the figure containing the numbers are removed and new boundaries set.

The two instances just mentioned carried the suggestion of novelty; but that suggestion is emphasized in the next item. Passing from arithmetic to geometry, Pascal refers to his work on tangents to circles (*tactiones circulares*, in the Latin text). He has found a generalized method of solving these problems that goes beyond all that the ancients had done, and beyond the work of Viète, who had restored the ancient work on the topic. But that is not all: Pascal has also generalized such contacts to a remarkable degree ("mais encore généralisés au point qu'ils supportent avec peine le même titre") (L102b; MIII033). He makes a similar claim for his work on the tangents to spheres (*tactiones sphaericae*) where, according to his indications, he has followed the same method as before, continuing thus the process of generalization. He adds a little compliment to himself, to the effect that his demonstration takes scarcely a single page. The

third item in this group, on the subject of tangents to cones
(*tactiones conicae*), shows the sequence at work in Pascal's mind:
it is a methodical march from circles to spheres to cones.

Pascal notifies the academy that in another *opusculum* he has
studied solid loci (*loci solidi*), or the problem of determining the
location of points with reference to conic sections. He says that
the treatise is complete in every respect. In presenting the next
item, on plane loci (*loci plani*), or the problem of determining the
location of points with reference exclusively to straight lines and
circles, Pascal touches on all the themes I mentioned above: the
explicit references to his results, to what was previously known,
to the novelty of his method, and to the advantages of his
approach. He has ready, he says, "... not only the loci that time
saved from the ancients, not only those that the most celebrated
geometrician of our age has mastered, after having restored
those of the ancients, but even more that were unknown until
now, which include the preceding and go far beyond them, by
means of a method that one may believe to be absolutely new,
since it gives new results by a way that is, however, much shorter
than before" (L102a; M111033).

Regarding conic sections, the next item on his list and a
subject that had long fascinated him, Pascal speaks expansively
once more. He has a complete treatise ("opus completum") on
these figures, including not only everything worked out by
Apollonius of Perga, but also innumerable other results. There
is a reference to his method, as he reminds us that he solved all
problems using essentially as his point of departure a single
proposition. It was already noteworthy to have so much come
out of so little; but Pascal adds that he made the basic discovery
when he was only sixteen years old.

Pascal mentions as the tenth item of his catalogue a "method
of perspective" ("perspectivae methodus"). No method that
has been or can be invented, he says, will be more advantageous,
since his new way depends on the intersection of two straight
lines only. Then he adds, in the same modest vein, that it is
absolutely impossible to be briefer ("sane nihil brevius esse
potest" (L102c; M111034)).

We reach something like a climax as Pascal describes his

achievement in connection with the calculation of probability, or as he calls it, the geometry or science of chance. It is, he tells us, a completely new treatise ("novissima tractatio"), one that deals with a subject absolutely unexplored hitherto. Chance or the fortuitous does not lend itself to treatment in terms of experience or of natural necessity. Reason has to work all the harder in the face of this challenge, he says. But thanks to geometry he has reduced chance or contingency to an art that partakes of the certainty of science, and it is progressing boldly ("audacter"). Joining the rigor of demonstrations to the uncertainty of chance, and reconciling two things so contradictory in appearance, the new discipline may take for itself the paradoxical, even stupefying, title of *aleae Geometria*.

This instance supplies a fine example of the way in which the art of discovery moves, at times and with good results, technical devices from one area to another. To deal with uncertain future events Pascal saw the possibility of transferring devices and demonstrative techniques of geometry onto a new terrain, into a new frame of reference, where they might replace ineffectual vocabularies based on common experience or on the notion of natural determinism. By selecting and refining a new and different set of terms for use on the subject-matter under study, he opened the way to truly novel discoveries. And, going hand in hand with the impulse to discover was the impulse to generalize, to formulate a new art and, as he suggests, a growing scientific discipline.

As he nears the end of this résumé Pascal reports that some current researches, though rather well in hand, are not finished nor, indeed, worth finishing; that his treatise on the vacuum will soon be published, though not before submitting it to the society for its approval: he had experienced the value and weight of its judgment in connection with the *machine d'arithmé-tique*, of which he had been the timid inventor ("quod timidus inveneram" (LI03a; MIII035)). Such are, he says in conclusion, the mature fruits of his "Geometria"; the author would consider himself happy, if, after having communicated those fruits to them, he should receive in exchange some of their works.

It is a fascinating list. These little paragraphs provide a very useful supplement to what we have been able to infer from an examination of the mathematical and experimental works themselves. They show us how Pascal himself liked to think of his achievements and discoveries, how he surveyed them in retrospect. Through the rhetorical flourishes and touches of vanity, we can discern once more, in a new and non-technical context, some of the recurrent themes in the working of his habit of invention.

He starts with an awareness – sometimes expressed in an explicit and detailed way – of what is known in the field of his particular inquiry and of what remains to be investigated there. He has a sense of alternatives to whatever is traditional in it, and this frees him for an original act of choice, a selection of new topics as sources of concepts. He knows how, once that selection is made, to specify the new ideas so that they may bring fresh light to the different levels of his problem. All of those operations are accomplished with a high degree of awareness regarding the successive steps of the whole process and the framework within which it takes place. He readily formulates the rules that underlie the operations, doing so with a comparative eye, for he constantly seeks a way of thinking about the problem that is easier, shorter, more general than anything known before. Then, from formulating the rules to composing a method is but a small step. On finishing his task, when he has shown us the problem, the solution, the operations, the rules, and the method, Pascal usually adds, not without enthusiasm, a note recalling the advantages of his inventions.

DISCOVERY AND REDISCOVERY

Pascal's art of discovery takes on an added note of complexity and interest if one considers it in a historical light. As we have noted, it represents a revolt against the scholastic way of approaching physics, which is ontological rather than mathematical. Pascal's way of thinking – and his view was shared by the scientific community in which he participated – has the character of a *jugement sans appel*: that earlier kind of physics and the terminology that supported it must go. We have, therefore – and obviously – a case of change by the introduction of a new set of concepts and heuristic devices intended to replace a lexicon incapable of explaining in a satisfactory way certain natural phenomena. But this process of discovery is not entirely pure. It depends on a return to the past and on a recovery of what some ancients thought about the physical world and the relation of mathematics to it. Pascal's mentality and discoveries do not come out of thin air; his work is unimaginable without the treatises of Euclid, Archimedes, and Apollonius. He finds, learns, and formulates an art, but in an important sense what he does is to *re*-discover some things already known and used brilliantly in Greece as early as the third century B.C. He and his scientific colleagues accomplished in their fields what others around them were doing in literature and in the fine arts: a leap back over medieval habits of thought to times in classical antiquity that offered congenial minds and models of achievement.

Still, one has to add a nuance to such statements. Pascal and his friends do not dismiss their predecessors among the ancients, far from it, but they do not admire them dogmatically, either. The competitive attitude that the moderns had toward one another – for an eloquent example of it, recall the matter of the *roulette* curve and the contest concerning it as instituted and recounted by Pascal – extended to their elders. The scientists of the seventeenth century thought of themselves, in effect, as being engaged with the ancients in something like intellectual Olympic games. Descartes and Pascal and Fermat meant not only to know and understand what the ancients knew and understood, not only to see if they could add something to the received knowledge, but also to surpass the old attainments. The element of reinvention or rediscovery, as I have called it, was genuine; it consisted essentially in restoring an ancient style of thinking in the study of mathematics and nature: that sufficed to create an attitude and a family of minds. But it left ample room for individual differences, as the stars of the "century of genius" determined exactly how they would redefine the generic style, and what content they would express within its limits. The example of Pascal shows how the two levels of consideration apply. He could learn from Archimedes ("O qu'il a éclaté aux esprits," he exclaims in the *Pensées*), and, at the same time, develop in remarkable detail his own conception of invention and demonstration. It is appropriate to notice, then, two aspects of change or novelty with regard to the art of discovery as applied by Pascal and his scientific colleagues: (1) change by revolution and replacement for scholastic or otherwise outworn habits of thought; and (2) change by original invention that begins with insights and principles recovered from ancient practitioners of arithmetic, geometry, and physics.

TWO *GENII*

The third sentence of the address to the "celebrated academy" of scientists, in which Pascal made an inventory of his accomplishments, contains a distinction that meant a great deal to him, I believe. He proposes, on the one hand, the "genium audax inventionis," the bold gift or capacity for discovery; only a few have it; and on the other hand, there is the "genium elegans demonstrationis" (L101b; M111031), the elegant or subtle gift of demonstration; even fewer have that. The two terms, when combined, produce a third possibility; and this double capacity is found in fewer still. Pascal plays with the conciseness of Latin as he indicates the distribution: *paucis*, *paucioribus*, *paucissimis*. Although, for delicacy's sake, he enters a disclaimer, it is obvious that he believes himself to be in the third category.

The distinction calls our attention to two fundamental intellectual operations, the first of which has been, of course, the subject of the present section. And the two are really distinct for Pascal. Finding out is not the same thing as proving, though the interrelation is close: the latter takes up and puts into proper sequence what is given in the former. Looked at in the general context of the arts of the mind, Pascal's ideas on invention and demonstration evoke the ghosts of two traditional arts: rhetoric and logic. (Actually the art of statement or interpretation, with which I began this whole discussion, serves to fill out something like a trivium, for it contains the rudiments of a grammar.) As I have said, each talent involved in the present distinction leads to the other. With an art of statement behind us, and now, also, an art of invention that selects and specifies viable concepts for use in those statements, we may go on to the art of establishing connections – sequences in things and consequences in thought and language – since that would seem to be the proper work of the *genium elegans demonstrationis*.

PRESENTATION (1)

ANOTHER OBJECT OF METHODICAL ATTENTION

After interpretation and recovery, after invention and discovery – but, it must be added, also in company with those methods – another basic intellectual technique emerges within the controlling perspective of geometric: the art of connection and presentation. Once again we must fix our attention on statements, though in a different way. We looked first at statements as items to be interpreted, as requiring a special kind of effort, so that one might see how the words carry meanings and how both words and meanings may be applied to things. In the art of discovery, statements reappeared, in a new guise, as dependent on conceptual elements or terms that had been found and specified to the needs of a particular investigation. In recovery and discovery one tends to examine and analyze single statements. But statements rarely occur in isolation; they appear much more often in the sequences of discourse; and in discourse what interests us and Pascal is precisely the pattern of relations that holds among statements or facts. Questions about these relations arise especially when the truth of a statement is contested. Then it becomes necessary to show that the statement really belongs in the discourse, that it does not contradict other things said, that it either stands on its own feet, in the light of its own *évidence*, or it needs another statement as its support, and that it occupies its rightful place in the flow of reasoning and language. It is the business of an art of connections to answer such questions.

Pascal surely felt and knew this concern for the texture of

discourse, not only in ordinary relations and conversation, but also and particularly in technical writing. For he was an extraordinarily competent constructor of technical discourse in geometry, in arithmetic, in physics, and even in mechanics – all related subject-matters, no doubt, all tied to mathematics and the study of the physical world, but still genuinely diverse. For such consistent and orderly discourse in all those fields to exist it seems to me that we must posit in Pascal's mind, as an indispensable precondition, as a scientific *idée de derrière la tête*, the awareness of an object of reflection and study common to those various fields. Here what I want to suggest is: *sequential ordering*. I mean a dynamic theme that may be exemplified in many ways: in a line of thought, in a succession of statements, in a series of events or movements. Then, in planning particular investigations, in reflecting on the results, and in putting them into writing, Pascal judges in the light of the basic theme; he composes variations on it, according to promptings furnished by the habit of presentation linked to that theme.

HOW THAT OBJECT IS CONCEIVED

The idea of truth stands in the background; I place that even before the idea of sequential ordering. And so the connections he seeks will be true, accurate, certain. That means that he must recall and obey the two conditions of truth in statement, that were so forcefully put forward in the letter to Noël. A statement is true independently and axiomatically or it has its force by a kind of contagion, by its relation to a prior truth. Obviously, though, we must narrow the focus. Pascal has an art and a habit of making connections, but what sort of connections? What special insight has been fruitful for him? The formula *antecedent–consequent* is useful again, and in two steps.

(1) The pair may be taken as designating an order of succession and presentation. If the first or initiating factor is given, the other must follow; and in such a case we have a true and indubitable sequence. We have referred to antecedents and consequents before, but until now they have appeared in a context either of the interpretation of statements or of the

discovery and specification of terms. The emphasis falls here on the fact of connection – and not only in a logical sense: the relation may also be temporal or spatial. At this juncture, then, Pascal's leading insight and the habit of mind associated with it would appear to bear on detailed acts of observing or assembling or expressing sequences, which he conceives originally or primarily as pairs in which the second member depends on the first by a logical or natural link.

(2) Of course, as he works with sequences and formulates discourses in the fields that interest him, he does not stop with two terms alone. He aspires to build long sequences; and, in accordance with his intuitions concerning *évidence*, each such chain can only be a series of connected pairs, every member of which functions, in a logical overlap, both as an antecedent and as a consequent. As each item in the long procession is established, it furnishes the point of connection for the next in line. Pascal performs many variations on this theme.

END AND RELEVANT OPERATIONS

In analyzing his approach to problems of connection and presentation we are fortunate in having a text that is very explicit. In the pages of *De l'esprit géométrique* he discusses openly and fully the characteristics of an art that is to be set in his intellectual armory, according to my general hypothesis, alongside those of interpretation and discovery. (Retrospectively, it throws much light on the other two.) Here he is perfectly straightforward as to his experience with books and men, referring to his emergent convictions, to a proper subject-matter or set of questions, growing out of that experience, to the need to define the operations suitable to the end sought; and we encounter here once more his tendency to move eventually into the formulation of rules, which are then brought together into a unified and complete art.

Two things stand out that clarify and confirm assumptions made in the first two sections of this chapter. First, Pascal offers primarily not a method written out on paper and designed to be examined there in detail but an ensemble of procedures that one may come to possess in a vital and personal way. Once attained, it lifts one above the level of accidental or irrelevant or routine operations. And that leads me to my second point: in *De l'esprit géométrique* Pascal returns again and again to the aim of the art he is analyzing. His conception of art is classical in its dualism; it consists essentially of means, but of course those means have no significance or value apart from the fact that they have been found to be effective in accomplishing a known and definite end. In the present instance, the end is connected discourse having the quality of certainty, whether one thinks of it primarily as language or as thought, whether the connotations are linguistic or mental; but the emphasis that Pascal puts here on the notion of end or aim helps us to do justice to a principle that was seen less clearly in our earlier discussions of his arts.

What are the operations that will lead to success in accomplishing the desired end? To understand the views of Pascal, it is well here to consider the two sources of operations that may be seen at work in these richly significant pages. The pair is a familiar one in seventeenth-century thought: one encounters it in literary criticism and poetic theory, when critics and readers presume to say what the poet is and does; one sees it in moral discourses, when theorists define the moral ideal of the *honnête homme*; one sees it in philosophy, when Descartes builds on it his notion of *méthode*. I mean the couple: nature and art. And so, likewise, some elements that Pascal needs here in the process of demonstration have their source in nature and a natural light. One receives them, one does not acquire them. They are indispensable, but not sufficient. But the rest is a matter of art, of conscious planning and technique. In discussing both factors, Pascal insists on applying a strict criterion of clarity: let there be no obscurity, no doubt about what comes from nature and what we add to it. As we undertake to demonstrate something, we must have a clear view of the conditions and requirements on each side.

In constructing a demonstration we must define and prove:

Cette véritable méthode, qui formerait les démonstrations dans la plus haute excellence, s'il était possible d'y arriver, consisterait en deux choses principales: l'une, de n'employer aucun terme dont on n'eût auparavant expliqué nettement le sens; l'autre, de n'avancer jamais aucune proposition qu'on ne démontrât par des vérités déjà connues; c'est-à-dire, en un mot, à définir tous les termes et à prouver toutes les propositions. Mais, pour suivre l'ordre même que j'explique, il faut que je déclare ce que j'entends par définition. (L349b; Mɪɪɪ393)

It is pleasant to note that, in a discourse about geometrical method, Pascal feels constrained to proceed reflexively and to write geometrically about geometry. He adds, immediately after the lines just quoted, a bit of justification for what he is about to say: "Mais, pour suivre l'ordre même que j'explique, il faut que je déclare ce que j'entends par définition."

DEFINING

Now we see one of the consequences of the controlling distinction mentioned above. Pascal explains the two indispensable operations by referring them in turn to what originates in nature and to what depends on art, method, or convention. Some terms are naturally indefinable, just as some propositions are unprovable. Such terms have a kind of obviousness about them, corresponding to an analogous quality in the self-evident propositions. One may try to justify them by definitions and demonstrations, but the effort is unnecessary and even vain, because what one ends with is less clear than what one began with. And since the meanings of these terms and the force of these axiomatic propositions will be givens in any discussion, they supply a basis for demonstration on which all may reach certainty and agreement. To proceed in this fashion at the outset is to follow the "ordre de la géométrie," which at one point Pascal characterizes as "cette judicieuse science"(L351b; Mɪɪɪ400).

In the presence of such terms and statements, all we can do is to recognize them, bring them out into the open, pay attention to them. The case is different with the terms and propositions that are not obvious: those who are engaged in the discourse have the responsibility of fixing their sense and status. The relatively passive attitude with regard to what is known by nature gives way to an active posture and attitude. Nonetheless, everything is uncovered, visible: indefinable terms will be indicated and all terms whose reference is not immediately clear will be defined explicitly, and once and for all. The meanings of terms, in genuine geometrical discourse and in discourse that aspires to its qualities, will not vary as the discussion proceeds. If we follow his advice and lock each term in a univocal sense, we may revert, at any point in the reasoning, to the agreed-upon definition for the term defined, so as to avoid any confusion as to what is being said and understood.

Early in *De l'esprit géométrique* he explains that in the act of defining one substitutes, for the sake of convenience and brevity, one word for a group of words; but he comments at once on the utility of always keeping in mind the possibility of a return to the full formula for which the term stands:

Rien n'éloigne plus promptement et plus puissamment les surprises captieuses des sophistes que cette méthode, qu'il faut avoir toujours présente, et qui suffit seule pour bannir toutes sortes de difficultés et d'équivoques. (L349d; MIII394)

Several times Pascal returns to this idea of substituting definitions for defined terms. Here, in another example, as he sums up the whole process of demonstration, he adds at the end a clause on the place of substitutions as elements in the process of producing a really convincing demonstration:

Et il est facile de voir qu'en observant cette méthode on est sûr de convaincre, puisque, les termes étant tous entendus et parfaitement exempts d'équivoques par les définitions, et les principes étant accordés, si dans la démonstration on substitue toujours mentalement les définitions à la place des définis, la force invincible des conséquences ne peut manquer d'avoir tout son effet. (L356d; MIII418)

THE NAME OR THE THING?

Implied in what I have just been saying is Pascal's way of understanding the classic distinction between a *définition de nom* and a *définition de chose*. The general context here is that of the operations, the mental activities, involved in the art of connections and sequential orderings. One of these, as we have seen, consists in defining, and the other in proving. It now becomes necessary to note the two fundamentally different ways in which terms may be defined. Both fit into a discussion of sequential ordering, in the sense that each in its way contributes to the beginning of the reasoning or demonstrative process. The great emphasis laid by Pascal on the topic of definition clearly comes from that fact: you must have secure starting points for your demonstration; without them the results can only be unsatisfactory. Now, the one kind of definition that really interests the geometricians, and consequently the kind that Pascal wants to discuss, is the *définition de nom*. As I have suggested, it is designed simply as a handy means of abridging the discourse. The process of nominal definition includes three steps: (1) one first designates clearly and unmistakably what the subject of the discourse is; (2) a descriptive formula is used to say that which has been designated or indicated, using always terms that are understood perfectly; (3) then, with that group of words in mind, one selects a single term for use instead of the group. Thus a *définition de nom* makes it possible to use one word for a train – which might be long – of descriptive words.

A definition of this kind does not say anything about the essence or nature of the subject indicated. That is the business of the *définition de chose*. And strictly speaking, this second kind of definition is, in Pascal's view, a proposition, and it functions like a proposition in the process of demonstration. If you pronounce the word *temps*, everyone knows, he says, what it is that you are designating, what you mean, by the term; but if you go on to add that time is a measure of movement, you have gone onto the terrain of essence or nature. Having gone beyond the simple designation of the word "time" or "temps," you have left the level of definition and put yourself onto that of demonstration. Your definition-proposition has to find a place then in the sequence of propositions that constitutes your discourse. It is subject to the conditions regulating the process of proving rather than the process of defining.

On the other hand, in proposing a *définition de nom*, one points to the subject of the discourse and identifies it in descriptive

formula involving more than one word; one makes no essen-
tialistic claims, no pretense of giving or knowing the nature of
the thing defined. Then, for the sake of saving breath and time,
and for simplicity's sake, one makes known what single word
will be used instead of the phrase. As the reasoning progresses,
one can always bring back the full formula and substitute it for
the single word that is being utilized. Incidentally, there are
difficulties in Pascal's exposition, assumptions, and details that
need development. For example, it is not always entirely clear
whether in a nominal definition he wishes to restrict our
attention exclusively to language, or whether he wishes to
include designation and reference. I have chosen the latter
interpretation, but have tried to keep something of his occasional emphasis on the essentially verbal character of these
définitions de nom.

I should like to stress, as Pascal does, that any attempt to say
what a thing is in essence moves out of the realm of designation
and description, and belongs to the demonstrative phase of the
discourse. One must not confuse the two operations of defining
and proving. He may say, as one consequence of his distinction,
that nominal definitions – the only kind used in geometry, he
asserts – are free (*libres*); the fact of their being drawn so plainly
and explicitly at the beginning of the demonstration precludes
any disagreement or contradiction. *Définitions de chose* enjoy no
such advantage. Since they have actually the status of propositions, it is perfectly possible for speakers and writers to be in
disagreement about them.

PROVING

If, to be satisfactory, the definitions require words that are
either clear in themselves or that are explained, what of the
propositions or statements that are to serve as principles?
Something quite like the same argument appeals to Pascal. One
will use in demonstration only propositions that are self-evident
or that have been proved already. The parallel is complete: use
terms that are clear or explained; use propositions that are self-

evident or already proved. With terms so defined and with propositions so established, he assures us that we have the grounding of the demonstration, the foundation of the edifice:

…il serait inutile de proposer ce qu'on veut prouver et d'en entreprendre la démonstration, si on n'avait auparavant défini clairement tous les termes qui ne sont pas intelligibles; et qu'il faut de même que la démonstration soit précédée de la demande de principes évidents qui y sont nécessaires, car si on n'assure pas le fondement, on ne peut assurer l'édifice… (L356c; Mɪɪɪ418)

Again a similarity presents itself. One avoids unnecessary clarification of terms, and, likewise, unnecessary establishment of propositions: why attempt to demonstrate something that is already clearly known? After we have completed the act of discernment, the act of seeing what is appropriate or – rather, necessary – for demonstration, Pascal urges us on to the operations required, using always the model of geometry and its characteristic sequences. We have demonstrated a proposition when we have shown it to be consistent with and dependent on clearly defined terms and obvious principles. Their light spreads over the whole process and settles on the conclusions.

According to his usual custom, Pascal undertakes at the end of the exposition in *De l'esprit géométrique* to condense things into rules. He manages to summarize all the operations that he has been describing and analyzing, along with the criteria supporting them, in a few short imperative formulas that cover the problem area and form something that is complete. As an introduction to the rules, he writes:

Il importe donc bien de les comprendre et de les posséder, et c'est pourquoi, pour rendre la chose plus facile et plus présente, je les donnerai toutes en ce peu de règles qui renferment tout ce qui est nécessaire pour la perfection des définitions, des axiomes et des démonstrations, et par conséquent de la méthode entière des preuves géométriques de l'art de persuader. (L356d; Mɪɪɪ418–19)

He gives three rules for definitions, three for axioms, and two for demonstration. Although the total of eight seems not a large number, Pascal wants to abbreviate still more. Three of the rules are not, strictly speaking, necessary, since they merely tell

us not to do superfluous things. The suggestion appears to be
that if some of those are done in defining and proving, the
process is not really vitiated; the demonstration will simply
include some uncalled-for furniture. If one subtracts those three
rules, the essential core is reached, consisting of five rules. They
are absolutely indispensable for perfection in demonstration.

It is interesting at this point to look back to what Pascal led
us to expect in the opening remarks of *De l'esprit géométrique* and
then observe what he has in fact done. Apparently, he had in
mind at the origin four distinct stages in presenting his "art de
démontrer": there would be treatments (1) of terms or
definitions, (2) of axioms or principles, then (3) of demonstrations – those three subjects as treated forming the first and
major part of the work – and finally (4) of what he calls a *suite
géométrique*. The explanation of *suite géométrique* would thus have
constituted one of the two main parts of the projected treatise.
He gives his outline at the end of the short introduction to *De
l'esprit géométrique*:

> Et parce que cet art consiste en deux choses principales, l'une de
> prouver chaque proposition en particulier, l'autre de disposer toutes
> les propositions dans le meilleur ordre, j'en ferai deux sections, dont
> l'une contiendra les règles de la conduite des démonstrations géomé-
> triques, c'est-à-dire méthodiques et parfaites, et la seconde compren-
> dra celles de l'ordre géométrique, c'est-à-dire méthodique et accompli:
> de sorte que les deux ensemble enfermeront tout ce qui sera nécessaire
> pour la conduite du raisonnement à prouver et discerner les vérités,
> lesquelles j'ai dessein de donner entières. (L348d–49a; Mɪɪɪ391)

Of the four subjects Pascal has spent his time and energy on the
first and the second, in particular; he includes some explanation
of the third – demonstration – though we are left, it seems to
me, to assume that in its specific operations it may be identified
in or extracted from the *Elements* of Euclid, or at least from the
study of geometrical treatises. He does not develop his thought
on the subject of demonstration; even more remarkable is the
fact that he gives almost no attention to the fourth stage,
concerning the arrangement of demonstrations into a satisfying
and complete order. After stating the rules of the method, he
comes back to the subject of that important second part of his

treatise, but once more, what we have is a promise, and it trails off:

Voilà les cinq règles qui forment tout ce qu'il y a de nécessaire pour rendre les preuves convaincantes, immuables, et, pour tout dire, géométriques; et les huit règles ensemble les rendent encore plus parfaites.
  Je passe maintenant à celle de l'ordre dans lequel on doit disposer les propositions, pour être dans une suite excellente et géométrique... Après avoir établi... (L357b; MIII421)

A remark in Pascal's defense or in explanation suggests itself at this point. In an intellectual project of this sort, the beginnings are of such importance that one needs, as a matter of sound procedure, to be prolix. These considerations furnish the grounding for everything else. Whatever he may have intended when he started *De l'esprit géométrique*, Pascal has at least established firmly the criteria of clarity, distinctness, self-evidence, and valid consequence that must regulate all the acts – from analysis to combination to discernment or refutation – that fall within the bounds of true writing or speaking (as Pascal conceives it here). He makes us thoroughly aware that everything must be done in the light of those values; and he shows us by general arguments and some examples what the elements of demonstrations look like when examined under that light.
  One can infer with some probability, I think, what Pascal meant by *suite géométrique* if we observe the sequences of topics that he builds up in his mathematical treatises. When he considers numbers, for example, in working with the *triangle arithmétique*, he arranges them in a table of *ordres* or series. He passes from a sequence of units $(1,1,1,1,1 ...)$ to the natural sequence of numbers, formed by the addition of a unit to each preceding term in the series $(1,2,3,4,5 ...)$; then to the sequence formed by the successive addition of each natural number to the preceding term, thus forming the "triangular" numbers in series $(1,3,6,10,15 ...)$; then, by the addition of each triangular number to its preceding term, we arrive at the order of "pyramidal" numbers $(1,4,10,20,35 ...)$; the same operation, applied to the pyramidal numbers yields the order of the

"triangulo-triangular" numbers (1,5,15,35,70...); after that
comes a sixth order (1,6,21,56,126...), to which Pascal assigns
no technical name; and so on to infinity.

We see even more clearly the tendency to lay out problems in
an orderly way, when he turns to demonstrations in geometry.
Take the case of the little work (actually the surviving remnant
of a much longer treatise) on the "generation of conic sections":
Pascal generates and defines them in a progression that goes
from point, to line, to angle, to closed curved lines, which give
the ellipse, then to open curved lines, which give the parabola
and the hyperbola. Or, in connection with the *roulette*, he seeks
centers of gravity, first, of curved lines, then of surfaces both
plane and curved, and then of solid figures. In every one of these
instances, which, I think, tell us something about *suites
géométriques*, there is a movement from simplicity at the outset of
a progression to complexity at its end. Of course, in extensions
of the geometrical method to matters other than mathematical,
it would be necessary to find something analogous to such
arithmetical and geometrical sequences of topics.

For another thing, we have to recognize that in *De l'esprit
géométrique* his mind is not focused simply on his main subject,
nor on the exact proportions according to which he might treat
it. At one point he engages in a long discussion of the difficulty
that some people have with the style of geometrical reasoning
and discourse. It could have become, but does not quite do so,
something parallel to the pages in the *Pensées* on the distinction
between the *esprit de géométrie* and the *esprit de finesse*. And the fact
that geometry does not try to define some of its most important
initial terms leads him into some reflections on the whole of
Nature, on its composition in terms of time, movement, space
and number; and from there the transition is not difficult to the
theme of the two infinites that characterize every one of those
basic dimensions of nature. And, as usual, he cannot touch that
string without doing a modulation into moral considerations,
for the infinites give us all a good lesson in humility.

THE ART OF SEQUENCES

I should like at this point to look through what Pascal is saying and doing and to comment on it in a slightly more abstract way, relating my remarks to the theme of sequential ordering, which is fundamental in the art we are discussing. His enterprise assumes, as a *sine qua non*, the possibility of arriving at the least parts or elements relevant to the problem at hand. It does not matter whether one is moving in a context that emphasizes things or thoughts or words. The process of demonstration or deduction cannot begin until absolutely basic atoms or ideas or terms have been found. Only after such an ultimate moment of reductive analysis and clear vision can one undertake with security the task of construction, the task of combining according to rule the basic elements (mainly linguistic in *De l'esprit géométrique*; but geometrical entities have least parts, also) into larger and larger wholes. Without this initial coming to rest we cannot avoid getting into the confusion of infinite regress; and Pascal evokes explicitly that possibility. By contrast, there is no closure in the other direction, for, strictly speaking, the conclusion of the deductive process never comes into sight. Although we require a fixed starting point, the other end of the line is open.

Surprisingly, in spite of all the arguments in its favor, the method of geometry is a second-best method.

Je ne puis mieux faire entendre la conduite qu'on doit garder pour rendre les démonstrations convaincantes, qu'en expliquant celle que la géométrie observe, et je ne le puis faire parfaitement sans donner auparavant l'idée d'une méthode encore plus éminente et plus accomplie, mais où les hommes ne sauraient jamais arriver : car ce qui passe la géométrie nous surpasse ... (L349a; Miii392–93)

The ideal would have been to define everything and to prove everything. But, as I have just said, there Pascal runs into the indefinables; or at least, into terms that are already clearer than any attempt at definition can make them; and exactly the same thing is true of certain propositions – the ones that have the force of axioms.

Actually it is well to keep in mind this precondition, so to say, that underlies all of what Pascal does in this text: an ideal performance would do one thing; but we have to be satisfied with something else, something less than the ideal; our efforts can never bring about a result that is truly comprehensive in definition and proof. However, we do have a kind of certainty above and beyond human opinion in the firmness and stability that nature makes possible, by the fact that we have immediate apprehension of axioms and primitive terms like "time," "movement," "space," and "number," which are, of course, the starting points of geometry.

As the constructive phase of the method takes over, Pascal must form his elements into propositions; and propositions, whether they are axioms or derivatives from axioms, will consist of terms assembled into units. From that point, and in succession, the last-arrived-at complexes become units. There is a certain ambiguity about them, in that what are in fact collocations of parts serve, on a new level of consideration, as elements. And these new elements are, in their turn, assembled into reasonings or demonstrations. Just as there are rules and criteria for the defining of terms and for the assembling of terms into propositions, there must be rules for arranging the propositions into demonstrations. These new rules regulate the process of establishing the connection, the sequential con-nection, between the axioms and the consequences. Pascal foresees the fourth and final phase of the method as the task of bringing together the demonstrations into the geometrical sequence. The demonstrations having now become building blocks in still another whole or complex, the next unit would appear to be a treatise, a complete technical account of the way in which the original problem has been analyzed and solved.

Obviously, certain criteria are presiding over the whole process, with its stages and decisions that have to be made to keep it going. They apply to the three phases of the process: first, finding the elements and examining them in themselves; second, differentiating them from other elements present in the problem situation; and then, third, combining them into a unit, a complex. Each of these operations requires a specific virtue: clarity in any view of the elements or ideas or terms seen in themselves, with reference to their designata; distinctness in any view of them that is collective, that takes up into a single glance the elements in their plurality. All possibility of confusion and ambiguity must really be avoided in those first two phases. As for the combined elements, in the third phase, there must occur a kind of transference of evidence from the principle that has been granted or proven already to the proposition that depends on it. Clarity, distinctness, coherence: those would seem to be the criteria presupposed by Pascal's conception of the method of geometry. The last presides over the act of combining terms and judging the links, the consequential links, between propositions; this is what brings into existence a demonstration; and it focuses our attention specifically on the importance of sequential ordering in this art of connections.

Perhaps we should note here the linear character of the demonstrative process: there is a definite beginning, leading deductively to something else in the middle, which serves in turn as the beginning for further deduction as one approaches the end. Pascal seems usually to be looking forward, once the foundations of the line have been laid; but there is no reason, in theory, to prohibit one from looking backward, or analyzing backward from conclusions to premises: the same notes of *évidence* and intelligibility would be found. It is a fact, however, that Pascal's mind seems to work here in a single direction – away from discovery and the proposal of alleged truths and toward the complex that he wishes to construct. Assembling statements into chains of demonstrated truths appeals more to him than the movement in the other direction, though, of course, the process of any axiomatic system like geometry is, and essentially so, both analytic and synthetic, since the two impulses imply each other in the combinatory process.

Pascal writes confidently about the completeness of his method, with which he is clearly well pleased. He believes that he has thought of everything. In the foreground he sets out the argument regarding the elements, the demonstrations, and the longer sequences. In the background his basic terms, taken together, form an ensemble very much like the general terminology that I have been using: end of the art – operations conducive to the end – rules guiding the whole process – method/art drawing the rules into a unified discourse – acquisition both by understanding and by doing. And the whole thing becomes really manageable as well as useful, since Pascal has reduced it to a bare minimum. But he includes an emphatic bit of advice: although one can get quickly some understanding of the art, one must make allowance for the time and effort required if one is to come to possess it as a habit. I am grateful to Pascal for stressing the point. It is, of course, a basic thesis of this book that one way to think of him is as an intellectual artist, and, indeed, as *possessing* several arts of the mind. And that word must be stressed not only in thinking about Pascal himself but also in describing – as I am attempting to do – his *art de démontrer*. He uses the verb *posséder* several times in *De l'esprit géométrique* in the sense intended here. Until the art or method has become a matter of habit, until one owns and controls it as personal property, it is not really useful.

MONTAIGNE, AUGUSTINE, AND DESCARTES

He says the same thing somewhat differently by suggesting the question, how can we identify those who actually have this competence as part of their intellectual equipment? There are three sides to the art, as it applies to the solution of any problem: one must, he says, know the principles, then grasp the consequences, and, finally, be able to answer objections. Can the person who has made a statement relate it explicitly to principles, to consequences, to a line of demonstrative thought? And, if someone proposes objections, can he draw actively on what he knows in order to respond? Pascal sees a great difference between something that is said and happens to make sense, on the one hand, and something, on the other hand, that fits into or comes out of a demonstration and has, moreover, the power to defend itself. Here his discussion leads to some remarkable allusions.

But first he imagines someone who might pose some objections to his method. Thereupon he begins a little exercise in reflexive thinking. He has himself just evoked a situation in which an assertion is made, explained, and then defended. Putting himself into that very setting and playing his own game, so to speak, he imagines three objections to the exposition that he has just made of the geometrical method. One might assert, in the first place, that there is nothing new in the method proposed. And again, that the method is simple and easy to learn. And finally, that the method is, in fact, rather useless, "assez inutile." Pascal's way of replying to the objections strikes me as discursive rather than systematic (his beginning led us to expect the latter), though he does begin obviously with the first of his points: that the method he is promoting has nothing new or uncommon about it, and logicians have said the same or similar things. Here his answer is plain and comes quickly: actually only a few possess the method; as for logicians, their remarks about the matters at hand seem to Pascal to be descriptive, haphazard, and scattered. (And I would add, they lack the *sequential ordering* that must be present if one is to take statements seriously.) Referring to readers or interlocutors who have accepted his principles, he writes:

Mais s'ils sont entrés dans l'esprit de ces règles, et qu'elles aient assez fait d'impression pour s'y enraciner et s'y affermir, ils sentiront combien il y a de différence entre ce qui est dit ici et ce que quelques logiciens en ont peut-être décrit d'approchant au hasard, en quelques lieux de leurs ouvrages. (L357c; MKⅢ422)

I wish to return in a moment to this opposition between logic and geometry. As for the second objection, that the method is easy to learn, the lines just quoted show how Pascal conceives the problem: one must grasp the spirit of the rules, let them take root in the mind, allow them to become stabilized there. Only the geometricians know and have the method thus as a habit. Sustained effort is required to reach that state; and it is not difficult to discern who has attained it and who has not.

Pascal refers us to Montaigne and the chapter in the *Essais* on "l'art de conférer," and specifically to the passage in which Montaigne shows how it is possible for someone to say something intelligent but without understanding by chance or simply from memory. He approves of the procedure suggested by Montaigne: test the statement; ask questions of the speaker; treat what he has said coldly, to see if he will stand by what he has said. (Incidentally, one thinks here of Pascal's own technique in the *Pensées*: this reads like a version of the *renversement continuel du pour au contre*, and of the lines beginning "S'il se vante, je l'abaisse" (L514c, f130; S86, f163).) This subject obviously fascinates Pascal. He does a sort of algebra in laying out the cases.

He has just dealt with the case of a single speaker who makes an assertion that is then questioned by a listener who tests the opinion. Now he proceeds to a more complicated example, but one that illustrates beautifully what he has in mind. It is the case in which we apply the test of sequential ordering apropos of what *two* people say, when they say apparently the same thing. The judgment of the case comes down to this: one of the speakers sees the consequences of what he says, but the other does not. And at this point Pascal introduces two names: Descartes and Augustine. He picks up two principles from Augustine, both of which Descartes could be thought of as affirming also. In this little scenario, Augustine simply said them twelve hundred years before Descartes. One of the statements is that matter suffers from a natural and invincible incapacity for thought; and the other is that "je pense donc je suis," – the affirmation of existence as recognized in the act of thought itself. This pair of affirmations is present in the minds of both Augustine and Descartes, but not in the same way, says Pascal. The difference is such that one may wonder to whom effective authorship is to be attributed:

En vérité, je suis bien éloigné de dire que Descartes n'en soit pas le véritable auteur, quand même il ne l'aurait appris que dans la lecture de ce grand saint; car je sais combien il y a de différence entre écrire un mot à l'aventure sans y faire une réflexion plus longue et plus étendue et apercevoir dans ce mot une suite admirable de conséquences, qui prouve la distinction des natures matérielle et spirituelle, et en faire un principe ferme et soutenu d'une physique entière, comme Descartes a prétendu faire. (L358a; MIII424)

In the mind of Descartes the statements have results: "une suite admirable de consequences." Descartes establishes – he does

not simply assert – the distinction between spiritual and material natures, and proceeds to draw out of it a whole physics, *une
physique entière*. Pascal takes care not to commit himself to
accepting that physics as true, limiting himself to saying simply
that Descartes was able to see the consequences of his principles.
Although here, it would seem, Pascal had an opportunity to
point out that the geometrical method can go awry when the
premises are doubtful or mistaken, he passes over it.

He continues to develop his example and his basic idea, now
with some imagery involving seeds and soil: while a thought
may bear no fruit in one mind, it may produce in another *un
arbre admirable*. Incidentally, Descartes had himself used the
metaphor of a tree for indicating the spirit and the outlines of his
system, where metaphysics corresponds to the roots of a tree,
physics to the trunk, and particular sciences to the branches. I
believe that this may serve as another example of what Pascal
means by the expression "suite géométrique": Descartes had
worked out – or intended to work out – a whole tree, a totalizing
series of demonstrations. As a final development of his train of
thought, in which he has been comparing two minds at work,
Pascal reverses the order of presentation. What may have begun
as a well-elaborated thought in one mind may be taken up by
a superficial and imitative mind, in which it loses its true
excellence and fruitfulness.

DISCERNMENT AND ASSIMILATION

The art or method of demonstration coming out of geometry
does not appear in the text in isolation. It is not possible to
conceive it correctly *in abstracto* without relating it to other
intellectual modes, nor can we understand Pascal's idea and use
of it without raising the question of how he relates it, for
example, to logic. In a way the answer is easy and categorical,
if one takes the words of Pascal at their face value:

La méthode de ne point errer est recherchée de tout le monde. Les
logiciens font profession d'y conduire, les géomètres seuls y arrivent, et
hors de leur science et ce qui l'imite, il n'y a point de véritables
démonstrations. (L358c; Mɪɪɪ425–26)

In another way the answer to the question is relatively complex, and of course mostly to the detriment or demotion of logic.

(1) As a start, Pascal notes that the logicians propound the distinction between definitions of words and definitions of things. He attaches great weight to this distinction, insisting that the failure to observe it leads to many errors in reasoning. However, in developing and explaining the distinction he takes as his models not logicians but geometricians: their way of defining words, and especially their *définitions de nom*, are the only ones we hear anything about.

(2) Furthermore, Pascal recognizes on a more general level that the logicians have treated the operations of defining and of proving – which are doubtless the two most important things discussed in *De l'esprit de géométrie*. Nevertheless, he repeats the argument that we have just seen apropos of the two ways in which terms and rules may be present in minds: either superficially, accidentally, and that is the case of logicians, or demonstratively, and that will be the case of Pascal's disciples, for their words and statements will have their proper places in the texture of geometrical or quasi-geometrical discourse.

(3) But that is not all. Like Descartes before him, Pascal does not miss the opportunity to state some objections to syllogistic reasoning, that center-piece of traditional logic. There are two things wrong with the syllogism. It leads to treatments of great technicality, and to the entry of much jargon into the discussion: Barbara, Celarent, and the like. Pascal has no patience with such complication; it runs counter to his constant tendency in thinking about method to simplify and streamline. In fact, and this is the second point, it is another instance of a misguided art trying to make over a nature really sufficient unto itself. What I mean is that for Pascal and for his Port-Royalist friends syllogistic reasoning, though reducible to a few rules – if one insists – is actually something that can be left to nature. Quite early in the text Pascal indicates his preference for geometry as the source of the *véritables règles*:

Et je n'ai choisi cette science pour y arriver que parce qu'elle seule sait les véritables règles du raisonnement, et, sans s'arrêter aux règles des syllogismes qui sont tellement naturelles qu'on ne peut les ignorer, s'arrête et se fonde sur la véritable méthode de conduire le raisonnement en toutes choses, que presque tout le monde ignore, et qu'il est si avantageux de savoir... (L349a; MIII391)

In a paradoxical way one of the assumptions of the method about which Pascal is so enthusiastic comes back to this, that it depends on syllogistic reasoning, that it assumes such thinking as a natural basis for all the rest. The *Logique* or *Art de penser* of Port-Royal shows how one should relate the various phases of thought. The first three parts of the work take up the usual topics in the usual sequence: conception, judgment, and reasoning; and the authors admit readily that they have borrowed much from Aristotle. But they have added a fourth part. After the traditional subjects, developed and expounded in the practical and popularizing way that is characteristic of Arnauld and Nicole, they present a concluding section on "méthode" and on demonstration in the geometrical mode. Indicating their source, the authors of the *Logique* mention Pascal's text, and it does appear to have furnished them with the outline and much of the substance of their treatment. We may conclude, I think, that syllogistic reasoning is unavoidable and prior to geometry, but insufficient for perfect demonstration.

To return to Pascal's argument: if geometry replaces logic as a source of the art of demonstrative thinking, that fact will have an important consequence. Other sciences have not been conceived, as to structure and content, on the model of geometry. As presently constituted they have in them a large portion of confusion and obscurity. Although the practitioners of these other sciences do not understand what their situation is, the geometricians can see clearly where the problems lie:

Je veux donc faire entendre ce que c'est que démonstration par l'exemple de celles de géométrie, qui est presque la seule des sciences humaines qui en produise d'infaillibles, parce qu'elle seule observe la véritable méthode, au lieu que toutes les autres sont par une nécessité naturelle dans quelque sorte de confusion que les seuls géomètres savent extrêmement reconnaître. (L349b; MIII391–92)

The well-being of the sciences appears to depend on their relationship to geometry and its way of thinking, if they are to avoid the consequences of that *nécessité naturelle*.

Although Pascal has in mind marking the differences between the method of geometry and that of logic or other scientific enterprises, he also sees another discipline, the *art de persuader*, where, rather than differentiate, he can assimilate – and, indeed, end by bringing that art more or less completely into the orbit of geometrical discourse. About half-way into the text, when the second main section begins, it becomes clear, unmistakably clear, that the *art de démontrer* and the *art de persuader* are identical, at least as to logical structure.

In other words, Pascal has decided to subordinate rhetoric to geometry. It is true that in this section Pascal evokes an interpersonal situation: he assumes a speaker and an addressee or interlocutor, evoking imagery and a framework that have not always been present in the first, and more scientifically oriented, pages of *De l'esprit géométrique*. Into this rhetorical situation, however, Pascal imports all of his principles and rules; or perhaps one should say, to be more exact, that into his preferred geometrical situation Pascal imports a few rhetorical circumstances and conditions. He expects to accomplish persuasion by the same means as those used for certainty and for excellent demonstrations in science or mathematics. Although the person I have called the "addressee" does not come into the argument as someone who is solving a scientific problem or preparing a technical treatise, the vocabulary is precisely the same as if he were doing so. As rhetoric all but disappears into geometry, the difference between demonstrating and persuading evaporates.

With a curious exception, however. There is a case where Pascal seems ready for once to admit defeat. He acknowledges that there is a way of persuading not based on quasi-geometrical reasoning. He even recognizes the possibility that it may have its proper technique and status as the *art d'agréer*, the art of pleasing. This is, though, an area into which he decides not to venture. He hesitates between asserting that such an art is purely and simply impossible and asserting that it is, at least beyond *him*. "I do not know," he says, "whether there is an art for accommodating proofs to the inconstancy of our desires": "...je ne sais s'il y aurait un art pour accommoder les preuves à l'inconstance de nos caprices" (L356b; MIII416). I suspect

that the important word here is *preuves*: if we give up on the use
of proofs, if we say that to demonstrate/persuade and to please
are radically different activities, we have certainly left geometry
behind. But it may be that we do not, for all that, take ourselves
entirely out of the realm of method. A moment later Pascal is
still revolving in his mind the idea of rules for pleasing, and of an
art that goes beyond all he has presented so far:

Mais la manière d'agréer est bien sans comparaison plus difficile, plus
subtile, plus utile et plus admirable; aussi, si je n'en traite pas, c'est
parce que je n'en suis pas capable; et je m'y sens tellement
disproportionné, que je crois la chose absolument impossible. (L356b;
MIII416–17)

A few lines down he backs away from this extreme conclusion,
suggesting that, if *he* cannot compose this art of pleasing, certain
people that he knows could pull it off – if *anyone* is capable of
doing it – thanks to their clear and abundant ideas on the
subject. This little discussion bears witness to the difficulty that
Pascal's geometry has in absorbing rhetoric *in toto*. In the classic
expositions of the art, it sought to persuade by a combination of
teaching, moving, and pleasing. Teaching can be assimilated
rather easily to the demonstrative or geometrical mode of
thought. The other two operations, non-rational by nature,
really have no place in it; they remain on the outside; and yet
Pascal knows very well that feelings and pleasure function
widely and effectively as means of persuasion. He must, in this
important digression, admit that his art of sequential ordering,
conceived and worked out in the spirit of geometry, has a rival
in another discipline, as yet unelaborated.

LOGICAL MECHANISM/MECHANIZED LOGIC

To conclude, let us go back to our starting point. In the very
first lines of *De l'esprit géométrique* Pascal told us that three things
could be done with truth: one may discover it, demonstrate it,
and discern or distinguish it from falsity. He quickly telescopes
the third of these into the second, and he decides that he need
not treat the first. (I hope that I have shown in my discussion of

his art of discovery that there is a sense in which he is very much preoccupied with finding truth, and that the care he shows in inventing and specifying the terms needed in his inquiries is a necessary precondition of his scientific achievement.) In the document that he is preparing, he intends to propose to us a way of dealing with statements that report on discoveries alleged to be true, though it is not yet certain that they are so. One is reminded of an earlier invention. Pascal had contrived a *machine d'arithmétique* that had succeeded admirably; and he now offers a method that is a sort of *machine de géométrie*. Using the former, we enter numbers; the machine processes them; and we read the correct answers on its dials. Using the latter, we put in definitions, axioms, and propositions; the logical machine processes them, according to five interlocking rules; and we can then run our eyes over the resulting sequence of logically certain conclusions.

I would not be able to speak in this somewhat far-fetched way of a logical machine if Pascal had not in the present context conceived serious thinking in general and demonstration in particular as activities made up of a succession of isolated, crystalline operations performed on terms having those same characteristics. And if he had not written in numerous passages about *l'esprit géométrique* in such an enthusiastic and dogmatic way.

Moreover, he presents his method as the *only* approach that will yield certainty in *any* human discourse. That adjective is important: near the beginning of his remarks on the *art de persuader*, he takes care, as usual, to leave God's initiative unbounded. Apart from that – and the untreated question of *agrément*, noted above – he seems to consider the applicability of the geometrical turn of mind to be unlimited. This is not a program just for mathematics or physics or specialized discourse. Without giving details, Pascal repeatedly speaks of occasions in which the need for his method has been illustrated. He makes no place for other kinds of discourse that might have other and proper criteria of composition: no history, no poetry, no political theory. He leaves no room for dialogue as a pluralistic exchange of ideas, that might be based on positions worked out from different principles; as I understand the consequences of his position, dialogue can have no place except in a narrative that might accompany a demonstration, or in a prelude to such a demonstration. Instead of possibilities and choices Pascal offers an extraordinarily penetrating grasp of one intellectual way, from which all else is deviation.

This habit of mind is not yet balanced against any real alternative, as it will be in the *Pensées*, where it is contrasted with the *esprit de finesse* and the *ordre du coeur*. Nor is there a suggestion of anything like the possibility of assigning it to a step on a hierarchical scale, as in the fragment on the three orders, where geometry belongs to the *ordre de l'esprit*. Pascal does, indeed, present the method as lying between two extremes, both quite unattractive: the extreme of demonstrating everything, which is not possible, and the extreme of demonstrating nothing, which fails to grasp the reality, the force, and the fruitfulness of self-evident beginnings and simple rules of combination.

PRESENTATION (2)

OTHER CONNECTIONS

At the time of writing *De l'esprit géométrique*, Pascal sees the operations and rules of geometry as constituting models for all discourse. In that perspective *demonstration* emerges as one of the fundamental terms. Sequencing becomes demonstrating. However, a word of caution: we must recognize the difference, clear from Pascal's practice, between demonstration as an intellectual process and demonstration as a product. In the latter sense it takes its place in something broader and more comprehensive. A demonstration is typically, as we have shown, a composition, a complex formed of elements; but Pascal does not conceive of it as an isolated whole. A sequence in its own right, it must find in turn its proper locus as an element in a sequence of demonstrations. The whole process stretches from the technical attention paid to the operations of defining terms and establishing axioms, to the act of formulating a demonstration, then to the orderly combining of a number of demonstrations so as to form a treatise, which is the final outcome envisaged by the scientific investigator. Presumably, in everyday extensions of the geometrical mode, one would stop somewhere short of turning conversations into treatises.

Pascal applies, of course, this technique of analysis, implication, and synthesis to problems in physics and in mechanics. In the former he seeks to establish connections in the operations of things by the systematic formulation of discursive sequences that permit *verification*. That notion has in physics a position comparable to that of demonstration in pure mathematics. The act of verifying a hypothesis presupposes obviously the habit of consistent thought, the *art de démontrer* – in order to formulate the hypothesis – but it requires also a supplement. For in the statements of physics, two sorts of error – outer as well as inner – emerge as pitfalls. One cannot be satisfied simply with the inner coherence of thought and language; one must eliminate contradictions with regard to things, and by that I mean one must be on guard against discourse that is irrelevant or inadequate to the physical bodies under study.

And thus we move from the pages on the geometrical turn of mind to those containing a "Récit de la grande expérience." Experimentation is actually a species of *verification*, or, more precisely, a means to that as an end; Pascal invents and executes experiments in order to verify suppositions. Perhaps we should line up the two complementary sequential orderings as follows: demonstration starts with premises, moves through a series of deductions, and ends in a product – the theorem, along with its train of proofs; verification starts with an hypothesis expressed deductively, moves through a series of experimental observations, and ends in a circumstantial, reasoned-out account – in fact, an instance of narration, a *récit*.

Finally, the art of sequential ordering appears in Pascal's approach to problems of mechanics, that is, in the practical applications of geometry and physics. The idea, the project, and the end-result in the case of the *machine d'arithmétique* provide a splendid example. One key concept here, as regards sequencing, is *construction*. For the machine to exist Pascal has to carry out a precise series of activities both mental and overt; and the undertaking involves also collaborating with craftsmen who work and assemble the materials and parts. Once more, we find ourselves in a sequential play of simples and complexes, of ends and means. In actual operation, the device presents itself as a framework within which, in an orderly sequence of actions and reactions, the parts – the wheels, the gears, the pins – move one another. In short, the aim of everything comes down to a matter of *mouvement réglé*, to use Pascal's own expression.

THE PHYSICAL APPLICATION

Before we can discuss in more detail the theme of sequential ordering as it applies to Pascal and the "Récit de la grande expérience," we must look into some prior conceptual activity that sets the stage for his coming down out of abstract thought into the real world and the data about which he intends to make descriptive and explanatory statements.

First, he assumes a close association between language and thought. He writes as if there were no need to trouble ourselves about a possible disjunction of the two; he uses them as linked and assimilated to each other. Instead, the distinction that he wants to keep in mind is the gap between language-thought on the one hand, and things on the other. One cannot, he obviously believes, trust language to reflect correctly what is the case in things. The whole purpose of the investigative process is to bring language-thought into some kind of adequate relation to reality outside the mind. Pascal cannot here take for granted an initial and trustworthy parallel between language and thought on the one hand, and, on the other, that to which they are applied: the relationship must be discovered, worked out, demonstrated. The significance of my remark may emerge if I contrast the situation in the scientific *récit* with that of the *Pensées*, where, with a basic idea as his touchstone for judgment of things and men, Pascal will use language in an ordinary way: "Il faut avoir une pensée de derrière et juger de tout par là, en parlant cependant comme le peuple." Whereas in physics thought and language have to be brought explicitly into a correct relation with an external and independent reality, in the apologetic enterprise – which is dialectical rather than demonstrative – thought, language, and things clarify one another simultaneously.

In the second place, a question arises concerning one of the factors just identified: how are we to conceive of the reality lying outside of the mind? Pascal is convinced that we must set aside a notion long accepted by the ancients and by their modern followers: the idea of Nature, the physical order of things, as endowed with senses and feelings, as capable of experiencing horror. For him, that is a required first step if we are to tailor our concepts to reality as found in Nature: it is essentially inanimate; and he substitutes immediately for the old notion a view that is essentially mechanical:

… car, pour ouvrir franchement ma pensée, j'ai peine à croire que la nature, qui n'est point animée, ni sensible, soit susceptible d'horreur, puisque les passions présupposent une âme capable de les ressentir, et j'incline bien plus à imputer tous ces effets à la pesanteur et pression de l'air, parce que je ne les considère que comme des cas particuliers d'une proposition universelle de l'équilibre des liqueurs qui doit faire la plus grande partie du traité que j'ai promis. (L221d–22a; MII678–79)

Thus, after the negation, which has to do with nature in general, Pascal's language becomes more specific, narrowing to the idea of nature as corporeal, indeed, as bodies, and – to complete the insight – bodies acting on one another.

An interesting *rapprochement* gives us an even closer look at Pascal's notion of body. As we have already noted, it is possible to recover one important example of the way in which he appears to have derived it. In *De l'esprit géométrique* a verse from Scripture – "Deus fecit omnia in pondere, in numero, et mensura" – authorizes him to say three essential things about bodies. (1) One can number them, separate them from one another, examine them in their multiplicity, with arithmetic as the source of principles. (2) One can trace out their dimensions, establish their extent, measure them, with geometry, this time, as the science in the background. And, finally, (3) one can take them as masses and weigh them, which means putting one body in balanced opposition to another; and as instances are added to instances one resorts once more to arithmetic and the measurements that it makes possible. In a real sense God has furnished the conceptual instruments needed for the *grande expérience* of the Puy-de-Dôme.

Pascal accepts and works out in his way the general tendency of his scientific contemporaries to mathematize nature; and in so doing, he is led like them to adopt the accompanying and analogous tendency to mechanize nature: those clear and distinct mathematical ideas, combined according to simple and explicit rules, have their counterparts in physical reality. By that stroke natural bodies are homogenized into quantitative being; that kind of being lends itself to division into assorted shapes and sizes; and they, in turn, can be plainly identified, arranged, and manipulated so as to permit precise observation regarding their mutual relations. Arithmetic has a particularly pervasive role to play in this scheme. At the beginning of the inquiry it provides the means of distinguishing individual bodies in a physical reality that would otherwise be confused or continuous. Then it lends devices and conventions by which one may make measurements, certifying by its numerical series and operations that clear and distinct ideas of quantity are available for interpreting the movements and interactions of the world's bodies.

Pascal reaches the logically final moment in the process of reflection that I am reconstructing here, when he posits – "... j'incline à croire" he says carefully in the lines quoted above – that the phenomena described and attested in the commonly performed *expérience du vide* have the status of a particular instance of something treated in hydrostatics, namely, the equilibrium of liquids. If we assume the two basic branches of mechanics to be statics and dynamics, it is interesting to observe that motion, *mouvement*, though obviously widespread in Pascal's nature and though subject to endless extension in the play of the double infinities, emerges primarily in his thought as a preliminary and relative phenomenon. It is a phase, something that takes place on the way to repose in an equilibrium. The problem area of physics on which he concentrates differs from that of Galileo, for example, who is intent on discovering the laws of terrestrial movement; and something similar can be said of Newton, who not only wanted to draw the movements of the planets into a system of orbits with no end of motion in sight, but even in the domain of mathematics itself invented a kind of calculation that gave him a key to the interpretation of quantitative changes and rates of change. For his part, Pascal, with the example of Archimedes behind him, sees a great opportunity for making progress in the field of statics, of movements on their way to rest in a balance, and for developing a revolutionary view of nature not as a necessary plenum but as an ensemble of bodies in space.

ANALYSIS AND EXPERIMENTATION

The analytical art now begins especially to come into play. If Pascal were doing geometry, the first act would be to define important terms once and for all, or, in some cases, to point out that one cannot really define certain terms, nor can one be mistaken about what they designate. When he turns outward toward things, what is the equivalent of clear, distinct, and univocal terms? It must be something like the irreducible identities and differences of such things as air and mercury, which (in a sense) assert themselves in an obvious way. The words "air" and "mercury" that we use to indicate them are thus free from ambiguity. In language and in reality Pascal establishes the only kind of starting points satisfactory in an analytical procedure: the least parts, the factors beyond which one cannot go. He introduces into his physics a phase comparable to that of definition in geometry.

As an analytically minded thinker he will not stop at this point; he is likely next to feel impelled to combine his elements into something larger. In language and thought Pascal may join ideas by means of a copula in order to form a proposition. Or, beginning with the two elements, quicksilver and air, he can move on to a combination that reproduces in things a balance similar to that achieved in a proposition: the two substances are arranged as opposed weights on the two sides of a center of gravity. They become equal parts of a third something, an equilibrium – which corresponds, in a way, to the balance of a subject and a predicate in a proposition. Out of this imagined equalizing of weights Pascal can formulate a hypothesis to be verified or falsified by experience. Not by just any experience, but only by the special kind to be had within the contrived framework of an experiment and the maneuvers that it allows. To show then that a balance is at work in the behavior of things, it will suffice for Pascal to show that if he makes a change in the weight of one of the two balancing elements, that change, that fact, will entail a related change on the other side, so as to re-establish the equilibrium.

And it is precisely here that we encounter once more and in a leading role, the notion of sequential ordering: a change of the weight on one side of the balance is followed by a related change on the other side. If you do *this*, you will note *that*. But notice that in this context Pascal's sequential ordering is not, strictly speaking, logical; it does not embody the sort of deductive relationship that he appreciates so much in *De l'esprit géométrique*. He is here tracing physical movements, events occurring in a temporal order. Instead of constructing logical demonstrations with their proper kind of self-evidence, Pascal now intends to observe sequences that impose themselves by another kind of *évidence*, that of sense perception. However, the change to a new sort of necessary succession – temporal rather than deductive – though important, does not erase the fact that what he wants to find in nature is a tight sequence. He reasons on the basis of something like the succession from axiom to dependent proposition in the geometry: the initiating factor in the process has the independent status of an axiom; it implies and produces the dependent event.

A RAPPROCHEMENT OF ORDERS

Let me now return to an earlier point: Pascal sees a constantly possible gap, an *écart* between language linked to thought on the one hand, and reality on the other. The hypothesis, as it assumes the image or model of the balance, and then the possibility of a change on one side that brings about a change on the other side, never leaves the sphere of thought. We do not yet know whether it corresponds to extra-mental reality, to the behavior of actual mercury and air. In physics and mechanics, the difference between sequences in thoughts-words and successions of events in things becomes crucial; in geometry it can recede into the background of the inquiry or even disappear as irrelevant. Pascal entertains the mechanical model in his mind, hypothetically, and approaches nature as a locus in which that model and its workings may or may not reside. And so the experiment he invented is designed to permit nature to answer the question "yes" or "no," as to the presence or absence in it of the model. In this part of his account he takes us to the alternative before him:

Je travaille maintenant ... à chercher des expériences qui fassent voir si les effets que l'on attribue à l'horreur du vide, doivent être véritablement attribués à cette horreur du vide, ou s'ils le doivent être à la pesanteur et pression de l'air ... (L221d; MII678)

In fact, at least two experiments are involved: there is what Pascal refers to as the "expérience du vide dans le vide"; and he recalls in the first part of the "Récit de la grande expérience" that he had already performed it for Périer. It would seem that on the small scale of that experiment Pascal had satisfied himself as to the truth of the matter. But it was a "petite expérience," if you will; it had nothing like the impressive scale and the paradoxical flair of the "grande expérience," carried out at the foot and on the top of a mountain, where Nature was summoned to reveal its way of working with the lightest and the heaviest of its liquids.

Je l'ai nommée la grande expérience de l'équilibre des liqueurs, parce qu'elle est la plus démonstrative de toutes celles qui peuvent être faites sur ce sujet, en ce qu'elle fait voir l'équilibre de l'air avec le vif-argent, qui sont, l'un la plus légère, l'autre la plus pesante de toutes les liqueurs qui sont connues dans la nature. (L221b; MII677)

Of course, Périer did succeed in finding evidence for the presence of the hypothetical model in nature. And not in just one instance: he confirmed the basic finding repeatedly. Pascal had foreseen the whole series; we can obtain the light we seek, he wrote in advance to his brother-in-law, if all the stages of his project can be executed accurately; the guiding idea is as follows:

C'est de faire l'expérience ordinaire du vide plusieurs fois en même jour, dans un même tuyau, avec le même vif-argent, tantôt en bas et tantôt au sommet d'une montagne, élevée pour le moins de cinq ou six cents toises, pour éprouver si la hauteur du vif-argent suspendu dans le tuyau se trouvera pareille ou différente dans ces deux situations. (L222b; MII680)

Pascal's correspondent carried out the instructions, and, in fact, enlarged them, not only performing the experiment at the foot and on the top of the mountain, but also repeating it at different sites at the top, at intervals on the way down, and at the end of the descent. Then the next day he did it at various elevations in Clermont. Thanks to all these re-enactments of the test in different circumstances, he established and extended abundantly a series of concomitant variations in the equilibrium of the two liquids. The principle had already emerged in the experiment of the vacuum in a vacuum, as Pascal reminds Périer:

Vous vîtes ensuite que cette hauteur ou suspension du vif-argent augmentait ou diminuait à mesure que la pression de l'air augmentait ou diminuait, et qu'enfin toutes ces diverses hauteurs ou suspensions du vif-argent se trouvaient toujours proportionnées à la pression de l'air. (L222b; MII679)

In the context of physical science these multiplied experiments correspond to the repeated exemplifications of mathematical principles in Pascal's treatises in geometry and arithmetic. They enter into an analogical series, each experiment adding another link to the chain of related events and another confirmation to the hypothesis.

Although one may think of Pascal's investigative process as a matter of defining an end – the establishment of necessary connections between phenomena – and then using the empirical means that give promise of realizing the end, such a statement tends to conceal the interesting particular activities that use terms and generate facts. These operations are so many in number that as one begins to make distinctions, the analytical art of connecting events and presenting arguments seems to break down into techniques of lesser scope, each of which has its own routine, its relation to others that come before and after it, and eventually its peculiar place with reference to the overriding aim.

Pascal's geometrical turn of mind invites this sort of excursion in search of least parts. Because of the way in which he separates mental processes (including those involving language) from processes occurring in things, he is led to practice an art of thinking provisionally or hypothetically (one must include the adverbs until confirmation has taken place). Here he formulates the proposition to be proved, that is, the sequential ordering to be sought in the world of bodies; then he invents the scenario of the experiment to be performed. Next, leaving the armchair, so to speak, he must arrange to bring together in accord with his purpose and in a real situation a complex ensemble of factors – of things, people, and instruments. Then, still another technique is called for, which selects, arranges, manipulates, observes, and measures the actions and reactions of the crucial factors in the experiment. And, finally, back in the realm of discourse, there is an art of conclusion, by which statements made in the earlier hypothetical mode become independent and affirmative; and usually, at the same time, Pascal shows their power of expansion in several corollaries and exploits their power of negation in passages calculated to refute the assertions of opponents.

Assembling the hypothesis, designing the experiment, arranging and proceeding step by step through it, assimilating the results into the body of justified knowledge: each of these operations and those immediately subordinate to them fall into line; and Pascal judges them all, as he goes along, in the light of analytical *évidence*. He also sees them in a definite perspective. On reading Pascal's triumphant *récit*, which upsets both common and technical views ("le consentement universel des peuples et la foule des philosophes"), one may lose sight of the important consideration that for him the "grande expérience du vide," though decisive with regard to a much debated question, belongs as one instance to a particular category of investigations: those having to do with the equilibrium of liquids, and it eventually must take its place in a larger sequential ordering, not of the parts of an experimental whole, as I have treated it here, but as a component part in a treatise on hydrostatics. It is subject to the enveloping drive of the art of connections, which characteristically starts from primitive elements and moves by a series of combinations to ever larger complexes.

VERIFICATION: A CONSTANT

The notion of verification plays such an important role in physics that one wonders whether it has any function in the more geometrical applications of the art of sequential ordering. Verification serves to bring the senses into the process of knowing where things are concerned. Is there anything like a check by the senses of what reason proposes in the course of a geometrical demonstration? In discussing *De l'esprit géométrique* I made no mention of verification: all the emphasis lay on demonstration. But I am inclined to think that one cannot dispense entirely with the notion, even in a purely geometrical context.

Pascal recognizes, among other powers of the soul, the faculties of reason, sense, and imagination. In experimentation he calls on the first two, and especially on the second, since it is via sense experience that we confirm or falsify what reason has elaborated. Given the psychological structure he has used, my suggestion is that imagination may function like sense where the problems under study do not require going outside of the mind in order for verification to occur. (In the *Pensées*, I know, the imagination is a *puissance trompeuse*, but even there it does not always deceive.) Although mathematical objects of thought do not fall under the senses, as Pascal might have said, they are not totally abstract; and they can be "visualized" by the imagination. If that much is granted, something like this follows. Geometry makes statements about figures and numbers (I am including arithmetic under geometry, as Pascal occasionally does); indeed, it constructs demonstrations about those subject-matters. Are the statements in question purely and simply elements in a demonstrative fabric? I think not: the statements apply to something, and it is precisely this applicability, this referentiality that leads me to suggest the place and existence of a kind of verification in his geometry. The reasoning may tend to rise into abstract mediation (in axioms, conventions, and propositional sequences), but, from time to time, one recognizes that the statements correspond to something – and I would say that in Pascal's mental scheme, they correspond to something that the imagination can "see" in a gesture of verification (which is not, after all, completely unsupported by sense, because visible figures and signs are present on the written page).

In other words, I think it is possible to move in two directions in considering Pascalian geometry and physics. In the analyses presented above, I have intended to show how some aspects of the demonstrative process as defined by Pascal (concern, for example, with definitions, undefinable terms, unproven propositions, and the like) reappear with physical connotations in the experimental side of his work and become noticeable in the "Récit de la grande expérience." Conversely, the epistemology of empirical physics has some points of coincidence with the process of solving problems in arithmetic and geometry. Reason supplies consistency in both physics and mathematics; for confirmation it needs sense in the former and imagination in the latter.

NATURE AS MACHINE

As we have already seen, Nature tends to become mechanized in the physical investigations of Pascal. He does something that his contemporaries liked to do. For Descartes, mechanics furnished the laws of nature, even of animate nature, as long as it was not rational; thus, animals and the bodies of human beings are machines. Newton does something quite similar: in framing his system of the world, he offers explanations and proofs in mechanical terms; and, indeed, it is a remarkable fact that he considers geometry itself to be something like a branch, a theoretical branch, of mechanics. The wedding of mathematics and mechanics appears less intended in the thought of Galileo: mechanical terms suggest in his mind a resort to causal explanations, into which he did not care to go; what he proposed to give was a reading of natural phenomena that would be expressed in the language of mathematics, rather than that of mechanics or in that of an exact parallel between the two.

In this seventeenth-century rebirth of Pythagorean and Archimedean approaches to nature, Pascal arrives at something rather like the view developed by Descartes. Getting rid of the *horror vacui* in nature has for him, as its logical corollary, a decision to approach Nature as bodies interacting in space; hence a natural allegiance to the mechanical sort of explanation, and its way of defining the *raison des effets*. He did not avoid causal explanations, as Galileo preferred to do. An important qualification should be added, in that Pascal implants in his quantitative and mechanical universe a disturbing factor in the two infinities, which are profoundly subversive to the aspirations of any system of thought that is based on univocal definitions and the strict application of the principle of identity. The infinities lead to unstoppable lines of paradoxes, along which bodies, numbers, spaces, movements are at every point simultaneously big and small. His insistence on these saves him from the dogmatism of Descartes, encourages in him a sense of the ultimate incomprehensibility of nature, and provides a lesson against pride on the part of man. Moreover, when the time comes for him to undertake his work on the ways of God to man, he is entirely capable, as we shall see, of using and generalizing an art of ordering that uses all the possibilities that may be had with analogical rather than univocal terms, with shifting rather than fixed meanings, with negations of negations, and with the fusions of contraries: in short, he exchanges the divisions and compositions of an extended geometry for the antitheses and reconciliations of a full-scale dialectic.

MATHEMATICS AS MACHINE

In geometry and arithmetic, one works with ideal entities, in an attempt to make justified statements about them; in physics, one works with objects in the real world, and one attempts to make verified statements about them. In geometry (to be specific) one constructs, with a compass and a straight-edge, the subject-matter of the science; whereas, in physics, the subject-matter presents itself as something given outside of the observer and not as a constructed object existing only in the mind. But there was still another possibility to exploit. It seems to me that, when Pascal as a young man turned to the project of the arithmetical machine, he already knew quite a lot about the art of connections and sequential orderings; and the terms we have been using had been specified in a different fashion. Instead of constructing a geometrical and ideal entity for study that would never leave the bounds of the mind, he had set about making, on the basis of an inner and rational design, a thing that would exist outside of the mind. And this thing that eventually did exist extra-mentally was a machine, put together out of corporeal parts, that had been shaped and fitted according to mathematical formulas: it was a mixed object, physical as to existence, mathematical as to structure. The paradoxical part of the project was, though, that this mixed object was not an ordinary tool, not something to be applied to something else in the physical world to produce an action or reaction; this object springing out of a brain into the real world had parts whose movements could be read as mathematical calculations. The parallels are so exact that one can hardly keep arithmetic and geometry from becoming mental mechanics, while the machine and, beyond it, the natural bodies in interaction that comprise Pascal's natural order behave, all of them, in the style of extra-mental, objective mathematics.

In my account, especially in what I have said about the process of conceptualization prior to his experiments, Pascal would seem to have been to a striking degree a philosophical idealist – someone who started with thought, with mathematical thought in particular, and who then accepted the mechanical implications of mathematical thinking, and who finally attributed to Nature and bodies those mathematical and mechanical attributes, all without ever facing the question: is the physical world really like that? Can one legitimately proceed from within the mind and move outward, implanting one's terms, so to speak, in reality? Did Pascal get the Nature required by his method, or the method required by his Nature? I suppose he might say that what he was doing was to discover in Nature what *is* in Nature: Nature presents itself as a machine; it works according to mechanical devices and elements and combinations; and all that he has done is to look up in the catalogue of machines a confirmable suggestion as to what the machine is – in this case the balance – that operates in the *expérience du vide*. Looked at from this viewpoint, the experiments allow Nature to tell Pascal what it is like, and to guide him in the task of locating a model that corresponds to a process observable in Nature. And he might add that, in so doing, it simply declares the handiwork of God, since he created it so as to be measurable, numerable, and ponderable. Consequently, there has been no unwarranted extension of a mathematical and mechanical art of connections into domains where something specifically different is required.

CONCLUSION

In the first part of this section, we have explored the way in which, starting from geometry and its deductive discourse, Pascal developed his conception of an art of connections based on the pattern of geometrical reasoning. After a rather short description of its workings, Pascal gives us to understand that about all that remains is for more people to learn it and use it. In that description and in what he actually does elsewhere, we can detect all the formative aspects of an intellectual art. Taking as its subject-matter connections and series of connections that are available for many different applications, the art has its typical procedures, which may be reduced finally to an ensemble of rules; however, those rules are conceived and used freely: one may be called upon to reformulate or modify them at any moment; and one looks constantly for new sets of circumstances in which to test their adequacy and fruitfulness.

In the second part of this section we followed Pascal into two extensions of his habit of connections. First, into the field of experimental physics, where he finds himself working out the consequences of that habit in a context that requires confirmed contact between the world of thought and the world of things – a concern only obscurely visible in pure geometry and arithmetic; he analyzes and manipulates in experiments bodies that have mass and, above all, weight; he presents his results in an explanatory narrative destined to fill a place in a complete and orderly work of scientific knowledge. Then, second, we moved into the field of applied and productive science, where Pascal makes use of the "lumières," as he says, of geometry, physics, and mechanics in order to produce a machine that can solve by a sequence of local motions the typical problems of arithmetic.

Mathematical sciences taken either (1) in themselves or (2) with reference to something else, that is to say, applied; then, applications that take the form (2a) either of investigating what is given in natural reality (2b) or of adding useful devices to the store of existent realities; or, finally, (2c) of introducing demonstrative texture into all or most of discourse: the program of study is comprehensive and impressive. But it is not exhaustive, for even though Pascal leans heavily on his geometrical model, he does not as a matter of fact think of it always as furnishing a schema of everything that may be known. It does not give him a truly inclusive view; it omits from consideration an important insight and a consequent distinction. Because of that distinction Pascal's way of seeing the world assumes a systematic character, and we can discern in it traces of the fourth and last intellectual method to be discussed here: the art of systematization. Along with problems of statement and recovery, of specification and discovery, of arranging and ordering, he deals with problems that arise when he attempts a synoptic view of knowledge. In the preface to the *Traité sur le vide* Pascal sketches with some development a truly comprehensive line of thought and exemplifies the relevant mental operations in a particularly explicit and enlightening way. Let us now turn to that text and the issues it raises.

INTEGRATION

THE PREFACE TO A TREATISE IN A SYSTEM

The art of sequential ordering, when fully extended and applied, results in the formation of structures, of bodies of knowledge that can be set down in treatises. As the activity of that art proceeds, another important problem arises – that of integration or systematization. It becomes necessary to deal with a complex situation in which several structures need to be related to each other. They may be actual sciences or ensembles of warranted statements on their way to attaining the status of sciences.

A good place to begin the discussion of this organizing process, as Pascal conceives it, comes in the *Préface* to the treatise on the vacuum. This document gives us a discursive treatment of the subject. Although it is rather short, it contains enough development to give a real sense of how the field of knowledge in general appears to Pascal during the time when he was especially concerned with mathematics and physics. But a word of caution is in order. The preface is written against a particular rhetorical background; it emerges in the context of an argument about the ancients and the moderns, and about the relevance of that distinction to the experimental work done in connection with the problem of the vacuum. Pascal is preparing to present his findings, his solution to the problem of the *vide*. Since he knows the climate of opinion in which his treatise will appear, he can anticipate the kind of opposition his views are likely to encounter. There will be, he assumes, objections from the partisans of the ancient way of discussing and settling the problems of physics. He foresees, as a result of this kind of disagreement and the cast of mind that it reflects, a serious obstacle in the way of scientific progress. This general issue is in the back of Pascal's mind; and since it establishes the immediate context in which he presents his ideas, it has a bearing on the question of how knowledge is to be systematized.

Pascal's experience in dealing with our present problem is perhaps nicely summed up for us in the two lists of sciences that he provides early in the *Préface*. He mentions – and that would seem to be the right word, since he does not work out in detail a schematism of the sciences – eleven sciences in all. The first group includes: *histoire, géographie, jurisprudence, les langues,* and *théologie.* Then, a few lines later, he offers a second list, consisting of: *géométrie, arithmétique, musique, physique, médecine,* and *architecture.* He adds a very useful tag at the end of this latter grouping: "... et toutes les sciences soumises à l'expérience et au raisonnement" (L230d; M_{II}779). The phrase – "and all the sciences subject to experimentation and reasoning" – would seem to indicate exactly the essential characteristic that Pascal has in mind for the entire second group – they all come from an orientation as to method that is empirical and rational.

TWO DIRECTIONS

His effort of classification goes in two directions, one leading to inquiries concerning nature and natural phenomena and the other to knowledge of what is to be found in books. Once the two subject-matters are distinguished, he can say something about the differing purposes and researches that are correlated with them. While the first group of sciences aims to break new ground, to discover the secrets of nature, to reveal its hidden workings, the second group aims to recover what is already known and exists now in written form, available for learning.

Pour faire cette importante distinction avec attention, il faut considérer que les unes [les matières] dépendent seulement de la mémoire et sont purement historiques, n'ayant pour objet que de savoir ce que les auteurs ont écrit; les autres dépendent seulement du raisonnement, et sont entièrement dogmatiques, ayant pour objet de chercher et découvrir les vérités cachées. (L230b; M_{II}777–78)

This division according to objects and purposes takes us to two stages even more basic: to the operations, which, as means, will accomplish the two objectives, and then to the faculties of the soul required to make those operations possible. The reference to memory and reasoning in the lines quoted shows us what to expect. Pascal could have made something else basic, something other than the knowing faculties, and worked away from that in his argument. He might have chosen to emphasize much more than he does the characteristics of the various subject-matters; he might have shown that their intrinsic characteristics and complexities laid down the rules for the rest of his analysis. Or, on another tack, he might have selected language as basic; then his analysis would have proceeded according to the way in which he conceived the nature and workings of language in the two areas of knowledge. That would have given, I should think, something rather like what we see in *De l'esprit géométrique*. He has chosen, however, to place the faculties at the center of attention. This choice does not mean that he will have little or nothing to say about subject-matters and language; but here, as indeed everywhere, much depends on what he takes to be primary and fundamental as opposed to what will as a consequence turn out to be secondary and derived.

Specifically, what does Pascal do? He analyzes the operations of knowing as involving mainly activity on the part of the reason and the senses. He makes some references to memory and will, *mémoire* and *volonté* (the latter comes into play especially in *De l'esprit géométrique* as an element in persuasion), and we shall discuss their role later. Pascal's way of conceiving the two main powers, and especially reason, leads naturally into a discussion regulated by a set of topics that is quite traditional: the faculty itself, its typical activities, the subject-matters covered or approached, and the products that result. Taking the faculty as a sort of root or source, one can detect in his argument a *va-et-vient* along the line thus indicated: faculty – operation – object of attention – purpose or product. His discussion adds details, formulas, and short developments to this skeleton, so that, as he proceeds, what seem at first to be unclear abstractions come to evoke precise phases of a methodical analysis. And when those factors have been made explicit, their interrelations clarified, and their functions explored, we have in front of us – in outline at least – the art according to which Pascal has systematized the various structures of knowledge that have been or may be constituted.

SOME EXAMPLES

Here are some examples of what I mean. (1) Regarding objects, we have already seen one important distinction at work here, that between nature and books as things that may be studied. And now, an essential detail: they differ as to accessibility. To understand the significance of this point, one must recall that, of course, the object to be known in books is not the books as such, with their tactile and visible characteristics. We want to become acquainted with their contents, with what they are *about* – and it is with reference to that question that the problem of accessibility to our knowing powers presents itself. In the case of nature, what we want to know is there in front of us, we have only to open our eyes and minds and take advantage of the immediate juxtaposition in which we find ourselves as knowers. When we open a book, the situation changes. Suppose that we want to learn about an event that took place a long time ago, or that we want to know about an institution that exists on the other side of the globe, or that we are reading the Bible for knowledge of God: none of these objects is present to us directly. We must turn to authorities (and, of course, their limits are our limits):

... il faut nécessairement recourir à leurs livres, puisque tout ce que l'on en peut savoir y est contenu: d'où il est évident que l'on peut en avoir la connaissance entière, et qu'il n'est pas possible d'y rien ajouter. (L230b; MII778)

It is important, for the development of Pascal's argument concerning the sciences in their systematic aspect that we grasp thus the ambiguity of the object term.

(2) Or take the notion of "operations": in the *Préface* Pascal is quite precise as regards the natural sciences and our efforts to discover the secrets of nature. He tells his reader that in such inquiries one should be involved in demonstration and experimentation. Mathematics and physics are obviously the disciplines that provide models for such activities. At one point

he goes so far as to say that the secrets of nature become progressively known to us as a result of experimentation and of that alone:

Les expériences qui nous en donnent l'intelligence multiplient continuellement; et, comme elles sont les seuls principes de la physique, les conséquences multiplient à proportion. (L231c; MII781)

However, in connection with the other side of his picture, Pascal is tantalizingly brief; he has practically nothing to say about the operations needed for the interpretation of books. He does point out the way in which one may mis-use activities like those that are appropriate in the sciences: he considers it a great mistake for one to introduce innovative and inventive reasoning into the domain proper to authority. He has in mind, of course, theology, where he has no patience with discourse that does not come from or rest on authoritative sources. In view of the fact that Pascal takes off in the *Préface* from the question of the *vide* and its implications for the future of physical science, it is not surprising that the problems bound to arise in the interpreting of books should seem rather far from his mind. We know that he will come to think deeply about those matters when he takes up and argues from the Bible, the writings of Saint Augustine, or the pronouncements of the Council of Trent, thus bringing into better balance the array of intellectual operations. Here he makes interpretation appear easy: one opens the books, one learns the contents, and that is about all there is to it, apart from minding the general caution against the presumptuous use of our powers when we turn to objects that happen to be inaccessible either in fact or by nature.

(3) Or, again, consider the notion of products, of the results that accrue in our scientific endeavors. On this point Pascal sees a real difference between the two types of knowledge and science. He imagines, it would seem, books on the model of recipients and containers; we can arrive at a grasp of whatever is therein, and, moreover, of *all* that they contain. There the books are, there we are, and it is possible for us to achieve, in a kind of transfer, a total and complete knowledge of what has been written in them. He concludes that such knowledge does

not progress; its status differs decidedly from what he sees in
mathematics and physics, which are cumulative. They build on
the past – on the parts of the past from which errors have been
weeded out – and they develop by adding demonstrated truths
to demonstrated truths. The process will have no end; there is
no chance that we shall ever reach a total knowledge of nature.
Pascal draws a distinction between the *science nécessaire* of
animals, which nature has granted them as a matter of
unchanging instinct, and the evolving knowledge open to
human reason. After emphasizing the limits of instinct, he
proceeds:

Il n'en est pas de même de l'homme, qui n'est produit que pour
l'infinité. Il est dans l'ignorance au premier âge de sa vie; mais il
s'instruit sans cesse dans son progrès: car il tire avantage non seulement
de sa propre expérience, mais encore de celle de ses prédecesseurs,
parce qu'il garde toujours dans sa mémoire les connaissances qu'il s'est
une fois acquises, et que celles des anciens lui sont toujours présentes
dans les livres qu'ils en ont laissés. (L231d; MII782)

Several lines later he adds, in a striking metaphor, that one can
sum up all of humanity as it seeks this kind of truth in the idea
of a single man, with the ancients representing this collective
man in his childhood, while we are the real ancients and we live
in a period of maturity that is and will remain open where the
accumulation of scientific knowledge is concerned. (Fontenelle
made much of this figure of speech in his *Digression sur les Anciens
et les Modernes* of 1687, as the "quarrel" between the two sides
indicated in his title was reaching the level of a polemic.)

   The emphasis in all of the foregoing falls on the future in store
for science and mathematics, but one must not lose sight of the
corrective balance that Pascal furnishes quite definitely in the
Préface even though it occupies less space than the passages he
writes in the expansive and optimistic key. This brings us to the
moment when we can see what is, in my opinion, Pascal's main
insight here, the one on which his classification of the sciences
finally depends. *Reason and sense have limits.* We glimpsed
something of this problem above, in connection with objects to
be known; we must now go further into its nature and
implications.

. POWERS OF KNOWING AND THEIR LIMITS

The argument leads us backward now along our line of discussion to the knower, because his equipment is what interests Pascal mainly, and it will permit him to say how, given our cognitive faculties, we may arrive at various kinds of stable and certain knowledge. He has no surprises for us here. The powers in question turn out to be those provided by the traditional philosophical psychology: reason, sense, memory, imagination, will. He treats them, however, in terms derived from an important distinction that – while focusing on reason for his present purposes – sets up a dichotomy. There are things of great interest to us that elude us, questions we can ask, the answers to which are inaccessible in the direct and immediate use of reason, the senses, or any of our naturally given powers. Consequently, knowledge falls into two classes: (1) that which is due to the operations of a knower's *own* faculties; and (2) that which is received, accepted, adopted on the basis of what someone else, using *his* faculties, has come to know. One may see the truth for oneself, without decisive reference to anyone else; or, in the second possibility, one "knows" or accepts as knowledge what someone else has known. Cognition occurs directly or indirectly; and in the direct mode reason and the senses investigate a subject-matter given in nature; in the indirect mode, they are absorbed in activities of reading and interpretation designed to recover a subject-matter set out in a written text.

In filling out the schematism that results, Pascal first presents a list of the sciences that result from someone else's knowing: history, geography, jurisprudence, languages, and theology – five disciplines in all. What they have to teach us we receive on the basis of and out of respect for the authority of the source. Pascal identifies this group as having to do with "quelque institution humaine ou divine" or with what he calls "le fait simple." In the latter category we can no doubt put those facts of history and geography, which because of their remoteness in space and time are beyond the reach of any knower here and now. Our only chance to learn such facts is from competent observers on the spot and at the time who have recorded what happened or what they saw. Jurisprudence, as a legal science, is similarly a matter of record, as are the grammatical aspects of languages. Some examples:

S'il s'agit de savoir qui fut le premier roi des Français; en quel lieu les géographes placent le premier méridien; quels mots sont usités dans une langue morte, et toutes les choses de cette nature, quels autres moyens que les livres pourraient nous y conduire? (L230c; M11778)

Since these sciences exist already in books, the task is to retrieve and to assimilate them; it seems fair to say that they put us into a posture more passive than active.

On the other hand, the knowledge gained from the other group of sciences comes from discovery rather than from recovery. Here there is a basic list of six (though Pascal leaves the end of the series open): geometry, arithmetic, music, physics, medicine, and architecture. (It is interesting to note the persistence of the old quadrivium in the first four of these and to recall that medicine and architecture might be found at the end of such lists at least since the enumeration of Varro, in his *Disciplinarum libri IX*.) Although in the following sentence Pascal is interested mainly in the theme of progress in the sciences, one senses a certain logic in the order of naming them:

C'est ainsi que la géométrie, l'arithmétique, la musique, la physique, la médecine, l'architecture, et toutes les sciences qui sont soumises à l'expérience et au raisonnement, doivent être augmentées pour devenir parfaites. (L231a; M11779)

Geometry and arithmetic would seem to be the fundamental sciences; then physics comes along essentially as an application of the other two to the physical world; and finally he puts in two other eminent instances of applied science in medicine and architecture. The list as a whole implies something like a movement from the simple to the complex, and from the theoretical to the applied.

THE RESULTING SCHEMA

Two things are happening in Pascal's project here. He is dividing up the world of knowledge, assigning subject-matters and disciplinary names, arriving at a schematism; that is one activity; but there are hints and at times more than hints of something else; he is not only grounding the sciences, he is also indicating, with varying degrees of emphasis, orderings and priorities. Note, for example, the way in which he defines our relations to predecessors (they may be ancients), tells us what we are to do now, and imagines the situation of those who are to follow. As Pascal judges the sciences, the concepts of past, present, and future serve as indicators of limits and of values. He thinks that we cannot really progress beyond what authorities (ancient or recent) have relayed to us where remote facts and acts or institutions are concerned. But in mathematics and in physics it is our task to confirm – or, if necessary, replace with something better – what our predecessors have asserted, and beyond that, to seek new knowledge that can be added to the old, for the steady perfecting of the sciences. Those who follow us will have, in turn, the obligation to judge our contributions and to add on their discoveries. As to the possibility of progress, Pascal clearly sees an advantage or a priority in those sciences that depend solely on the exercise of our natural faculties.

However, we can have no doubt about the way in which he defines the special status of theology in the group of subject-matters that fall under the rule of authority.

Mais où cette autorité a la principale force, c'est dans la théologie, parce qu'elle y est inséparable de la vérité, et que nous ne la connaissons que par elle… (L230c; MII778)

Incomprehensible things – the most incomprehensible things, Pascal says, in order to sharpen the paradox – though clearly recognized as such from the natural point of view become entirely certain in the supernatural light of the Bible and of theology; and, conversely, the most plausible things in ordinary experience may become entirely uncertain, when one shifts into the religious perspective. We see another instance of this kind of arranging by priority when Pascal points out the confusions and errors that result if we move from one of these disciplines to the other without recognizing that we are crossing important boundaries. Authority, if asserted purely and simply in physics, leads to timidity and bad science; innovative reasoning, unaware of its limits and used outside of its proper domain, leads to temerity and bad theology. And so, although the possibility of progress without end constitutes an impressive feature in the quantitative and physical sciences, the pre-emptive certainty of the Bible and of theology reverses the standings in a striking way.

The situation of the disciplines with regard to their sources of certainty may be summed up in a little table:

Sources of certainty

A. REASON (plus SENSE, as required),
   working in:
1 arithmetic, geometry
2 physics
3 medicine
4 architecture

B. AUTHORITY, OF TWO SORTS:

   DIVINE, based on the Bible, Fathers, and Councils; found in
1 theology
   HUMAN, found in
1 geography
2 history,
3 jurisprudence
4 language

That would appear to be the position at which Pascal has arrived in thinking about the organization of the disciplines, though it misrepresents somewhat the effect he seeks in the *Préface*, where the principal thrust goes into defining exactly the completely secondary or tentative role of authority in the sciences and with affirming in their case the primacy of reason and sense, of demonstration and experimentation. Actually, I do not think it an exaggeration to say that divine influence and initial permission extend to the mathematical and scientific use of reason: we come back to the fact that Pascal had it on biblical authority that God created all things in measure, number, and weight.

DISTINGUISHING AND ARRANGING THE SCIENCES

To complete our grasp of Pascal's procedure in organizing the sciences here we need to define further the criteria, largely implicit in the text of the *Préface*, according to which operations of knowing are carried out and the results put into place. As we saw above, he finds himself involved in two kinds of activities, one that might be called differentiative or scope-setting, for distinguishing the kinds of sciences under the two sources of certainty, and the other that might be called architectonic or value-setting, for defining their interrelations and relative positions. He applies his criteria – which become visible, I think, in the precepts and examples or in the ends and means he proposes – on two levels, first within each of two groups, and then with reference to the two groups taken as such.

The best way to proceed here may be to put the argument in terms of suppositions. If we want certain knowledge, what must we do? We must attend to two sources of such knowledge: reason and authority. And, if these are the two possibilities, what characteristic and specific things must we have and do to go forward? We need the instruments that will allow us to divide the sciences into two groups and then make sub-divisions within each of the groups: Pascal posits first the distinction reason/authority, which derives from a consideration of knowing faculties, and then makes distinctions derived from the characteristics of the various subject-matters. Then he has the equipment he needs for taking care of the differentiative or originative phase of his effort to classify the sciences.

Furthermore, if we want to put the disciplines on a scale, we must have terms for rankings: for the sciences based on reasoning and experimentation, Pascal uses, it seems to me, pairs such as simple/complex, pure/applied, theoretical/ practical. For the areas where we must receive and accept statements on the basis of credibility, of *who* said them, Pascal falls back on terms derived from the character of the subject, like "fait simple," or "quelque institution," and on the radical division as to source: human or divine. Then, with regard to final ranking, if we engage in sciences of quantity and of physical nature, our own powers and discernment must come first, and Pascal posits the priority of reason (with the assistance, where relevant, of empirical observation); but if we seek knowledge of objects in fact inaccessible to our powers – or by nature beyond them – we must rely on others, and Pascal is prepared to accept here accounts provided by authorities, and the contrast human/divine reappears, completing the integrative or architectonic phase of his argument.

He has in mind also advice regarding confusions and perversions possible within this basic framework. Commenting on the distinction between the two sorts of sciences, he writes:

L'éclaircissement de cette différence doit nous faire plaindre l'aveuglement de ceux qui apportent la seule autorité pour preuve dans les matières physiques, au lieu du raisonnement ou des expériences, et nous donner de l'horreur pour la malice des autres, qui emploient le raisonnement seul dans la théologie au lieu de l'autorité de l'Ecriture et des Pères. (L231a; MII779)

What he fears most particularly here concerns what happens in physics. He emphasizes that we should not abandon entirely in physics our consideration for authority; what we need is not respect pure and simple and blind, but respect that may be allowed to stand until the old has been confirmed by demonstrations or experiments (at which time authority becomes unnecessary). Ancient doctrines regarding, for example, the nature of the Milky Way or the incorruptibility of beings beyond the sphere of the moon had a claim to our attention until the telescope showed the former to be composed of stars, and until the observation of changes in comets made the latter untenable. Rather than have the status of indisputable principles, such views are subject to the rules of rational evidence.

Pascal does not develop here an argument for the proper use of reason in the domain of authority. But I doubt that he meant to exclude it on principle. He works, as often, toward a balance between extremes, so as to avoid unthinking attachment to either of the sources of certainty. In fact, the second paragraph of the *Préface* consists of this sentence: "Ce n'est pas que mon intention soit de corriger un vice par un autre, et de ne faire nulle estime des anciens parce que l'on en fait trop" (L230b; MII777). From what we know from other places of Pascal as an elucidator, an advocate, an apologist, and a critic, it is clear that reason has a great deal of legitimate work to do outside of the sciences: in identifying, at the outset, proper authority, in interpreting and extending the content of what one takes on faith and by authority, and in making the discernment of truth from error. In short, the two main terms, "reason" and "authority," undergo at his hands a sort of *dédoublement*, and take on by turns a primary and an ancillary status in his reasoning; each may appear in the area of the other, but in a limited way.

TOWARD AN ART OF INTEGRATION

I have attempted in this section to review the fundamental operations, the basic procedures that permit Pascal to distinguish and then to unify the sciences. Taken along with the criteria that he applies, they bring us to an approximation of his way of working. However, they do not exhaust what I am calling his art of systematization. For an adequate view of that, we must include, it seems to me, the set of topics proposed above and arranged along the fruitful line consisting of faculties, habits, activities, objects or subject-matters, and final products. Pascal's effort to classify and to integrate the sciences becomes possible against this background and through the interplay of those factors.

Of course, the *Préface* is just that; it is not a treatise; it is not even a completely composed preface; and Pascal worked into it some strongly rhetorical elements. His design includes appeals to three sorts of readers: to the generally curious, but mainly to the learned, some of whom he knows are positively inclined toward his inquiries, some negatively. He draws up a rapid survey of the disciplines and sciences as a means of accomplishing his main objective, which is to present methodically, against that sketched-in background, his experiments and conclusions regarding the *vide*. But even with these restrictions, we recognize in these pages Pascal's usual clarity, penetration, and consistency. At a time when his scientific interests were at a peak, they serve to bring into a single view, with indications of specific differences as well as of interrelations, the different parts of his intellectual universe. They will assume further meaning when we shall have occasion to see them in connection with his complex "art de persuader" and with the synoptic scheme of three orders that emerges in the *Pensées*.

CHAPTER 3

Multiplicity, unity, and dialectic

INTERPRETATION

A CHANGE OF DIRECTION

The preceding analyses grew out of the fact that Pascal is wonderfully competent and innovative when he works in the geometrical mode and according to the intellectual habits rooted in that mode. He grasps the implications of that way of thinking for the mental activities essential to his inquiries: recovery, discovery, ordering, and systematization, each of which takes on its particular identity and coloration in the light of the mode chosen as dominant. Conceived and applied in the geometrical perspective – which includes modifications that adjust it to the requirements of experimental projects – the basic activities are expressed, as is appropriate, in univocal language and in demonstrative discourse.

Of course, that is not the only mode in which Pascal excels. He is adept in at least two other major arts of the mind, (1) dialectic and (2) rhetoric. To look forward for a moment: with a grasp of the way in which Pascalian dialectic proceeds – it does not develop independently but presupposes geometric and sometimes builds on it, usually by contrast – and after studying the principal aspects of Pascal's rhetoric, we shall eventually be able to draw these different orientations into a single and cumulative picture. Our present purpose, however, is to understand and reflect on the first of the remaining pair of disciplines. The sense of the contrast between the preceding *esprit de géométrie* and the dialectical habit of mind will become clearer as we proceed. And, regarding my vocabulary here, I should like to point out that, although Pascal does not use the traditional term "dialectic," the formulas he uses to describe what he is doing show clearly the degree to which he understands not only the basic requirements of this new method but also how to apply it effectively, how to specify it to different circumstances.

In fact, for him the change of intellectual style is correlated with a change in the problem-area, or, more precisely, in the scope of the area of interest to him. To this point we have observed him as he deals with Nature, studied mainly in its quantitative and mechanical aspects and according to the disciplinary norms of mathematics or of mathematical physics. Now, however, adding an important new dimension, he becomes acutely conscious of the relation that inquiries of that sort have to an attitude centered on problems of morality and religious life. Nature and natural science are infinite, even infinitely interesting – or should I say, puzzling – but they and those who study them depend finally on a Person who transcends the physical universe as its author and end. Preoccupation with scientific problems may present an obstacle to progress in the scientist's understanding of himself, of others, and of the situation of Christian doctrine in the contemporary Church.

The drive for unification typical of this new way of looking at oneself and the world calls for a mode of discussion essentially different from that of geometry, though, as I have said, Pascal sees at certain moments important interrelations between the two. The new predominance of dialectic has many consequences for the main intellectual operations discernible in the works and, therefore, for the habits of thought, the arts that initiate and guide Pascal's creative activity. We have seen how the geometrical mode leaves its marks on statements, concepts, sequences, and systems constructed in its proper sphere of application. Here, in like fashion, the distinctive signs of his dialectical method appear in a pervasive way.

TEXTUAL BASES

The non-mathematical and non-scientific works to be considered here are all clearly concerned with morality and religion. The topics they treat vary a great deal, but I believe that every item on the list has a place, finally, in the same basic perspective:

> *Sur la Conversion du pécheur*;
> *Entretien avec M. de Saci*;
> *Abrégé de la vie de Jésus-Christ*;
> *Ecrits sur la grâce*;
> *Comparaison des chrétiens des premiers temps avec ceux d'aujourd'hui*;
> *Prière pour demander à Dieu le bon usage des maladies*;
> *Trois discours sur la condition des Grands*;
> *Ecrit sur la signature du Formulaire*;
> *Les Provinciales*;
> *Les Ecrits des curés de Paris*;
> *Les Pensées*.

To the foregoing we should add a group of letters written by Pascal to friends and to members of his family.

Apart from variations in topics discussed, the texts differ in several other ways: (1) as to length and discursive complexity: we go from personal letters consisting of a few lines to sustained arguments of the kind found in the polemical texts; (2) as to degree of finish: from a complete document like the *Prière pour demander à Dieu le bon usage des maladies* to a collection of fragments (as in the *Pensées* or, a more extreme case, in the *Trois discours sur la condition des Grands*, reconstructed in part from accounts composed by others); (3) as to character of the addressee: at one end of the spectrum, what seem to be summaries of meditations and notes for Pascal's own use (as in *Sur la Conversion du pécheur*), then correspondence with family members or with friends, involving many instances of spiritual direction, and after that, near the other end of the line, elaborately conceived works – adversarial or apologetic in nature – either published or intended for publication (such as the *Provinciales* and the *Pensées*).

THE RANGE OF TOPICS

Given, then, a group of texts similar as to the perspective in which Pascal composes them, let us now focus on matters of interpretation and statement, putting ourselves on what has traditionally been the terrain of grammar, conceived broadly as an art of recovering and expressing meanings and their referents. We soon become aware of the fact that Pascal is using, as he moves from situation to situation, a distinction that he found indispensable in the *Préface* to the treatise on the vacuum: the opposition between what we can learn from authoritative sources and what we can learn from direct experience. In the context of the *Préface*, we saw that Pascal tended to separate sharply the two kinds of knowledge or discovery, allowing a great degree of independence for reason and the senses in physics and related sciences, but limiting there the place of authoritative pronouncements, which have only a provisional status that is always subject to revision. In the sphere of dialectical reasoning he shows continually a tendency that stands in sharp contrast: authority has the final word.

The facts and statements with which Pascal is concerned here fall into two broad categories, quite like those of the *Préface*, that is, between those that have been recorded in written sources and those that serve for the interpretation and expression of direct experience, between recorded facts and encountered facts. But the remarkable novelty before us consists in this, that the facts of experience cannot be rightly interpreted unless they are considered in the light of what is furnished in authoritative texts, such as the Bible, the writings of the Fathers, the decisions of Church Councils. Whether seen introspectively and reflexively or taken as facing outward to social contacts, to a vision of Nature, or to an encounter with God (who is, actually, both in us and outside us), human life will be truly understood only when judged and expressed in the light of principles accepted on the basis of faith and authority. This means that reason and sense undergo a radical change of status, becoming insufficient by themselves as sources of true judgments, though they do have value in preliminary or auxiliary ways.

I have just suggested something of the wide range of reflection and statement in which Pascal is involved: situations like those in which the human subject (1) studies itself, in Christian variations on the ancient theme of *gnothi seauton*, or (2) relates itself to others in a view of social existence, or (3) sets itself off against the rest of creation and the spectacle of the physical universe, or (4) turns itself decisively to God as its beginning and end. This division provides us with one way of showing the diversity and, incidentally, the interrelations of the statements that Pascal finds himself continually interpreting and expressing as he takes up these lines of thought.

INTERIM CONTEXTS

I have two preliminary remarks to offer here. In the first place, these pairings – of the self and some topic for exploration – and the statements that arise from them belong to contexts, to which one might assign, respectively, adjectives such as: moral, social, scientific, and theological. In other words, my fourfold list evokes fields of discourse open to Pascal – places of departure, exploration, and return for his affirmations and arguments. His facts and truths are not free-standing: they depend in a fundamental way on the terrain where they appear and develop their implications. Already in his preface to the treatise on the *vide*, Pascal has offered us one set of disciplinary reflections that show how his mind works on the problem of grouping and ordering the sciences. Several times in the *Pensées* he suggests another way in which to go about the task. For example:

Vanité des sciences.
La science des choses extérieures ne me consolera pas de l'ignorance de la morale au temps d'affliction, mais la science des mœurs me consolera toujours de l'ignorance des sciences extérieures. (L503a, f23; S46, f57)

Or, when he is inclined to make light of technical or methodical discourse, he turns again to morality, but puts with it two other disciplines:

La vraie éloquence se moque de l'éloquence, la vraie morale se moque
de la morale ... Se moquer de la philosophie c'est vraiment philosopher. (L576d, f513; S346–47, f671)

And yet, in the second place, although Pascal appears to
think of these suggested frameworks as being distinct, as having
their typical problems and lines of argument, it is essential to
understand that all such differentiations are local and
contingent, for the fourth context or field, that of the human
being in his relation to God, contains the terms, notions and
statements to which all the rest are finally referred. Previously
made statements will be true or false according to their
agreement or disagreement with what is said – authoritatively
– about God, his providence, his revelation, his Incarnation, his
Church; and if an occasion arises – as in the fragment on the
three orders – for declarations made elsewhere to be set in
order, we find them located on an exhaustive scale that has been
laid out in view of that reference point.

TRUTH AND VALUE

Pascal thinks that his statements have a serious claim to our
attention because they are true. We are never far from his basic
allegiance to truth, and his concern for finding it, justifying it,
and distinguishing it from error. At the same time, neither are
we far from his preoccupation with the good, with what is to be
sought and what is to be avoided. This holds especially in
Pascal's dialectical way of thinking, for in that mode it is not
really possible to separate truth and value: true statements
embody and express values, while values elicit statements and
establish their truth. Truth and value – or truth and good, to
use language more idiomatic to Pascal – cooperate and, at the
last, coincide. When, for example, he meditates on the order of
his apologetic argument, he writes:

(1) Partie. Misère de l'homme sans Dieu. (2) Partie. Félicité de
l'homme avec Dieu.

autrement

(1) Part. Que la nature est corrompue, par la nature même. (2)
Partie. Qu'il y a un Réparateur, par l'Ecriture. (L501d, f6; S42, f40)

In the first way of expressing his thought, he puts the emphasis on the side of value, of absence or presence of the good in the condition of man, though he surely implies that he will make descriptive, objective, true statements about that condition. In the second version, he formulates two propositions and adds notations as to the sources in which he will seek justifications for making those two statements. Human nature, when approached according to a natural light (" par la nature même ") reveals the truth of its corruption, that is to say, its lack of value; and the restoration of value, by virtue of the Redeemer, has its guarantee of truth in Scripture, in what God has said and done.

One may express the basic point somewhat differently in this way: "truth" and "value" or "good" have a reciprocal relation. Truths have immediate consequences for action and morality; and values or goods have immediate consequences for the pursuit of truth (whether in the relatively narrow confines of science or in the broader moral and religious problem areas). The possibility of error and evil is implied in all of this; they lie everywhere in the shadow of the positive terms; and Pascal finds frequent occasions to point out deviations from the truth and the good, perceived in his various adversaries, or, for that matter, in anyone (including himself). He has much to say, for example, about concupiscence and imagination as sources of error in statements, in thought, and in behavior.

In physics, if one sets it for a moment in contrast with knowledge of morality, the interrelation of fact and value works on two levels. As he goes about investigating natural things, with their parts, mechanisms, and processes, Pascal surely recognizes that the conclusions he reaches have a kind of independence apart from the opinions and passions of the investigator. And there, precisely, we are on the first of the levels I mean: in the act of setting up the difference between scientific and objective statements as opposed to interpretations imbued with wishes or other subjective states, Pascal makes a choice, introduces a value, marks a certain category of statement with a positive coefficient. But he moves everything onto another level, it seems to me, when he asks us to see where our dispassionate science will lead us. If we accept the invitation he

proposes in the fragment on the "Disproportion de l'homme,"
if by observation and imagination we go far enough up into
Nature's silent spaces beyond the stellar universe or far enough
down into its infinitely divisible recesses, we end in aston-
ishment; we cannot help wondering about ourselves and our
place on such a stunning scale of reality. Scientific objectivity,
itself based on a determination of value and then deployed in
the fruitful study of Nature, takes us eventually to questions
concerning the limits of human existence, and makes explicit
our desire for a place where our impulses to seek the truth and
to possess the good may come finally to rest.

A DUAL SUBJECT-MATTER

These facts and values that interact, this familiarity with the
wide range of beings explored, from self to fellow-men to Nature
to God, plus the activities implied in the effort to capture such
a vision in statement – all that suggests and requires, it seems to
me, some comprehensive insight. Irresistibly there comes to
mind the little remark from the *Pensées*, the one that begins "Il
faut avoir une pensée de derrière, et juger de tout par là ... "
(L510d, f91; S74, f125). Although I am aware of the difficulty
of saying what the insight is here (Pascal's mind will always be
out in front of us) and of the risks (one may easily fall into too
much or too little specification), I think that we must attempt to
formulate it.

Let us say that Pascal conceives the reality to which the
activities of language and thought must attain as being
essentially *double*, and, as a corollary, that he traces out
everywhere in greater or lesser detail the consequences of that
consideration. This is something that affects all aspects of the art
of statement whose main features I am undertaking to make
explicit here. What is said, thought, and designated must reflect
or adapt itself to this duality. The terms that constitute it are,
quite simply: (1) God, and (2) everything else. In the universe
of Pascal, we begin with a *two*; and, as human creatures, our
proper destiny is to end in a union, in a *one*. Of course, he
develops and qualifies each of these polar terms. He may take

the "everything else" as creation, with insistence on its essential dependence on God; and, again, that creation may be further specified, as he isolates and identifies the human creature apart from all other creatures; and then he must formulate the relationship holding between two persons, one divine and the other human. Here is how Pascal defines in the *Ecrits sur la grâce* the view held by the disciples of Saint Augustine in regard to human nature as God sees it:

Ils considèrent deux états dans la nature humaine:
   L'un est celui auquel elle a été créée dans Adam, saine, sans tache, juste et droite, sortant des mains de Dieu, duquel rien ne peut partir que pur, saint, et parfait;
   L'autre est l'état où elle a été réduite par le péché et la révolte du premier homme, et par lequel elle est devenue souillée, abominable, et détestable aux yeux de Dieu. (L312d; Mɪɪɪ787)

Or, still on the side of creation, he may wish to stress that a great event has occurred in it, the Incarnation. At that point the possibility and conditions of salvation enter the scheme, topics abundantly discussed in the *Ecrits*; and along another line of thought, there comes a complete revision of human possibilities for knowledge, as is attested by this from the *Pensées*:

Non seulement nous ne connaissons Dieu que par Jésus-Christ mais nous ne nous connaissons nous-mêmes que par J.-C.; nous ne connaissons la vie, la mort que par Jésus-Christ. Hors de J.-C. nous ne savons ce que c'est ni que notre vie, ni que notre mort, ni que Dieu, ni que nous-mêmes. (L550a, f417; S40, f36)

And he can engage in the same kind of development on the left-hand side of the picture: God eludes us, but by this or that paradox we have some inkling of his nature: he is hidden and yet revealed, just and yet merciful, transcendent and yet intimately present to us, providential and having a plan for his creation and yet allowing for the exercise of human freedom.

Many such elaborations of the original distinction appear in the whole list of documents where, as I see it, Pascal gives free rein to the impulse to think in the dialectical mode. The reality that underlies the process of interpretation and statement has two dimensions, with each side of the couple serving to make the other intelligible. If we go on to conceive the opposition in personal terms, we must say that each one seeks out the other: movement appears in the scheme. Pascal invites the human person to set out on an ascending path that complements and meets the descending movement coming from God (understanding always that the overriding initiative and power lie on the divine side). In *Sur la Conversion du pécheur* he traces, stage by stage, the ascension of the soul from things of this world to the throne of God; here are a few lines regarding the end of the journey:

Cette élévation est si éminente et si transcendante, qu'elle ne s'arrête pas au ciel: il n'a pas de quoi la satisfaire, ni au-dessus du ciel, ni aux anges, ni aux êtres les plus parfaits. Elle traverse toutes les créatures, et ne peut arrêter son coeur qu'elle ne se soit rendue jusqu'au trône de Dieu, dans lequel elle commence à trouver son repos et ce bien qui est tel qu'il n'y a rien de plus aimable, et qu'il ne peut lui être ôté que par son propre consentement. (L291b; MIV42)

Consequently, in language and statement one is always dealing with an antithesis, the emphasis falling on one or the other aspect according to the context – or, perhaps, falling equally on the two, if the argument requires; but never is the one held strictly apart from the other. For a particular purpose Pascal may speak as he does in the *Pensées* of "l'homme sans Dieu" and "l'homme avec Dieu" as though he had in mind a separation. But note that he cannot define the first of those two régimes without a reference to the other; and, furthermore, those whom he places in the first category are still subject to the action of grace.

CONSEQUENCES FOR MEANINGS

In this discussion of certain grammatical points that arise in the dialectical mode we find ourselves dealing with three factors: terms, meanings, and their applications. So far we have been examining the last of these, considered as subject-matter. But what are the consequences of Pascal's basic insight for the other two? I believe there are three main lines of development:

(1) He must engage in a kind of thinking and interpretation that is figurative: the notion of "figure" is absolutely necessary

if we are to grasp at all adequately the objects before us, which have always two aspects, connected both intimately and dynamically. Our reflection may begin in confusion, failing in the first moment to achieve a proper discernment, but Pascal intends that we should eventually manage to draw the veil aside, so as to see the other side of things, and finally to recognize the priority of the hidden sense. Late in 1656 in one of his letters to the Roannez, Pascal works out three variations on the theme:

Toutes choses couvrent quelque mystère; toutes choses sont des voiles qui couvrent Dieu. Les Chrétiens doivent le reconnaître en tout. Les afflictions temporelles couvrent les biens éternels où elles conduisent. Les joies temporelles couvrent les maux éternels qu'elles causent. (L267c; MIIII1036–37)

This passage, coming near the end of the letter, states the general principle and applies it to moral experience. A few lines earlier Pascal uses it in connection with the Bible:

On peut ajouter à ces considérations le secret de l'Esprit de Dieu caché encore dans l'Ecriture. Car il y a deux sens parfaits, le littéral et le mystique; et les Juifs s'arrêtant à l'un ne pensent pas seulement qu'il y en ait un autre, et ne songent pas à le chercher, de même que les impies, voyant les effets naturels, les attribuent à la nature, sans penser qu'il y en ait un autre auteur... (L267c; MIIII1036)

The reference here to "nature" and its hidden "auteur" may be easily attached to another passage in the same letter concerning the "Dieu caché":

Si Dieu se découvrait continuellement aux hommes, il n'y aurait point de mérite à le croire; et s'il ne se découvrait jamais, il y aurait peu de foi. Mais il se cache ordinairement, et se découvre rarement à ceux qu'il veut engager à son service. (L267b; MIIII1035)

Start with afflictions and joys, with Scripture, with Nature, with God Himself: in every case Pascal thinks it necessary to look for a second, less apparent dimension; and to fail to reach that second aspect condemns us to error. Every important term in Pascal's discourse bears thus an ambiguity, and this is the logical origin of the tendency to figurative or analogical interpretation so basic in Pascal's moral and religious thought. I believe that his frequent search for what he calls the "raisons des effets" reflects a similar – or indeed the same – purpose. In all but the last of the passages quoted, the direction taken by his argument runs from the inferior sense to its higher analogue.

(2) Pascal devises an important counterpart that shows up in the descending movement characteristic of grace or inspiration. This kind of meaning or perception, which is given by God, obtains in the many passages where Pascal interprets biblical prophecies – or, indeed, engages in a bit of prophetic thought and speech of his own; and it has its place in the mind of any faithful Christian. In such cases, Pascal exemplifies the reverse of figuration: instead of going from the lower to the higher meaning, he and the prophets are led by the spirit to insight regarding the letter.

(3) In the third place, and generalizing from the preceding, we may draw attention to a constant feature of Pascal's thinking in these dialectical writings: the resort to analogy. Since the universe shows everywhere the marks of a pervasive structure, since everything apart from God belongs in the same general order, it is inevitable that thought in the dialectical mode should be fundamentally analogical. Pascal has before him in the temporal order a reality wherein differences are neither total nor final; and as he moves from one subject to the next, he has no difficulty in making transitions (however difficult they may be at times for his readers), because he knows that he will find, along with difference, some degree of likeness. The new subject can only be another instance of letter and spirit, of reality and figure. Every partial context must reproduce in some way the nature of things as it has been established in the whole picture. A particularly good example of what I mean may be seen in the strict parallel that holds between the religious life of the individual and the religious life of the race – or of the Church. Again, in one of the letters to the Roannez, Pascal defines the analogy with great clarity:

Je lisais tantôt le 13e chapitre de saint Marc en pensant à vous écrire, et aussi je vous dirai ce que j'y ai trouvé. Jésus-Christ y fait un grand discours à ses Apôtres sur son dernier avènement; et comme tout ce qui arrive à l'Eglise arrive aussi à chaque Chrétien en particulier, il est certain que tout ce chapitre prédit aussi bien l'état de chaque personne, qui en se convertissant détruit le vieil homme en elle, que l'état de l'univers entier, qui sera détruit pour faire place à de nouveaux cieux et à une nouvelle terre, comme dit l'Ecriture. (L265b; MIII1029)

In every context Pascal sees the same structures, the same intermittences, the same episodes of conversion and aversion. Choices and sequences reported in the Bible are re-enacted again and again, since the divine plan is working itself out in individuals, collectivities, and Nature.

CONSEQUENCES FOR LANGUAGE

Designations and meanings have parallels in language, the material out of which statements are made. When working in the dialectical mode, Pascal introduces us to problems quite different from those of geometry and physics. In the sciences, his basic attitude toward language is highly prescriptive; discourse must be fashioned according to agreed-upon rules of definition and combination; he has little or no patience with ordinary usage; and if we do not accept and observe the rules, what we say is simply disqualified. Instead of promoting such a radical reformulation of language Pascal adopts now a very different attitude. Inclusive rather than exclusive, it willingly takes off from ordinary language, explicitly setting aside the model of geometry. Rather than insisting on clarity and order from the beginning and always, it allows for confusion at the start. In fact, the essence of the interpretative procedure here would appear to be the gradual clarification of language; one progresses into the light, reaching it at the end of the process, not at the outset. At any rate that would be the experience of the person Pascal addresses in his apologetic vein; while his own attitude, his own state of mind comes out, I think, in this little fragment:

Raison des effets.
    Il faut avoir une pensée de derrière, et juger de tout par là, en parlant cependant comme le peuple. (L510d, f91; S74, f125)

Here "effets" would seem to apply to the speech according to popular usage; then the "pensée de derrière," along with the judgment of everything that accompanies it, would constitute the "raison" lying behind and explaining the speech.

Although a highly developed sense of the sequence and of the structure within which statements must fit goes, as we have shown, with the "esprit de géométrie," Pascal finds himself in the context of dialectic, very often engaged not in assembling a demonstrative argument but in making a crucial discrimination, in uncovering and expressing in a paradox the contrarieties that define moral and religious reality. Paradoxes are rare in mathematics and physics, because figures and things, triangles and mercury, are what they are, and what they are is single, not double. Their natures are not inherently contradictory, whereas the human subject is large and small, wretched and great; Jesus Christ is God and man; God is merciful and just. If, in science, a contradiction in statement usually signals an error, it is required for truth in morals and religion.

As discourse proceeds in the dialectical manner, statements tend to separate into two kinds: those located on the plane of literal meanings (and the attempt will always be made to go beyond their limits) or those occurring on the plane of additional and figurative meanings. One thinks again of the great distinction between the situation of man "sans" or "avec" Dieu. Two indefinitely large fields of statement are set up by those two prepositions. In the first, under the sign of proofs "par la Nature," propositions tend to arrange themselves in oppositions, in ambivalent pairs. But the final development of the arguments may turn out to be a situation where two extreme and therefore only partially true positions give way to a third position – with corresponding statements that set forth the whole truth of the matter in question. Pascal offers a fairly spectacular example of this procedure at the climax of the *Entretien avec M. de Saci*. After setting forth for M. de Saci the theses of Epictetus and Montaigne so arrayed that each position destroys the other, he adds triumphantly:

De sorte qu'ils ne peuvent subsister seuls à cause de leurs défauts, ni s'unir à cause de leurs oppositions, et qu'ainsi ils se brisent et s'anéantissent pour faire place à la vérité de l'Evangile. C'est elle qui accorde les contrariétés par un art tout divin, et, unissant tout ce qui est de vrai et chassant tout ce qui est de faux, elle en fait une sagesse véritablement céleste où s'accordent ces opposés, qui étaient incompatibles dans ces doctrines humaines. (L296d; M$_{III}$153–54)

One could cite many other examples of this reconciling technique, especially from the *Ecrits sur la grâce* and from the *Pensées*. An interesting variation occurs in Pascal's general approach to the task of harmonizing the Old and New Testaments: he finds that statements made on one side of the opposition – the Old Testament – must be treated figuratively, but on the New Testament side they must be taken literally; the idea of interpreting Jesus Christ figuratively shocks him.

In any case, it is clear that statements made under the sign of geometry have to find their exact place in a demonstrative sequence, each one having, so to speak, a coefficient that fixes its relation to a statement that precedes it and to another that follows it. But relations among statements made in the dialectical perspective depend less on a sequential order than on a diagram of forces that sums up contrasts, priorities, and reconciliations. This will be a matter for longer treatment when we consider Pascal's art of presentation.

GENERAL AND PARTICULAR PREDICATION

If we observe for a while the stream of his language, we begin to see certain regularities in the subjects about which Pascal makes predications. For one thing, they take their places along a scale of generality going from the unique to the universal. Let us start with the latter end of the line; it is frequent and characteristic in great blocks of Pascalian discourse. "La condition humaine," man in general, man with his weaknesses and aspirations – unqualified by social or historical arrangements or circumstances – there you surely have one of Pascal's favorite subjects. In this context, his statements illuminate great sectors of human experience; they assume something of the force of scientific generalizations, the resemblance becoming especially clear as we read the confrontations that Pascal works out from time to time between man and the whole of Nature.

Particularizing tendencies in statement are no less characteristic, however. Pascal may concentrate, for example, on the
various situations of his contemporaries as they are distributed
over the scale of the seventeenth-century French social hierarchy. And he can study their manners and those of other
nations in a comparative light, concluding vigorously against
the arguments for anything like the existence of a universal
justice.

Another kind of particularizing statement, dogmatic rather
than skeptical, occurs when Pascal turns to reflect on his own
activities, his health, his attitude toward his personal moral
situation – there the incomparable document is the *Prière pour
demander à Dieu le bon usage des maladies* – or when he addresses
and advises others on their personal needs and spiritual welfare,
as in the correspondence with the Roannez. Statements of this
kind are quickly caught up in a typical feature of Pascal's
language and thought in the dialectical mode: the tendency to
make a leap from individual destinies to parallels in the history
and destiny of the human race. Every present situation in the
life of every one of us has a definite relation to something in the
Bible, to some event or episode in the great narrative stretching
from Adam to Noah to Moses to Prophets to Jesus Christ, and
thereafter, to something in the history of the Church. Our
ontogeny as individuals repeats in a way our religious phy-
logeny. In the "Mémorial," after evoking the God of the Bible
(as opposed to the God of the philosophers and savants he
writes: "Je m'en suis séparé." Immediately thereafter he sees a
parallel from the book of Jeremiah: "Dereliquerunt me fontem
aquae vivae." Twice he writes, "Jésus-Christ," and then, in a
series of verbs – "Je m'en suis séparé, je l'ai fui, renoncé,
crucifié" – he interprets his personal experience against a
biblical background (L618cd, f913; Mɪɪɪ FCR50; S432, f742).

Or, again, there is a type of historical writing to be found in
the "Comparaison des chrétiens des premiers temps avec ceux
d'aujourd'hui." Pascal describes and analyzes two historical
realities, in fact: the serious discipline of the former, who
received baptism after long instruction, and the superficiality of
the latter, who tend to be baptized as infants and then never to

mature in faith and action. Moreover, the nature of the historical statements is noteworthy, for Pascal is writing about two groups, not two individuals; and the facts summarize collective phenomena. After a single introductory sentence, itself cast in the form of an opposition, Pascal offers a series of parallel statements:

On n'entrait dans l'Eglise qu'après de grands travaux et de longs désirs.
On s'y trouve aujourd'hui sans aucune peine, sans soin et sans travail.

On n'y était admis alors qu'après un examen très exact.
On y est reçu maintenant avant qu'on soit en état d'être examiné.

On n'y était reçu alors qu'après avoir abjuré sa vie passée, qu'après avoir renoncé au monde, et à la chair et au diable.
On y entre maintenant avant qu'on soit en état de faire aucune de ces choses. (L360ab; MIV54)

The rest of his argument follows the same plan, though each of the propositions is developed more fully, and the antitheses are built up into paragraphs. Finally, and in another vein, Pascal produces a remarkable instance of historical writing in the *Abrégé de la vie de Jésus-Christ*, where he assembles from the various gospel accounts a numbered sequence of particular events running from the beginning to the end of the life of Christ.

THE OUTLINES OF AN ART

Clearly, when Pascal switches into the dialectical way of thinking, an art of interpretation and expression consonant with that mode comes into being. All of the necessary signs or ingredients are present in the documents, it seems to me, and sufficiently worked out to permit an analysis. First of all, Pascal's experience – both vicarious (through reading) and personal – provides the basis with which to begin. Visible in and through the texts under discussion, this experience covers a period of approximately twelve years; it concerns not only theoretical problems but also relations with people – with people present in the roles of family members and friends, with nuns, scholars, and priests at Port-Royal, with a widening circle of readers. It is experience mobilized for use according to varying aims: communication, persuasion, polemic.

However, Pascal has a habit in decisive moments of considering everything from a single point of view, that of strict Augustinian Christianity. As he moves in that perspective toward the formation of the art of recovery and statement that I am outlining here, a process of conceptualization begins; it leads to an insight concerning the subject-matter of the art and what it is that he will want to interpret or express. The central problem concerns God and His creation. In that creation human beings stand out as having a measure of knowledge and even of freedom – freedom that is real though hard to define within the divine plan and ultimately mysterious; but in its exercise a determination is made that decides within limits how the human subject will relate itself to God. However, the main point at this juncture is that the dialectical way of thinking, as it plays over Pascal's experience, brings him to a dualistic view of reality as a whole.

All this has consequences, as I have shown, for interpretation, for repossessing and expressing what is known – in other words, for two characteristic activities of a grammatical art, activities that involve statements, meanings, and applications or designations. We may separate the three factors temporarily and by an analytical effort. However, since the basic drive of the dialectical mode is toward unity, we find Pascal treating them as implying one another and working in parallel. His work of interpretation starts from a duality noted in things, primarily, but echoed and embedded equally in thought and language. He tends in statement, therefore, to cast the questions he raises and the answers he gives in the form of oppositions, antitheses, paradoxes.

In the negative phase of the argument, he makes us constantly, even painfully aware of a doubling whereby each important term entering into the process of statement has two semantic colorations, both unfavorable. The *Pensées* furnish the obvious example: "l'homme" with his concupiscent "misère" and his prideful "grandeur." In the positive phase of the argument, Pascal introduces another doubling, this time between an unfavorable and a favorable sense. Thus, as he moves the argument from the terrain of "sans Dieu" onto that of "avec Dieu," the opposition lies between a negative view of man as an unresolved paradox and a positive view of man as a creature whose aspirations toward truth and good have come to a right focus on the True, which happens also to be the Good.

Or again, for another example of this contextual variation in the semantic value of terms, note the case of "imagination": the fragment having that word set off as a kind of title (L504b, f44; S50, f78) describes at length the misdeeds of that "maîtresse d'erreur et de fausseté"; but in the fragment on the "Disproportion de l'homme" (L525d, f199; S125, f230), it would have been impossible for Pascal to achieve the effects he desires in his evocations of Nature without calling on the imagination for help: "Mais si notre vue s'arrête là, que l'imagination passe outre, elle se lassera plutôt de concevoir que la nature de fournir." In other words, the elements out of which statements are made take on distinctive and specific characteristics as Pascal exercises his dialectic. In order to make paradoxical assertions he must have recourse to ambiguous terms with senses that evolve as the contexts change.

In a different connection above I quoted a little sentence, simply put, but rich in implications, that attests to what I mean to say: "Il faut avoir une pensée de derrière, et juger de tout par là, en parlant cependant comme le peuple." All of the factors are there, thought (in "pensée" and "juger"), things or subject-matter (in "tout"), language (in the phrase "en parlant comme le peuple"). His art of interpretation and expression goes forward in a way that keeps them all in proper relation simultaneously. As I have suggested, Pascal's project requires some initial ingredients – such as a body of diverse experiences, a regulating insight, a grasp of its corollaries, a pertinent framework of discourse; and as the art begins to function, it offers guidance to Pascal in determining the senses of statements, those encountered in books or conversations and those serving as expressions of his own judgments – all within a totalizing view of God and his creation.

GEOMETRIC AND DIALECTIC

In the régime of geometric Pascal hemmed in his language with quite explicit restrictions and rules. Likewise, he adopted a strict posture with regard to thought, or, to stay closer to his idiom, our thinking faculties. When he worked on problems involving numbers, figures, or liquids (in arithmetic, geometry, and physics, respectively), he was opposed to any intrusion of opinion, imagination, or desire. He prescribed the exclusive use of reason and of sense, and more specifically, of the former as subject to the rules of deduction and of the latter as subject to experimental techniques. Similar precautions prevailed as he defined subject-matters: in the mathematical and scientific mode, he considered quantities and things *ad hoc*, apart from God – in fact, isolated even from the whole of Nature. And I might add that in his physical inquiries he regularly homogenizes things, reducing them to two quantitative aspects, weight and shape, and achieving thus in the physical world something like the stability of univocal definitions.

In the dialectical mode we find differences everywhere. Instead of obliging us to learn a new and logically impeccable language, Pascal allows us to start from everyday usage; indeed, he does so willingly, in order to make the most of its grasp of ordinary affairs. Instead of limiting us to highly methodized uses of reason and sense, he has the same openness, the same willingness to begin where readers and interlocutors already are, and to work away from that, without insisting on preliminary *évidences* and conventions. Instead of narrowing the focus to a few kinds of things – or aspects of things – he takes a panoramic view; the universe from top to bottom is made accessible to everyone who is seeking to make correct discriminations and true statements. Instead of presupposing a clearly bounded structure into which every affirmation or negation will find its proper and sequential place – the "ordre de l'esprit" –

he selects another possibility, based on the notion of an end that is always kept in sight as one discourses freely and digressively on topics related to that end – in other words, the "ordre du cœur." In Pascal's succinct formulation: "Cet ordre consiste principalement à la digression sur chaque point qui a rapport à la fin, pour la montrer toujours" (L539d, f298; S175, f329). Contrasts such as these in the group of documents under study here indicate unmistakably that Pascal has deliberately set geometric aside. In its place he has perfected and used a new habit of intellectual performance, based on transcendental rather than on analytical principles: in short, a dialectic, with its own way of defining terms, justifying assumptions, laying out procedures, and reaching the truth.

INVENTION

TWO PRELIMINARY REMARKS

We have just examined some important facets of an art of methodical interpretation and statement, as it appears in a number of Pascal's works that treat questions relating to man, world, and God; and we have noted the need always to keep in mind the local context or framework within which statements occur. However, Pascal focuses, from time to time, on something that is, in a sense, more fundamental than either of those two parts of his analyses: the selection of terms, that is, of the elements that will enter into the composition of statements. As he works with these smaller units, he develops and exemplifies an art proper to the task of finding and specifying them.

One can certainly relate this art to rhetoric; in fact, I am convinced that it is an essential part of rhetoric, though I do not think it necessary to enter here on a detailed justification for that assertion. Let it suffice to say that I shall not here approach the problems of rhetoric in exactly the way chosen by Pascal in his pages and reflections on the "art de persuader." His position on that topic is discussed in a later chapter of this study. For my present purpose I shall concentrate on a particular operation, invention, which is the first of the traditional five activities –

invention, disposition, expression, memory, and delivery – assigned to rhetoric. Invention is, indeed, the starting point, the *sine qua non*, of the whole process that brings a discourse into being.

Let me add one further preliminary remark in order to clarify the limits of my discussion. Insofar as rhetoric and, in particular, one of its major processes are involved here, they take on a particular bias, since they fall in the domain and under the principles of dialectic, whose purposes they serve. On some occasions Pascal conceives of rhetoric as arguing from positions justified by a dialectic as he undertakes projects of communication and persuasion: that seems to me to be the case in the *Pensées* and to some extent in the *Provinciales*. There rhetoric is in charge, so to speak; it borrows principles and distinctions from dialectic, which has an ancillary role. Here, however, I want to show Pascal taking up into ongoing dialectical inquiries the intellectual activity of invention, along with some of its devices; in other words, he inverts the relationship just indicated and redefines the rhetorical technique so as to make of it the *ancilla*.

A WIDESPREAD PHENOMENON

The problem with which we must begin, as we undertake to discern and define the habit of inventive thought discernible in the texts before us, is that of divergent opinions, disagreement, dispute, controversy. Pascal seems to thrive in situations where contradictions abound, sides are taken, and clashes occur. The disagreement with Father Noël over the *vide*, like the lengthy exchanges in connection with the contest over the *roulette* curve, show to what acuteness and intensity Pascal could rise when facing opponents in physics and mathematics. In our present context, the first thing likely to come to mind is the running conflict in the *Provinciales* between the Jesuit and Jansenist points of view and their partisans. It is remarkable not only for the complexity of the issues treated but also for the emotional tone of the discussion, the vehemence that becomes all the more extreme as the quarrel moves from episode to episode. In the *Écrits sur la grâce*, where so many of the theses advanced in the

Provinciales have their theoretical justification, Pascal often finds himself in the position of someone surveying disagreements, at times minor but more often rich in consequences, and undertaking to bring them to a resolution. He has a great deal of self-confidence in such circumstances, a belief in his ability to work through the difficulties and to make his way – taking us with him – to the truth that has been obscured in partial and partisan statements.

In the *Ecrits*, for example, he analyzes a scene that has more than one historical level: he shows us an earlier picture, to which the Post-Reformation situation is closely analogous in structure. When he looks back to Augustine and his polemic against the Pelagians and the Manichaeans, he finds a striking resemblance to the conditions that followed on the Council of Trent, where Molinists and semi-Pelagians are pitted in theology or in action against Calvinists and Lutherans. At several points in the *Ecrits* he draws up little tables in order to sum up and to relate the various positions.

Or, again, in the *Pensées*, as he introduces his reader to the truth about the human condition, Pascal makes distinctions at one moment between the *opinions du peuple* and the opinions of those who think themselves superior, at another moment between the attitude of an indifferent or hostile *libre penseur* and that of a seeker, and at still another moment between simple, unquestioning faith and the faith of a Pascalian seeker who has made an elaborate preparation for belief by using his reason to the limit. Even clearer is the dispute that he evokes on the level of philosophical doctrine between the dogmatists and the Pyrrhonians (the conflict is closely related to the positions attributed to Epictetus and Montaigne in the *Entretien avec M. de Saci*). Later – still in the *Pensées* – passing to the level of religious discussion, he must take up the interpretation of the Bible, and that leads him to the opposition between the Christians and their reading of the Old Testament – as prophetic – and the Jews and *their* reading, which lacks the keys provided by the *figures*. Or, again, take the fragment on the old and new Christians, those of the first centuries of the Church as opposed to those of Pascal's day.

In more personal documents, such as the letter to his sister Gilberte and her husband that contains his reflections on the death of their father, we find something similar: Pascal builds up an opposition between the sadness of the event as seen in merely human terms and its positive, consoling aspect as seen in the light of faith. And again, when Pascal decides to compose a prayer on the right use of illness, the paradox, the potential disagreement, is embedded in the very title of the work. Finally, in the lines where he states his position regarding the signing of the formulary – regarding the five allegedly heretical propositions allegedly found in the writings of Jansenius – Pascal places himself in complete disagreement with his friends at Port-Royal; in his view, to sign the document without explicit restrictions would leave intentions and understandings ambiguous, even abominably so.

THE USES OF TOPICS

Such disagreements provide a fertile soil for the art that I wish to discuss here. In their more developed forms, they occur, let us say, between positions that come into existence within a framework, which may be a structure taken to be representative of a discipline or – something less formal – a context that supports a coherent line of thought; and within that structure certain parties have made or are making statements that contradict one another. We may take one further step, however, and examine the elements out of which such statements are formed: the terms and concepts at issue. If we look back at our list and observe Pascal's usual practice, we find him, I believe, concentrating regularly and explicitly on *ambiguities* as lying at the root or origin of disagreements. Then it becomes possible to isolate, from case to case, what was an object of particular attention for him – and the subject-matter of a technique designed to remedy the difficulty. And we have some chance of grasping the characteristic role of invention in Pascal's dialectical discourse.

At the start of a typical instance there is a confused situation that he intends to clarify. The two (or more) parties to the dispute mistakenly think they are talking about the same thing. However, that ambiguity, that shadowy subject – in spite of the negative connotations it may later have – is a positive precondition, a *sine qua non*: without it as a basis and without the peculiar stimulus it offers there would be no discussion. It suggests to us Pascal's oft-repeated formula, *raison des effets*, and the cause-seeking attitude that goes with it. I am inclined to think that the fundamental insight in the art we are studying here occurs at the point where the subject-matter to be investigated is finally conceived as a *topic* that is unstable, a subject only apparently shared that is being discussed in only apparently shared meanings. When that degree of understanding is reached, it seems fair to say, Pascal has a grip on the *raison* that will explain eventually all the *effets* observable in the discussion. Sometimes he works with a topic in the sense of a general notion, such as *libre arbitre* or *grâce*; at other times he may treat what we might call in a stricter sense a subject, when he has in mind some thing about which predications are being made, as in the case of the Bible, or Nature, or, of course, human nature. And so the act of inventing requires at the outset the discovery of a bone of contention.

In the *Ecrits sur la grâce*, Pascal moves steadily from some opening remarks to the statement of a basic question on which there is disagreement:

...il est question de savoir:
Si ce qu'il y a des hommes sauvés et damnés procède de ce que Dieu le veut ou de ce que les hommes veulent. (L312b; MIII784)

He brings the question of salvation into sharper focus in a restatement:

C'est-à-dire que:
Il est question de savoir si Dieu, se soumettant les volontés des hommes, a eu une volonté absolue de sauver les uns et de damner les autres...
Ou si, soumettant au libre arbitre des hommes l'usage de ses grâces, il a prévu de quelle sorte les uns ou les autres en voudraient user, et que suivant leurs volontés il ait formé celle de leur salut ou de leur condamnation. (L312b; MIII785)

Then, taking further control of the situation in its logical aspect, Pascal rises to a synoptic view:

Voilà la question qui est aujourd'hui agitée entre les hommes, et qui est diversement décidée par trois avis.

Les premiers sont les Calvinistes, les seconds sont les Molinistes, les derniers sont les disciples de saint Augustin. (L312b; Mɪɪɪ785)

The third opinion he refers to – that of Augustine and his disciples – will be developed after a more elaborate presentation of the difference between the Calvinists and the Molinists.

SOME BASIC OPERATIONS

Actually, as my example has just shown, Pascal's intuition of what the issue is in a particular discussion is so sure that he spends relatively little time in describing the confused situation that he has encountered, though details may follow in his analyses. Rather he quickly sets himself and us down in the presence of oppositions like those just noted. To make a rapid statement of an issue is, in fact, one of the basic operations of the habit of mind I am discussing here, and the result is a platform, a *known* – and for practical purposes, *accepted* – basis on which the process of invention can work.

The next phase begins with the attempt to deal with the difficulty; in fact, the operations of the art of invention comprise precisely those mental activities that are required for the movement from some initial confusion to a clear view of what is at issue. After defining the opposition and restating it in various ways, Pascal moves in the direction of two outcomes.

(1) He may bring the argument to a point where he simply leaves the antithesis, having drawn it into sharp focus; he shows the opponents in a continual match of pulling and tugging. An example: Pascal has a very serious interest in the problem of knowledge, and we know from the *Pensées* how he poses that. The question or topic comes to a head in connection with the possibility of knowledge that is *certain*, and he sees here that there may be progress if we fix our attention on the antithesis underlying the controversy between the Pyrrhonians and the

dogmatists, those opponents and proponents of certainty in knowing. After a paragraph in which he shows the former combating the "principes" of the latter, Pascal surveys the whole scene:

Voilà les principales forces de part et d'autre, je laisse les moindres comme les discours qu'ont faits les pyrrhoniens contre les impressions de la coutume... Je m'arrête à l'unique fort des dogmatistes qui est qu'en parlant de bonne foi et sincèrement on ne peut douter des principes naturels. Contre quoi les pyrrhoniens opposent, en un mot, l'incertitude de notre origine qui enferme celle de notre nature. A quoi les dogmatistes sont encore à répondre depuis que le monde dure. (L515a, f131; S88, f164)

He does not provide immediately a solution to the controversy; and like our predicament in the face of the famous wager, each of us is *embarqué*:

Voilà la guerre ouverte entre les hommes, où il faut que chacun prenne parti, et se range nécessairement ou au dogmatisme ou au pyrrhonisme. (L515a, f131; S88, f164)

This final situation, this unending battle, is obviously what he calls elsewhere a "renversement continuel du pour au contre" (L511a, f93; S74, f127).

Within the perspective of moral and religious thought, Pascal not only observes such *renversements*; he will on occasion engage in them deliberately, and be entirely candid about his strategy, as the following fragment testifies. It comes in the context of an alternation between abasing and exalting the possibilities of human nature.

> S'il se vante, je l'abaisse.
> S'il s'abaisse, je le vante.
> Et le contredis toujours.
> Jusqu'à ce qu'il comprenne
> Qu'il est un monstre incompréhensible.
>
> (L514c, f130; S86, f163)

Or, see the case at the end of the fragment on the disproportion of man, where Pascal leaves him surrounded by unresolved infinites and extremes – in Nature, in his own mind, in his own constitution as mind *and* body.

(2) As a matter of fact, Pascal rarely stays at the point of an argument where the antithesis or difference or difference of opinion is in suspense. Almost always he goes beyond such a movement between poles; indeed, that *va-et-vient* becomes itself a basis, a platform on which to formulate a stronger and a more acceptable position. He will want at least to establish a priority and say that one of the two possibilities is preferable to the other, in so doing defining for us the terms of a hierarchical way of thought. In the *Comparaison des chrétiens des premiers temps avec ceux d'aujourd'hui* he presents his comparison point by point, in a series of numbered paragraphs. Again and again he underlines the articulations by phrases like: "Dans les premiers temps..." followed soon after by "... au lieu qu'on voit aujourd'hui," or "Dans le temps de l'Eglise naissante..." followed by "au lieu qu'en ce temps..." Here is a little passage that exemplifies the structure and sums up the argument at the same time:

De là vient qu'on ne voyait autrefois entre les chrétiens que des personnes très instruites;
  au lieu qu'elles sont maintenant dans une ignorance qui fait horreur. (L361a; MIV55)

Of course there is no doubt as to which of the alternatives Pascal favors; he wants a return to the ideas and habits of the early Christians.

What happens more frequently is this: Pascal looks for – and I mean to suggest by that expression a moment in the line of invention – some way of turning the two-term dialectic of antilogism to a three-term dialectic of synthesis and rec-onciliation. And he usually locates a suitable device, a com-prehensive third term, which, when developed discursively, makes it possible for him to combine in a kind of balance the virtues and strengths implied in the original pair of terms, while discarding their disadvantages as extremes.

In the passage quoted above concerning the three views on the subject of God, man, and grace, Pascal leads us first through the opposition of the Molinists to the Calvinists, and then to the opposition of Augustine to the other two. That is how this three-term argument, this *triplex ratio* works. In the *Entretien avec M. de Saci* we have in a very pure form the characteristic structure of this kind of development, even though we cannot be absolutely sure that the argument reproduces words written by Pascal. The partisans of Epictetus (they know about the duties of man but fail to see his impotence, his inability to accomplish them) and the partisans of Montaigne (they know all about the weakness and impotence but do not stress sufficiently the duties) sink into unresolved disagreement – or, as the text puts it, into "une guerre et une destruction générale." Neither side has a position that can stand alone, nor can the disputants locate any means of reconciliation. At this point, Pascal brings in the truth of the Gospel:

C'est elle qui accorde les contrariétés par un art tout divin, et, unissant tout ce qui est de vrai et chassant tout ce qui est de faux, elle en fait une sagesse véritablement céleste où s'accordent ces opposés, qui étaient incompatibles dans ces doctrines humaines. (L296d; MIII154)

He disarms the tension between the antithetical terms – here personified in the two writers – and defines a situation in which these two sources of energy and arguments, instead of being directed against each other, come to a focus with reference to a third term and the position announced by it.

Pascal is a master of this process whereby a confused debate comes to be clarified and shown to be susceptible of a solution. He controls easily every phase of it, from the moment of identifying the ambiguous original topic to the appearance of the carefully selected and conceived pairs of terms, to the revelation (sometimes sudden: Pascal does not disdain effects of suspense and surprise) of the key term, the *tertium quid*, thanks to which one may arrive at an adequate view of the debate and of the issue that informs it. This pattern has somewhat the form of a table containing a few reference points; it is simple and diagrammatic at first, but complex and rich as it picks up synonyms, antonyms, and associations. As a technical lexicon it presides, in a sense, over the activities involved in working out the details of vocabulary and statement in Pascal's discourse. Invention in its most precise and specific sense is found here, it seems to me, in these operations whereby Pascal transforms ambiguous topics into terms and concepts, clarifying, dividing, and unifying them so as to end with the tools required for his inquiry and for communication of his results.

The analysis of topics and terms proceeds, uncovering as it goes more proliferations in the lexicon with which Pascal may do his work. While these two- and three-term operations accumulate, he studies the data before him, which have begun to fall into groups or series. He must then find a way to arrange these complexes appropriately. It is fascinating to watch him locate answers to this problem: he has recourse to what we might call "levels," but to Pascal the word that renders best his meaning is, no doubt, "ordre." In other words, he invents terms that function not as means of discursive development, but as indicators of contexts or levels on which the discourse will unfold. Then the antitheses and paradoxes that he has defined may be disposed on the degrees of a scale, on the steps of a progression.

In the *Ecrits sur la grâce* it would be quite impossible for Pascal to make sense of the sorts of grace and of the contrasts and oppositions to which they give rise if he could not draw on the notion of two differing orders of causality, the human and limited versus the divine and unlimited. I do not mean that he wishes to reduce to insignificance the human factor; rather he recognizes, and attributes reality to, two kinds of causal action. That reality is attested by the care with which he analyzes the obscure experience of "double délaissement," in which God and man forsake each other: there he comes to grips with a breakdown in the mysterious kind of cooperation which should be the norm.

For another example, this time from the *Pensées*, we may consider Pascal's fundamental insight as he approaches the interpretation of the Old Testament. He sees the key to understanding the behavior of the Jews and, more specifically, the rejection of the Messiah in the simple but far-reaching device of "figures," that is, of the two levels of sense – literal and spiritual – in the Old Testament texts. By keeping constantly in mind this contrast of the letter and the spirit and the projection of the latter via the former, Pascal is able to treat details and ensembles of details that would otherwise present serious problems.

Also in the *Pensées*, and this gives us his most inclusive scheme, he develops the idea of three orders or domains of being and knowledge. For the dialectical mode of thought to work effectively, divisions must be made in the continuum of reality and experience; and it is precisely the function of these levels to indicate fields of application for the dialectic, fields in which the original acts of invention will show forth their consequences. Moving in his reflections from one to another of these " ordres," Pascal sees as he looks around an indefinite number – I think one may properly say, an infinite number – of paradoxes to consider on the successive planes of bodies, minds, and hearts; but banking on the power of his initial distinctions, he is confident of being able to approach appropriately the problem posed by each thing, idea, or impulse of charity.

Pascal takes his distinctions very seriously, but he does not turn them into separations, however much one may be inclined to think that he does, as when he emphatically puts infinite distances between the three orders. Distances notwithstanding, he introduces an extraordinary set of analogies that hold among the orders (we shall have to consider them later in some detail). Likewise, as I have suggested above, his opposition between the divine and the human, as it opens up in the *Ecrits sur la grâce* entails an essential interaction between the two; and the level of the spirit, with its special senses, cannot be explored unless one presupposes something definite provided by the letter of the text.

The pages entitled *Sur la Conversion du pécheur* show in a spectacular way the degrees through which the soul moves in its quest for the true good, the *véritable bien*. It comes to understand the distinction between good that is unstable and good that is durable, between partial goods and the sovereign good. Leaving the former behind:

Elle le cherche donc [le souverain bien] ailleurs, et connaissant par une lumière toute pure qu'il n'est point dans les choses qui sont en elle, ni hors d'elle, ni devant elle, elle commence à le chercher au-dessus d'elle. (L291a; MIV42)

At this point the ascension really begins:

Cette élévation est si éminente et si transcendante, qu'elle ne s'arrête pas au ciel: il n'a pas de quoi la satisfaire, ni au-dessus du ciel, ni aux anges, ni aux êtres les plus parfaits. Elle traverse toutes les créatures, et ne peut arrêter son cœur qu'elle ne se soit rendue jusqu'au trône de Dieu, dans lequel elle commence à trouver son repos et ce bien qui est tel qu'il n'y a rien de plus aimable, et qu'il ne peut lui être ôté que par son propre consentement. (L291a; MIV42)

In the remaining lines of the text, Pascal tells how the soul, in the presence of God, unable to form an idea of itself that is base enough or an idea of God that is exalted enough, considers him in his immensity – actually Pascal uses a plural expression, "des immensités qu'elle [l'âme] multiplie"; and finally, after further devout reflections, it recognizes that it must worship God in its status as a creature, give thanks to him as one indebted to him, satisfy him as one who is guilty, and pray to him as one who is indigent.

INVENTION VS. INTERPRETATION

While engaged in the kind of invention we have been discussing – movement from ambiguity to clear distinctions, thence to resolutions, the whole procedure shifting from one level to another within the bounds of a scheme that sets priorities – Pascal presupposes the answers to certain questions concerning semantics. In an important sense, what happens in the context of discovery or invention is that Pascal either revises the received ensemble of terms, meanings, and applications or, in extreme cases, replaces it with another. The distinctiveness of the intellectual operations is striking, if one recalls, as a contrast, what is required in the art of interpretation.

There Pascal takes up, let us say, a passage from an Old Testament prophet or a document issued by the Council of Trent and undertakes to recover from the text at hand a sense already fixed by context and by authorial intention. Definitions, choices of vocabulary, conventions of reference have been made independently of what Pascal, had he been the author, might have done. Coming along *ex post facto*, he must reason out the way in which the semantic variables were fixed by the person or persons who wrote the text. This sort of analysis and inference is assumed by, but differs from, what occurs in the art of invention: there Pascal undertakes to locate, without losing sight of what he knows from the exegesis of texts, another lexicon, another and different ensemble of terms that – he thinks – applies more suitably to the problem at hand.

The new devices being sought and determined may not differ completely from those already in use; it may not be necessary to discard them, only to modify them. But, in any case, the emphasis shifts as Pascal goes from interpretation and restatement to invention and novelty. In the former, he centers his attention on the work or text before him; as an already determined entity it serves as the primary source of answers to the questions he wishes to ask regarding the language and thought embodied in it. In the latter, the aim is not merely to understand a text or problem in itself, but to go beyond that, to free oneself from a particular set of discursive conditions, felt to be inadequate. Then the emphasis falls on difficulties and sources of difficulties – on topics and on the search for new devices of inquiry that can be used on a subject-matter no longer to be viewed as something inevitably fixed but as a site of possibilities.

THE RIPPLE EFFECT

Pascal uses linguistic elements (which I am calling terms) and intellectual elements (which I am calling concepts); and of course these two are correlated, so that terms represent or evoke concepts. Such a selection of terms and concepts is indispensable as one prepares for an inquiry into the facts of a problematic situation. By means of these elements, he can formulate true statements. But he does not – in fact, he cannot – make these statements in an unqualified, virgin territory: instead he composes them in the light of a framework to which they are relevant. And the final result of these activities is a position, a more or less completely filled-out and realized construction.

What becomes apparent now is the influence that makes itself felt elsewhere when changes are made in the elements selected for the basis of the discourse. It is easy to see how shifts in terms and concepts – as constitutive elements – affect immediately and radically what happens on the level of statements and judgments. Perhaps the effect of change is harder to grasp on the level of the overall framework in which statements are occurring, but it occurs, because of the mutual implication in which framework, statement, and vocabulary are involved. New expressions and concepts generate and are generated by new frameworks. In my discussion I have concentrated on the invention and specification of terms as materials of statements; however, frameworks or contexts are in a similar sense elements subject to the process of invention; and it would have been possible to start at the other end of the line and work backward – analytically – from framework to that primary level of expression and thought, where terms and concepts first emerge. The abstractness of this account is forbidding; let me relieve it by an example.

In the *Ecrits sur la grâce* Pascal traces much of the theological disagreement in question to the topic of human nature. The people against whom he writes – the pessimistic Protestants and the optimistic semi-Pelagians or Molinists – tend in opposite ways to a simple view of that nature. They define it without proper recognition of its complexity; and that leads them astray, into positions quite different from the Augustinian account. The truth of the matter is that a great transition has occurred; we must think of human nature not as locked in some original ontological charter but as characterized by two states; it now exists in the second and inferior state of the two, with traces, recollections, and tendencies left over from the first. The erroneous formulations of the Molinists overemphasize the former state, while those of the Calvinists go to the opposing extreme.

Pascal has changed both the data and the boundaries of the discussion. He has pointed out the difficulty arising from the equivocal notion of human nature: it must not be treated as simple; and even where the complexity introduced by original sin is recognized – as it is, in fact, by all parties in the dispute – extreme commitments are to be avoided. By setting up an opposition of two terms that he defines as extremes, Pascal makes a start in bringing order into the controversial situation. To each of the contending positions he attributes thus a certain unity, and, in addition, a definite relation to the other, a relation that is not simply confused and controversial. His way is clear then to introduce a third term, along with the position that it unifies, and to locate that term and that position between the other two as a mean or balance. Within the inclusive framework constituted by his final outline of the situation, Pascal can develop statements that will show the consequences of taking each of these three paths. He can give us a true description of the present state of mankind, stressing the corruption of the will; he can tell us, in some detail, how that is related to the preceding Edenic state, and then what must be done now, if we are to approximate a return to the former state of oneness with God.

THE ROLE OF THE KNOWN

The activities of invention and discovery presuppose prior knowledge and data, things known in advance and taken – by some, at least – as settled. After all, Pascal's innovations are, in a significant way, reactions; they consist of rejoinders to something pre-existing. It appears that the operations of the rhetorical art depend ultimately on the grammatical art of recovery and interpretation as a *sine qua non*. How could he proceed in the *Provinciales* without his exegesis of the books of casuistry, or in the *Pensées* without his exegesis of the Bible, or in the *Ecrits de la grâce* without his exegesis of the Bible, of certain texts of Augustine, and of a series of Tridentine pronouncements?

This listing suggests the need for more precision in defining Pascal's relation to the known and to the past, as they emerge from written works important to him because of their authority.

Such works do not serve simply to furnish a launching pad for flights of intellectual discovery. If we set aside the casuistical writings, the sources just mentioned actually provide the correct terms and the true doctrine that Pascal will use in identifying various errors. There is thus a species of the known that he is careful to recover and to maintain as it is. The rest of what is known – I am thinking specifically of the terms and positions proposed by the Molinists and the Calvinists – undergoes a significant transformation.

In short, he looks at the known in ways that are distinct: on the one hand, he tends to see it as fixed, as interesting in itself, as coherent and providing a view of reality that may be true. However, as soon as doubts arise as to the truth of something alleged to be known, what is thus given falls under the light of invention and its art: it becomes background or tradition, to be tested by new devices of demonstration and discernment. As we observe Pascal's practice, the contrast seems to be between something determinate – the past as it presents itself for interpretation – and something that may become other than it is – the past as it presents itself for alteration.

I think it valuable also to note the difference in his typical attitudes regarding invention itself as he shifts from geometric to dialectic. Geometrical and quasi-geometrical discourse focuses, when it turns to the past, on errors to be avoided and on occasional examples of demonstrative thinking that may be attached to what is being discovered and demonstrated in Pascal's own day. However, the dialectic of moral and religious discourse makes use of orthodox *and* unorthodox positions and viewpoints. The former style of thinking looks for signs of potential contributions to the sequence of theorems that have been justified compellingly, the latter for obscure or mishandled materials that need new modes of exposition and application. The former is essentially analytical and exclusive in impulse, the latter essentially integrative and assimilative. The former looks to the joining of links in a sequence of warranted truths; the latter to the reconciliation of opposed views and the formation of an articulated body of doctrine.

The point becomes particularly clear in regard to the theme

of progress. In mathematics and science, he tends to stress advances in the disciplines, along with anticipations of future progress; in his theological thinking, he seeks his terms and conceptual bases retrospectively, never losing sight of past truths and always using them as the criteria by which to judge new statements. I do not mean that no progress occurs in the latter area: since the beginning of the Church the development of doctrine has gone forward in the findings of Fathers, Councils, and Popes. Of course, Pascal does not think of himself as authorized to engage in the kind of "inventions" and pronouncements that they have made; what he does undertake with confidence is the effort to find better ways of understanding and applying what has been established as true.

MEANS AND A METHOD

At the end of the process we have been describing, Pascal has brought into being a set of instruments for the study of a disagreement or a controversy. They make it possible for him to identify the problem and the source of the dispute, to move toward mutual intelligibility for the two sides, and to shift into serious inquiry leading to a solution. In addition, with these devices – since they involve concepts and language – Pascal is able to explain himself to his readers and communicate the results of his work. May we not also speak of a certain sharpening of perception, which accrues both to Pascal and to his audience? His art of invention has, I think, this subjective aspect, because the procedures it defines and guides are interiorized. As a new turn of mind replaces an old way that has shown itself to be a hindrance, he and we see things not seen before about the problem being studied.

To recall in this way the concerns of perception, inquiry, and communication that, taken together, make up the complex objective of the art we are surveying here, implies of course that Pascal has been involved in a search for means whereby to realize that end. A number of purposive operations serve precisely as such means. He may begin with a sort of oscillation in the presence of disagreement and confusion: a looking from one side to the other in a dispute, a looking back to identify the source of the difficulties, and a looking forward to possible elucidation. With that as a basis, Pascal goes on to an insightful grasp of the ambiguity that is entangling the disputants in misunderstandings. At some point in the process – I do not mean, incidentally, to imply a temporal sequence so much as a process that is logically consistent as a whole – he analyzes or divides the underlying topic, which has been obscured by the ambiguity, into two- and three-term arrangements that throw light on what is happening in the discussion and suggest ways in which progress may be made toward agreement. As the inquiry goes ahead, he may find it advisable to invoke levels or "ordres" that emphasize the truly basic distinctions and provide space for series of oppositions and resolutions as his argument takes shape. Innovation in terms and concepts leads obviously to innovation in what will be said; and it may require adjustments in the general framework within which the whole discussion takes place.

Here, as suggested above, we need to keep in mind not only the effort of invention, but also the art of interpretation and the estimate it has furnished of what is already known (or at least accepted as known). In that prior process Pascal has recovered from one or more authoritative texts a *single* set of questions, devices of inquiry, arguments, and answers. But invention complicates the picture, for he is often engaged precisely in showing that a previously received position is inadequate and leads to error and controversy. He must, in such a case, (1) either make partial changes in the given semantic framework (2) or substitute a new one for it.

There appears to be an affinity between rhetoric of the sort I am describing here and the dialectical mode of thought seen in Pascal's moral and religious writings. I have preferred not to treat rhetoric here in the usual way, as an art of persuasion, requiring an analysis that reasons back from desired effects in an audience to rules concerning the details of the proposed discourse and the character of the speaker. It has seemed to me more pertinent to look at the typical sequence of operations in rhetoric and to ask where along that line the emphasis falls when

Pascal is engaged in dialectical inquiry. The obvious answer is, I think: at the beginning, at the stage of *heuresis* or invention. Rather than being concerned with the tastes and principles – or prejudices – of an audience, he wants to find some devices for inquiring into the nature of his subject-matter and for making true statements about it. Later, of course, those statements may go beyond the inquiry and become relevant to an apologetic or a polemical argument. With terms and concepts defined, with priorities settled, with hierarchical devices laid out, he (and we) are in a position to understand the schematism underlying what will be said or written.

And yet, however indispensable the contribution of rhetoric may be, it is only a beginning, only one voice in the counterpoint of the intellectual arts: Pascal's innovative terms and statements occur not in isolation but in a fabric of logical connections and reasoned-out discourse. That fact leads us into another set of questions, and onto the field of another art, that of sequential orderings. We have encountered it before in connection with geometry; here it appears in the sphere of the dialectical mode and its distinctive tendencies.

PRESENTATION

THE PROBLEM OF CONNECTION

In an important group of works by Pascal, the arts of grammar and rhetoric, along with their typical subject-matters and results, emerge in a climate where the dialectical mode of inquiry is predominant. Their essential operations, interpreting and inventing, take on meanings and functions that are specific to dialectic. In order to understand what Pascal has done, it seemed useful to list at the outset a wide range of documents concerning a wide range of moral and religious experiences and problems. In investigating the relevance of the arts to that list and its contents, we have seen that, at a decisive moment of insight, a particular object comes to the center of attention – an object proper to one or the other of the two arts in question – plus an intuition regarding the correct procedure for treating that object. When examined in detail, Pascal's practice then seemed to lend itself to further analysis into phases and operations characteristic of the two arts.

Continuing in the dialectical perspective, I should like now to pass for description and comment to a third art. It is a species of logic, a particular technique of making connections and sequences. In applying it, Pascal turns sometimes to language (as in the close analysis of the reasoning in certain documents issued by the Council of Trent), sometimes to things (as in the evocation of Nature in its infinite entirety), and sometimes to thought and attitude (as in the steps to be followed by his reader in the debates concerning efficacious grace or – and here action as based on thought has a large part to play – in the path toward belief in the *Pensées*). Indeed, the first point to be kept in mind here is the broad extension I am giving to the idea of logical connection; this initial ambiguity will make it easier, I think, for us to identify Pascal's preferences and usage.

BACKWARD FROM CONCLUSIONS

Now, since Pascal establishes connections in order to make clear how two items are joined, or how one follows from the other, I propose that we begin at the end of the process. If we think first of his conclusions, we may be able to determine more easily how the evidence has worked and how the steps taken in order to get to the conclusions are parts fitting into logical wholes. In the works, *opuscules*, and other documents treating of morals and religion, Pascal comes to conclusions about a long list of subjects.

He settles in his own mind and attempts to settle in his reader's mind issues arising from topics such as these: the two great commandments of God; the present state of human nature; the ways of God in his dealings with mankind; the total pattern of human history; the unity of the Bible; the confusions of philosophers; the doctrines of Manicheans, Calvinists, and Augustinians regarding grace; the mathematical dimensions of Nature; the plans of the Jesuits; the state of his father after his death; the original and ancient process of becoming a Christian; the right way to think about his illnesses.

When viewed as statements, some of the conclusions are quite elemental: they concern particulars, even individuals. Pascal gives precise reports on what Escobar or Diana or Bauny have proposed as probable opinions on questions of allowable Christian conduct; he consoles himself and his sisters on the loss of their father; he judges his illnesses in the light of his past life. But his focus can shift from such particular facts to what one might call extended facts that spread over space and time. Take, for example, the collective fact that appears when Pascal sums up the mentality and régime of the first Christians and then sets them alongside a contrasting but similarly conceived picture of his contemporaries and their behavior. Or – and in this case the stress lies on a sequence in time rather than on widely shared attitudes – Pascal can sum up in a single view the whole sequence of events since the founding of the Church to the seventeenth century; and, beyond that, it is not hard for him to use his beliefs and his reading of the Old Testament so as to see the whole of human history as forming a single vista.

The conclusions vary widely not only along the scale from particularity to generality; they also make connections having striking differences in status or modality. He shifts easily, as he goes along, from simple affirmations or negations about what is the case (the Lutherans deny free will) to what was the case (St. Augustine rejected the equivalent of the Lutheran thesis apropos of the Manichaeans), to what will be the case (Pascal's explanations of what the Council of Trent meant in some of its pronouncements will make the issues and the doctrinal resolution clear to his correspondent) to what ought to be the case (the Protestant heretics, who are children gone astray, ought to come back to their mother, the Church) to what must be the case (all must accept the fact that "les justes" do not always have the special help, the "secours spécial" necessary for accomplishing divine precepts), and so on. In fact, one of the advantages of taking the dialectical path in reasoning lies in the possibility that it gives Pascal of either insisting on or gliding over such distinctions as he moves from one context to another.

Coming as they do at the end of a process of connection, these conclusions point backward to their origins or bases. Not, however, to the objects and deductive procedures of geometry or to the problems and experimental observations of mathematical physics. Rather, it is clear that Pascal is asking and answering questions on the basis of his interpretations of the Bible, of key works by St. Augustine and other Church Fathers – and of his own experiences and observations.

The field that concerns us here includes, then, orderings that occur in regard to many sorts of data – linguistic, mental, real, practical – and assertions that spread over the whole scale of degrees of generality, that have varying force and coloration according to the mode of statement. Exactly how Pascal goes about treating these data so as to perceive and to produce a distinctive kind of logical sequence is what we now need to examine.

PASCAL'S CONCEPT OF ORDER

Connections involve the imposition of an order, and as is known, *ordre* is one of Pascal's favorite notions. The term occurs in his works that deal with problems of arithmetic and geometry, and also in his works of physical science, of mathematical physics. But he refers many times to "ordre" in the *Pensées*, as well. In fact, it might be useful to recall the senses that the word usually has in Pascal's thought. I would propose three possibilities. (1) First, the idea of command or commandment, an imperative; and this meaning is perhaps the least important, the least technical, the least instrumental and useful in our present analysis, though it may, by connotation, suggest divine *préceptes* or commandments, which are essential elements in Christian theology. (2) The second definition of "ordre" for him would be something like "domain," "terrain," in other words, the field of attention or inquiry. This is perhaps the final and the most significant of the senses that the term may have. We shall have occasion to come back to it when we treat the problem of dialectical integration. (3) Then, thirdly, "ordre" means "sequence," or "arrangement"; the implication being of something given simply, and then of an activity that arranges or has arranged those data into a satisfying pattern.

Incidentally, it has often been remarked that Pascal, who

clearly gave so much thought to the notion of order, obviously had much difficulty in bringing some of his own works into final and complete versions. But this paradox applies, it seems to me, to the order of whole works: there the structure and unity may be elusive for him and for us. In local contexts, however, and where his arguments are viewed as micro-structures entering into the texture of his discourse, he is quite successful. Even in his longer presentations, the outlines of what he wants to do are there – it is simply up to us to find them and attempt to follow out in accordance with them the branchings of his thought.

Our emphasis here on conclusions as furnishing the keys to logical connections is especially relevant to Pascal's use of the dialectical way of proceeding in the areas of morals, philosophy, and religion. His commitment to this purposive, end-seeking mode means that he will not often turn to other types of sequencing, even though he knows them, and has on occasion used them with great skill.

For example, he will not seek the kind of reasoning characteristic of geometry or empirico-metrical science: for that one must have the habit of mind of those who study quantity and its connections either *in abstracto* or – to go from the mathematician to the physicist – in Nature and natural mechanics; the readers Pascal has now in mind are not likely to have that kind of *esprit*. But, and this is something much more important, such deductive connections do not fit the subject-matter, do not inhere in it. Of course it will not be surprising if some vestiges or recast elements of this kind do find their way into our present documents (as, to mention the *Pensées*, in the *pari* or in the fragment on the *disproportion de l'homme*).

Nor do we expect to see him adopt the point of view of scholastic metaphysics and use the language of form and matter, substance and accident, natures and operations. To Pascal such terms, being obviously unverifiable as to their reference, would be useless in tracing and reporting the sequences he sought to discover in mathematics and in physics; then, being obviously and fatally obscure, they would serve only to confuse discussions of morals and religion. Though one must add that we meet here and there in the stream of Pascal's thought, bits and pieces left over from the old tradition (note, for example, the concept of human nature defined univocally, and specifically, of human nature as implying a soul that may be anatomized into powers of knowing, desiring, imagining, and remembering).

Nor, again, do we expect to find Pascal practicing the sort of order – or disorder – that he associates with Montaigne and the Pyrrhonians: the end-point of such reasoning consists in a juxtaposition of view points, a blank opposition even. I say, "end-point," but, as Pascal works over this situation, he finds in it movement without end – and therefore something that he can use in his own arguments as the "renversement continuel." And so it is clear that this kind of logic, though not acceptable in any final sense in Pascal's moral theorizing, has a role to play at the start of many arguments. It belongs, in fact, to another – the skeptical or suspensive – species of dialectic: the point is that for the Pyrrhonians it is final, but for Pascal it can only be preliminary and propaedeutic.

THE FUNDAMENTAL INSIGHT

If the foregoing possibilities are not of the essence and can have only complementary parts to play in the present art of connections, how may we define the logical insight that appears to guide Pascal? The best way to begin, I think, is to recall something absolutely fundamental. As an Augustinian, he subscribes to this principle: "Unless you believe, you will not understand." By faith he knows and in part (at least) understands two things: (1) that the universe in all its diversity has a single source of being and intelligibility, and furthermore, (2) that this source (which happens to be a triune Person) is also the end, the *point d'aboutissement*, of any sequence on any level of reality, whether it be corporeal, mental, or spiritual.

Let us take this twofold truth, with its terms and the movement that is implied in it, as forming a model for what we are likely to observe elsewhere, in less inclusive contexts, as Pascal undertakes to establish connections. I mean that Pascal reaches the end-point, the conclusion that unifies his vision, only after a preparatory phase, only after passing through an argument or area in which the presence of that unifying principle is felt not at all or only partially, and in which, consequently, he is especially conscious of a multiplicity. Furthermore, this region makes for intellectual discomfort; multiplicity takes on the aspect of a problem; it stimulates him to look for some means of using the diversity, of making it a springboard for movement toward and into the zone of some kind of unity or reconciliation. I should add that the multiplicity usually presents itself as something more intense than a collection of different items: it often has the form of an antithesis, and that brings Pascal's attention (and ours, as readers) to a sharp focus.

In other words, the moment of insight here, with regard to logical connections in dialectic, comes to Pascal when he becomes aware of contradictions and of something that may be done about them – *with* them – taken *as pairs*, that is, without simply discarding one of the elements as a mistake. In short, a connection may be established between them. To this sense of a complex starting point and movement away from it, two further elements need to be added, in order to complete the scheme. First, the negative implications: I have already given an indication of them in pointing out above that Pascal is unlikely, in this dialectical mode, to look for sequences like those of geometry, of physics, of Pyrrhonianism. We can now see why they must be ruled out: precisely because of the dogmatic attitude toward contradiction that characterizes them. As a matter of sound procedure in the two sciences, contradictions are eliminated rather than retained or reconciled; and in the vein of skeptical thought or discourse they are multiplied without resolution. Second, and this time the implications are positive and related to uses: Pascal sees the possible fruitfulness of this approach; he catches sight of a very broad field – it includes morals, eloquence, philosophy, and religion – that appears to lend itself to exploration when one's impulse is to find contradictions and to formulate sequences as one treats them.

In the development of this complex insight, that is, in the actual process of stating and justifying conclusions, Pascal behaves so often in essentially the same way that we can recover

rather easily and state in an outline the steps through which he
goes habitually. He selects, first of all, a subject, something of
current interest or doctrinal importance on which to focus his
procedure. Second, he locates in the subject a stimulus to
further activity; and here he is likely to find some multiplicity,
some puzzling accumulation of data. As the third step, he brings
into play a recurrent set of logical devices, which he applies to
the details presented by the problem before him. The fourth
moment or phase is reached when he has formulated the
connection or sequence or unity resulting from the entire series
of operations. Detailed examples of the process are not hard to
find.

In the group of works being considered here, Pascal chooses
as starting points subjects like man (with his behavior and
condition in the universe), Nature (with its extent and
underlying features), the Bible (with its peculiar history and
parts), the notion of grace (with the problem of defining its
nature and effects). Merely to mention the topics in this way
suffices to indicate the potential multiplicity of aspects that will
appear as Pascal examines these subjects. They suggest at once
contrasting viewpoints, ideas, statements. And Pascal makes it
his task to turn, by the devices of his logic, that potential
diversity into something strikingly real.

THE TREATMENT OF GRACE

In the *Ecrits sur la grâce* Pascal takes up a role in a discussion that
involves many people, and soon he sets in motion one of the
relevant operations for establishing connections. I mean that he
recognizes and makes explicit some divisions in the multitude of
people expressing opinions on the subject of grace. Two groups,
apparently different and yet somehow similar, appear: the
Calvinists and the Lutherans. Then, dipping retrospectively
into the history of Church doctrine, he calls up another group,
the Manichaeans. In so doing, he shifts from the first necessary
step in the mode of his dialectical logic, where he has identified
a multitude, to the second step, where the multitude is divided
– at least tentatively – into three distinguishable groups. But,

and this is more important in the dynamics of the argument, the three distinct groups soon find themselves united into a company larger than any of the constituent groups; and then Pascal is ready to propose the principle that makes them one: an extreme view of fallen human nature that eliminates freedom of the will and denies all positive capacity for goodness.

Now notice that Pascal must retrace his path and do another variation on the same logical theme. He makes preparatory groupings among the members of another multitude, and once more he discerns three subdivisions, consisting of the semi-Pelagians, the Molinists, and the original Pelagians, who are located retrospectively, as before. These three groups form a second sizeable party different from the first.

So far what Pascal has done is more or less a matter of common sense – of dialectical common sense, I think one should add – but it serves an important function, since it establishes the basis for everything else. Pascal now has put before us two groups of speakers and writers, and the moment has come to shift to another operation, one in which he shows clearly what defines each group and then what the relation between the two groups must be.

They are different, I have said. But not merely different: a simple difference would have no motive force in Pascal's argument. The second group must be partisans of a doctrine, of an approach to grace, that forms an antithesis when set alongside the position held by the first group. They must hold an extreme view of human nature in which freedom of the will is emphasized and with it an effective human capacity for goodness. The two positions do not point away from each other; in fact, they imply each other; and to conceive of one is to engage in the operation of defining the other. Thus, Pascal's logic aims to produce a connection in which one extreme implies another extreme, and the two views form a keenly felt paradox, a situation that seems to demand some further step.

At this juncture, he is well along in the process of clarifying and unifying the *données* of his problem, and he has led us to a critical moment in his presentation. On each side of the question of grace, we see a multitude that has turned out to be ambiguous, since it lends itself to division into distinct groups; and these groups are ambiguous in their way, since they may be understood as sub-groups that fit – on one or the other side of the argument about grace – into a comprehensive, totalizing group. Each party is at the outset a multitude, then a collection of three groups distinguished (though rather vaguely), then a single party united by a particular thesis concerning grace. The question for Pascal now becomes, in the face of this opposition that he has brought about between rigorists and laxists with reference to grace: is it possible to continue the logical drive toward unification?

However, at this moment in the process, which is not without its elements of suspense, Pascal may shift into a mode in which rhetoric seems to take over. He may engage in restatements and amplifications in order to emphasize the basic opposition and the fact that each side thinks it has the truth of the matter, so much so that convictions on the opposing side must be eliminated. This exclusiveness in the two rival claims has its importance, of course, for the argument. But, as I am suggesting, such developments do not really change the way in which Pascal has posed his problem. They serve to repeat and sharpen the array of terms, statements, and viewpoints.

It is conceivable that the rhetorical gambit would be presented as a way of heightening the force of a conclusion, and we might simply be left with the paradox. Pascal sees the picture, however, as one in which the two parties are engaged in mutual destruction. And any mere survey – whether simple or heightened for effect – of the situation, followed by retention of the two possibilities, he finds unacceptable. For him it is a challenge; he does not like the idea of setting up a dilemma and then leaving it as undecidable.

What are his choices? Here we may return to a distinction I made in the preceding chapter between two- and three-term heuristic figures. Pascal takes the latter possibility, turning the opposition between the rigorists and laxists into another pattern. Each of the two positions – which seemed to be pure – becomes under his gaze ambiguous in a new way; each has a positive and a negative aspect to it, something to keep and something to set

aside. Then, a third something becomes possible, an intermediate view that collects the positive aspects into a core of
truth. In the final phase of his argument, therefore, Pascal
establishes a figure consisting of three parts, all defined with
reference to one another, and all implying one another, though
the last to be found, the comprehensive part, has a special and
regulative status.

In a sense, all of the foregoing analysis, which sums up an
argument spread over many pages, is a preparation for two
passages that I should like to quote. In the first Pascal makes
clear how he understands the doctrine of grace reached by the
Council of Trent; in other words, he intends to formulate here
the third position to be set off against the two antithetical theses.

Concluons donc de ces décisions toutes saintes: que Dieu par sa
miséricorde donne quand il lui plaît, aux justes, le pouvoir plein et
parfait d'accomplir les préceptes, et qu'il ne le donne pas toujours, par
un jugement juste quoique caché. (L348a; MIII722)

In the second passage, which follows immediately, he puts the
third position into place and completes the logical structure that
we have been describing.

Apprenons par cette doctrine si pure à défendre tout ensemble la
puissance de la nature contre les Luthériens, et l'impuissance de la
nature contre les Pélagiens; la force de la grâce contre les Luthériens,
et la nécessité de la grâce contre les Pélagiens, sans ruiner le libre
arbitre par la grâce, comme les Luthériens, et sans ruiner la grâce par
le libre arbitre, comme les Pélagiens. (L348c; MIII722)

A final sentence insists on the necessity of holding all three
positions regarding human nature, grace, and free will in a
proper balance, if one is to reach the truth.

Et ne pensons pas qu'il suffise de fuir une de ces erreurs pour être dans
la vérité. (L348c; MIII722)

SOME ANALYTICAL GROUNDWORK

At times Pascal calls on geometric to lay the groundwork for his
theological reflections. In the third volume of his edition of the
Oeuvres complètes Jean Mesnard has explored this subject as a
pendant to his brilliant recovery of the chronological order in

which the *Ecrits sur la grâce* were composed by Pascal. In what follows I should like to discuss this presence of geometric in connection with one important problem, the accomplishment of divine precepts. Geometric functions as a partner, an *ancilla*, in the movement toward the later stages of an essentially dialectical position in theology. The case illustrates quite well, I think, the kind of cooperation possible among the arts of the mind as Pascal understands and uses them. I shall have occasion, in a later chapter, to develop the point further in my treatment of Pascal's rhetoric.

We may usefully remind ourselves here of the distinction with which he opens *De l'esprit géométrique*. In regard to truth: one may discover it, demonstrate it, distinguish it from error. Pascal chooses not to say anything about the first of those topics – it has already been adequately treated, he says. He concentrates on the other two, which quickly become practically identical, for, as Pascal understands them, the third is included in the second. Any demonstration found for a truth can then be used as the criterion in making discernments of error: by simple comparison one can determine whether the opposing view has, to justify it, anything like the same proofs as the truth that is being defended. In other words, geometry – and geometric or quasi-geometry – are for Pascal associated above all with demonstration and its requirements.

However, in matters concerning grace, he cannot simply declare the meanings of the main terms, nor can he proceed by asking that they be granted by a convention – either of which would be procedures acceptable in a mathematical discourse. His situation is quite different from that of the researcher in mathematics. Here he cannot do what he advocates in the fragmentary *De l'esprit géométrique*: define all terms that can be defined, take the undefinables – like "time" and "movement" – for granted in their natural, universal senses, and exclude everything else. He must allow ambiguities as such into the body of his account, make them explicit, study their backgrounds and consequences, and finally resolve the paradoxes they pose. His situation is more like that of the physicist; but, instead of having external Nature as the rule against which to measure his discourse, he must square it with what is given in authoritative sources.

As an exegete Pascal concentrates on linguistic units lying in a limited range that includes primarily words, propositions or statements, and passages. He is not greatly concerned with the particular economies or organizing principles of the works from which he draws passages and lesser units. Treating them like quarries, he takes out small blocks of text, excerpts, for analysis in the light of the current question that he wants to answer, extracting from those materials one or more propositions, which are then resolved into their component terms.

The notion of sense appears at this point, and right away, as I see it, Pascal must grapple with two properties of the terms he encounters: ambiguity and synonymy. He strives to resolve the former and, where appropriate, to establish and to affirm the latter. In ambiguity, one word or term has multiple meanings (at least two); and satisfactory explication of the discourse is possible only when the different meanings have been isolated. They are usually related – instances of pure equivocation hardly cause difficulty – so that one meaning may be mistaken for the other. In synonymy, one meaning or sense finds expression by means of more than one word; and satisfactory explication of discourse requires that such equivalences be indicated. In sum, the interpreter must be aware in his vocabulary – and in that of others – of apparent unities that are real multiplicities (single words with more than one meaning), and apparent multiplicities that are real unities (different expressions for the same senses).

Such is the problem at the lower and simpler end of the range where Pascal works. However, moving on to propositions, he finds himself asking exactly the same questions: is the statement susceptible of more than one sense? (Note the analogical extension of the sense of the word "sense": it now refers to *propositional* meaning, and not to that of simple terms.) And, if one is examining two statements, are they really distinct or are they merely two ways of saying the same thing? The next step is easy, and Pascal takes it, treating larger units in parallel with the smaller ones: a single passage may be interpreted in more than one way; and several passages drawn from an author (St. Augustine, for example) or from several authors (St. Augustine and other Fathers) may be shown to have the same sense. The first task in a theological discussion, as Pascal appears to have conceived it, is to sort out the realities and appearances, the identities and diversities, in the semantic behavior of such units of discourse.

The next steps in Pascal's procedure move away from interpretation onto the terrain of reasoning, of what would be – in a strictly geometrical situation – demonstration. Propositions become in this new context the units that, properly speaking, serve as the bearers of truth or falsehood. In demonstrative discourse, the propositions in question have either (1) axiomatic value, as when, for example, they are taken from authoritative texts (or may be reduced to propositions found in those texts) or (2) inferred value, as when support may be located for them in authoritative sources. Such backing may include arguments of a logical sort, estimates of what the writers intended, or considerations of context and sequence – what Pascal calls the *suite du discours*. If he can find in his sources either the proposition in question or the materials for constructing it, he thinks he has corroborated it.

The situation is not always so simple: more often than not he has in mind contentious opponents and their propositions, as well as the one that he favors. Here we recognize – to return to the original triple distinction mentioned above – the impulse toward *discernement* of error: it does not suffice to prove one's own favored conclusion; one must also make clear that in the relevant texts there is no justification for what the opponents are saying. And when their assertions may be arranged – in one of Pascal's very common patterns – so as to form an antithesis, the geometric inspiration begins to give way to dialectic and its characteristic process of reconciling contradictions.

SUBJECTS, PREDICATES, AND ADVERBS

Let us look at one of the important texts on which I have been basing my analysis. It is found in what Pascal was apparently preparing as a *discours* (rather than a *lettre*) on the subject of efficacious grace. At the outset, one must have firmly in mind that the principal topic is the *impossibility of accomplishing the precepts*, the impossibility for man of carrying out the commandments laid down by God. Pascal aims above all to show that the Council of Trent, and before that, the Church Fathers, took a position, in fact the same position, on this subject. They said something about it; they intended to say it; and they said it over and over again.

As Pascal reports them, the words of the "SS. Pères" and of the Council are: "Les commandements ne sont pas impossibles aux justes." But he goes on to say that these words may receive two senses:

Le 1. Qu'il n'est pas impossible que les justes accomplissent les commandements.

Le 2. Que les commandements sont toujours possibles à tous les justes, de ce plein et dernier pouvoir auquel il ne manque rien de la part de Dieu, pour agir. (L335d; Mᴵᴵᴵ748)

Pascal's first reaction is, thus, to clarify an ambiguity: one set of words has two senses – and, as I suggested above, "sense" is not restricted to a single term; it is attributed, in accord with the flexibility I mentioned above, to the next larger unit of expression, the statement or proposition. Note that another transformation has occurred also, this one based on synonymity. The original statement, which was a single clause, has been expanded into a complex assertion: "Qu'il n'est pas impossible que les justes ... " and the second phrasing "Que les commandements sont toujours possibles à tous les justes ... " leads to an even more complicated rewording that we are invited to take, at least for argument's sake, as being equivalent to what the Fathers and the Council thought and wrote.

Of course the aim is to discriminate, to identify the correct ("véritable") sense, the meaning really intended by the authorities who have been invoked. The first way of discernment plays on the proposition itself and the terms in which it is expressed. Pascal falls back on what he calls the "simple intelligence de la langue." He sees no rules of grammar entitling anyone to assert that the two propositions are equivalent. To say that the commandments of God are not impossible for the righteous is not the same as saying that the righteous have invariably and without need of anything else from God the full power to accomplish the commandments.

The disputed propositions all have the same subjects – God's commandments – and the same predicates – "possible" and "impossible." The problems begin because three adverbial modifiers are available: never, sometimes, and always. These modifiers may be – and are – applied to the two predicate adjectives, so as to produce a situation that may be summed up as follows:

possible – never, sometimes, always;
impossible – always, sometimes, never.

This way of enumerating the cases leads us to the recognition of some equivalences:

never possible *equals* always impossible;
always possible *equals* never impossible;
sometimes possible *equals* (or at least *implies*) sometimes impossible

Unless one keeps all of these in mind, the argument in this text will seem more difficult than it really is (which is quite enough).

In keeping with his sharp eye for synonymy, for standing above a meaning and seeing the different ways of rendering it, Pascal often puts the various theses in the form "It is possible that the righteous..." and "It is impossible that the righteous ..." In these cases "It is possible that" and "It is not impossible that" are equivalent in sense; and each of them is subject to the adverbial variations noted above: "It is possible always, sometimes, or never that..." and "It is impossible always, sometimes, or never that..."

THE RESULTING TABLE

This ensemble of propositions can be seen at a glance, along with their mutual relations and their partisans, in this table: The commandments of God are:

possible
- never (Lutherans, Manichaeans)
- sometimes (Pascal, the Council, the Fathers)
- always (Pelagians, semi-Pelagians, Molinists, Jesuits)

or

impossible
- always (Lutherans, *et al.*)
- sometimes (Pascal, *et al.*)
- never (Pelagians, *et al.*)

Although Pascal does not schematize the situation in quite this way, I think it follows his thought closely, respecting, first, his concern for clarifying points of ambiguity and synonymity, and second, his keen awareness of a basic requirement for proof: until plain and distinct propositions are before us, we cannot know what it is we are called upon to prove or disprove.

By referring to this table we can locate at once all the points of departure and return of Pascal's wide-ranging arguments. For example, the Council of Trent said, in its refutation of Lutheran views, that "Les commandements ne sont pas impossibles aux justes." Unfortunately, a crucial adverb is missing. And yet the most important point that Pascal wants to refute is the claim that this statement means: the righteous have always ("toujours") the power of accomplishing the commandments. To refute Luther it is enough to show on proper grounds that the righteous *sometimes* have the effective power of action; and Pascal considers it an illicit extension of meaning to understand, as his opponents do, this power as being present *always*.

Also indicated in my table is the fact that Pascal understands the three theses as falling into a pattern according to which one statement stands between the others as a mean between extremes. The middle position, since it has something of the other two without falling into their exclusions, is privileged; it even begins to take on the force of having been proved, precisely because it can occupy that place. Syllogistic reasoning is not involved here; for that, two antecedent propositions would be needed to provide the warrant – via a middle term – for a third and consequent proposition; nor does the Pascalian figure have the force of a geometrical deduction. Here, as dialectic reasserts itself in the dominant role and proceeds to use materials shaped by an excursion into geometric, the relation of antecedent to consequent does not disappear: it is redefined. The two extreme views function as antecedents in that they provide elements or tensions with reference to which the equilibrium of the comprehensive – and thus consequential – thesis may be established. Simultaneously, the contrasting schools of thought are firmly distinguished and the battle lines drawn in an unmistakable way.

FROM SELF-STUDY TO THE HUMAN CONDITION

In dealing with the nature of grace and its bearing on human nature and freedom Pascal goes out of his way to make the pattern of his reasoning clear, setting down at frequent intervals brief outlines and summaries – sometimes in tabular form – of the contrasting views. He uses the same type of sequencing in a number of other important instances, and they give a good idea of his skill in adjusting the formula to circumstances. Far from being schematic in a simple way, the procedure is flexible and lends itself, in Pascal's hands, to the analysis of quite diverse problems.

I should like now to propose three other subjects, involving not the collection and ordering of theological opinions but the arrangement into a particular pattern, inspired by dialectical reasoning, of theses useful in defining certain beings. The three are: man and mankind, the Bible, and external Nature.

The Pascalian concept of the nature that underlies the condition and behavior of the human creature comes progressively into the foreground in the opening chapters of the *Pensées*. There we can watch the very genesis of a dialectical argument, based as before on the movement from multiplicity to unity. The presentation of the process in plain stages results perhaps from the fact that a rhetorical situation is foreseen and outlined in the *Pensées*. Pascal intends to address someone in the hope of leading that person to the point of assuming a faith-seeking posture; and since he wants to show that the aim proposed is not contrary to reason, he pays particular attention to the articulations of his argument, moving from the restless multiplicities of moral experience to his schematism of inner harmony and unity.

In four chapters on "Vanité," "Misère," "Ennui," and "Raisons des effets," Pascal assembles fragments containing examples of behavior related to those ideas. His procedure consists, first, in evoking for us a problem area in which many data, many details are visible. Then, with all that characteristic human activity before us, Pascal can start the logical sequence and begin the search for something that will summarize and clarify the substance of those opening chapters. As readers we may be in something of a quandary at the sight of all the evidence that has been laid out before us; and we may feel some suspense as to what Pascal will use as his logical principle. Then it emerges: *misère*, the *misère de l'homme* is the inclusive term that sheds light on all those vanities and inconstancies. When put into place, it brings to a close the first episode of unification in this particular argument.

In "Grandeur" the assembling of data begins again, and this time Pascal sets forth notions, actions, tendencies that are associated especially with thought, and with the degree of distinction or dignity that it confers on human beings. And there is another motif that runs through this second current of behavior – pride; pride and thought are, so to speak, subsidiary means of unifying the materials that Pascal works with in this second phase of his case. As we know, however, the term that finally comes to the fore and effects the unification of this line of reasoning is the *grandeur*, the *grandeur de l'homme*. At this point a logical leap occurs, and the peculiar sort of inferential force that informs dialectic makes itself felt. Pascal is able to derive *grandeur* from *misère*: the fact that we *know* we are wretched testifies to our greatness. To affirm pertinently one of the two terms serves as a warrant for affirming the other.

With the two tendencies in hand, and with his two unifying labels, Pascal can advance to the next stage, "Contrariétés," in which he illustrates and emphasizes the antithetical relation that holds between the two sides. Once more the opposition embodies the logical force that makes this part of the argument compelling – and baffling, for these alternate lines of thought and conduct inhere in one and the same human nature. But the situation does not end in either dogmatic assertion or skeptical despair, though Pascal understands those attitudes as possible outcomes, one being Stoic in inspiration and the other Pyrrhonian. Instead, after reiterating the opposition so as to bring us to a sense of extreme tension, he prepares to build on it. Rather than treat the conflict by elimination – by choosing one thesis over the other – he looks for some way to hold and assert both at the same time: the truth will be found in a paradox that is puzzling but intelligible.

Two questions arise: what is the explanation of this peculiar conflict in human nature and its tendencies? And, is there a remedy for it? At this point Pascal enjoins the reader of his *Pensées*, "Ecoutez Dieu." As to origins, the intermittences of moral life derive from original sin, that first turning away from God, that decision on the part of man to think and act as if he were the center of things. The mystery of original sin is the *tertium quid* that makes it possible to understand our simultaneous misery and greatness: the former because of the fallen state of human nature, and the latter because some obscure recollection and evidence of the Edenic state remain in us. In a sense original sin mediates between the two tendencies of *grandeur* and *misère*, for it marks the transition from the one to the other.

However, since the explanation does not provide a remedy, Pascal proceeds to another three-term argument. The comprehensive principle is the same as before: after first asking his reader to listen to God and the message of original sin, now Pascal wants him to turn to God. That means reorienting the mind and the heart, so as not to pull against each other but to focus, both of them, on the same divine end and providence. Then some discernments can be made, some positive counterparts to the opposed terms (and realities) can appear: instead of *orgueil* on the side of *grandeur* there is *humilité*, and instead of *paresse* or *concupiscence* on the side of *misère* there is *mortification* or *pénitence*.

La vraie religion enseigne nos devoirs, nos impuissances, orgueil et concupiscence, et les remèdes, humilité, mortification. (L529d, f216; S140, f249)

At one point Pascal establishes a correlation between the two vicious tendencies of human nature, the positive counterparts of those tendencies, and two aspects of God's nature.

Comme les deux sources de nos péchés sont l'orgueil et la paresse Dieu nous a découvert deux qualités en lui pour les guérir, sa miséricorde et sa justice. (L599a, f774; S320–21, f638)

The function of God's justice is to cure our pride, that of His mercy to invite us to action and good works.

From the apologetic point of view, if the lines of thought and conduct indicated by these counterparts are stabilized – and Pascal thinks that he can contribute persuasive arguments for the mind and effective advice for the heart – the way will be prepared for grace and belief.

For the same pattern of reasoning expressed in slightly different language we may wish to look back at the *Entretien avec M. de Saci*. There Pascal personifies the two sides of the argument in Epictetus and Montaigne, and he states the final resolution with beautiful clarity.

De sorte qu'ils ne peuvent subsister seuls à cause de leurs défauts, ni s'unir à cause de leurs oppositions, et qu'ainsi il se brisent et s'anéantissent pour faire place à la vérité de l'Evangile. C'est elle qui accorde les contrariétés par un art tout divin, et, unissant tout ce qui est de vrai et chassant tout ce qui est de faux, elle en fait une sagesse véritablement céleste où s'accordent ces opposés, qui étaient incompatibles dans ces doctrines humaines. (L296c; Mɪɪɪ153–54)

It is interesting to note the way in which, as Pascal goes along, the principle used for unification in one moment is found to be incomplete and questionable in the next. He can explain one lot of behaviors by *misère* and another lot by *grandeur*; each produces

on its line a synthesis, but of temporary value only. The trouble
is that both make exclusive claims, and when Pascal looks at
them in the light of his basic logical pattern, he finds that each
side, though it has a positive aspect, is incomplete taken by itself.
He then shifts to another level of unification, where the new
connecting term or position comes into play and brings into a
proper equilibrium the partial truths contained in the preceding
formulation of the problem. Shifts of this kind in the status of
key concepts (and the doctrines determined by them) are a
typical feature of Pascal's dialectical thinking. He knows how to
make use of them not only to arrive at a logical closure but also
to keep up the interest of his reader, who, after the effort of
following an argument to a stopping point, finds that he is in for
more suspense, that what he has just grasped leads on to
something else.

THE UNITY OF THE BIBLE

A third example, in connection with the Bible – especially
important because of its constant and unavoidable presence in
the background of Pascal's thinking – will show further how the
same basic pattern of reasoning takes on distinctive traits as
Pascal's mind turns from one center of interest to another.

I should like to emphasize that I shall not undertake to treat
here matters of texture, that is, matters having to do with his
way of interpreting details and particular passages of the Bible.
It would certainly be possible to do so. Starting with Pascal's
commonplaces – such as the one that he provides in serial
fashion thus: "Morale./Doctrine./Miracles./Prophéties./Fig-
ures." (L549a, f402; S36, f21) – we can locate the origins of
statements and arguments that have been gathered up into
proofs of various kinds. Such as: quasi-geometrical (rather rare,
but still serviceable, as in the fragment on the *pari*), or syllogistic
(inevitable, since Pascal thinks this species of reasoning to be a
natural process, as in the proofs of the falsity of non-Christian
religions), or pragmatic (common, involving direct cause and
effect relationships that are usually dependent – as in miracles
– on the power and authority of God); and finally, dialectical

(very frequent, and quite characteristic of moral and religious works). This last sort of proof or sequence is, of course, the one being analyzed here; and we need to recognize Pascal's insight: he saw that, quite apart from the usefulness of dialectical devices in interpreting short or relatively short texts taken from the Bible, they had great value in dealing with the structural characteristics of the Bible as a whole.

Pascal works out the arguments concerning grace and human nature in four stages, from the identification of a manifold to assembling into groups to definition of conflicts to discernments and reconciliations. However, in the Bible much of the preliminary work has already been done: Pascal has in front of him a book that is already divided into two books – the Old and New Testaments. Great complexity remains within each, but the data concerning God and the human race have already been sorted into two lines so as to form, apparently, a single account. In a sense the first two steps of the dialectical process have been accomplished; what Pascal focuses on is the third in the series, where he indicates the great cleavage – alleged, at any rate – in the Bible, and the resulting inconsistencies in the two parts. Regarding the Old Testament, a number of people, including both authors and interpreters, made and read prophetic statements to the effect that a great event was part of God's plan: the coming of a Messiah. And they were convinced that the event had not yet occurred. Regarding the New Testament, Pascal sees another group of people (again, authors and interpreters) who insist that what was prophesied had indeed taken place.

In the face of these antithetical claims, Pascal wants to know (and to show us) how one can make a unified account of what is proposed and narrated in the two sets of documents.

Ainsi pour entendre l'Ecriture il faut avoir un sens dans lequel tous les passages contraires s'accordent; il ne suffit pas d'en avoir un qui convienne à plusieurs passages accordants, mais d'en avoir un qui accorde les passages même contraires. (L533a, f257; S152, f289)

Pascal actually extends to every author and book the rule he is following:

Tout auteur a un sens auquel tous les passages contraires s'accordent
ou il n'a point de sens du tout. (L533a, f257; S152, f289)

Such an absence of unified sense you will not find in Scripture,
he assures us, or in the prophets: they had too much "bon sens"
for that.

In conformity with his habit, therefore, Pascal looks for a
third and inclusive line of thought. A long search is hardly
necessary; the needed principle is already known: according to
one set of partisans, which includes Pascal, Jesus Christ stands
at the center of the two Testaments.

Le véritable sens n'est donc pas celui des juifs, mais en J.-C. toutes les
contradictions sont accordées. (L533a, f257; S153, f289)

Both books point to him as the key in exegesis and the link
connecting the two narrative accounts. Pascal states his solution
in a different but equally succinct way as follows:

Tout ce qui ne va point à la charité est figure.
    L'unique objet de l'Ecriture est la charité.
(L535b, f270; S160, f301)

We must recognize, nevertheless, a real problem, since the
custodians of the original Testament see no reason to believe
that the Messiah has arrived; for them the meaning and the
events of the second Testament do not continue and complete
those of the first.

In such a situation, as we have seen with the topics of grace
and the human condition, Pascal studies the opposed sides and
seeks to discern in each a duplicity, an ambiguity that conceals
something that is wrong in part and right in part. The solution
to the conflict begins to appear when he succeeds in distinguishing the partial truth from the rest in each case, opening the
way to the phase of his argument in which he can combine and
reconcile. As he studies the Bible, Pascal has in hand a
hermeneutic device that will solve his double problem of action
and sense, of narrative and interpretation: the notion of *figure*.
Of course he did not invent it: he had the examples – to
mention only two – of St. Augustine and St. Ambrose, who had
shown what could be done with it in the interpretation of
Scripture. The tack taken by Pascal, based both on evidence in

the Bible itself and on the work of commentators, leads him to assert that the Old Testament is the seat of two senses. One of them has, indeed, some truth in it, but the other is true in a more complete way, in that, without discarding entirely the first meaning, it unveils and justifies a meaning that takes us one step closer to a total view of the Bible.

Pascal argues that Jesus Christ, the disputed personage in the account, is indeed the promised Messiah and will be recognized as such, if one realizes that the prophets did not mean the arrival of a worldly king who would accomplish his work of salvation by worldly power. Actually, Christ himself spoke in this figurative mode, making a distinction between those who are free in spirit and those who are not, between the true bread of heaven and that which is merely physical, between Israelites who are true and those who are not. There is thus created an ensemble of terms carrying double senses, one literal and the other spiritual. Read in this allegorical fashion, the Old Testament states valid prophecies for which corresponding realizations may be sought.

What of the New Testament? How should it be treated so as to adjust its meaning and account into a single pattern? Here Pascal pictures to us a very special situation. To change the New Testament, to allegorize the role of Christ, and to hold, for example, that what he did with regard to "la charité" must be set aside in some sense: that would be horrible.

La charité n'est pas un précepte figuratif. Dire que Jésus-Christ qui est venu ôter les figures pour mettre la vérité ne soit venu que mettre la figure de la charité pour ôter la réalité qui était auparavant, cela est horrible.

Si la lumière est ténèbres que seront les ténèbres? (L611a, f849; S222, f430)

It is all right for the Old Testament to be ambiguous, but, in Pascal's view, he must safeguard the literality of the New Testament. In this application of dialectical sequencing, therefore, we detect a curious irregularity: one of the two sides of the basic paradox requires no preparation for the next and integrative stage of the argument. The New Testament contains no tentative sense that recedes in favor of another and final sense.

From this vantage point, Pascal can find the Bible to be entirely coherent, for it makes a promise and the promise is kept; and it proposes a narrative of God and the human race that stretches, without interruption and with Jesus Christ at the center, from the creation of the world to the founding of the Christian Church. The force of the argument depends on the logic of the dialectical pattern, whereby two groups of terms and actions are first set in paradoxical opposition to each other, and then modified semantically by reference to a third factor so that the contradiction becomes only apparent. Except that in this case one of the sides of the paradox is given at the outset in the state needed for the resolution of the difficulty.

THE DISUNITY OF NATURE

There is one other context where Pascal illustrates in a striking way, I think, how he can adapt his basic art of sequential ordering: in the evocation of Nature, of the whole natural order, which occurs in a fragment of the *Pensées*. The title, if one may call it such, that he gives to his text is "Disproportion de l'homme" (L525d, f199; S125, f230); we shall see how this phrase in fact points to the conclusion of his reflections.

It would be possible to work out here a detailed analysis of the way in which Pascal's logical trope arises and develops in all its stages. However, I wish to concentrate on the later parts of the argument, where there is much to discuss; and so I shall simply outline the first steps in the argument. At the opening of the fragment the whole of Nature – "la nature entière dans sa haute et pleine majesté" – comes on at once; Pascal calls it up in quick panoramic strokes. But the more or less undifferentiated whole gives way to something more accessible, as he invites us to turn our gaze in a particular direction. We do not know it at this point, but he already has in mind the opposite possibility and intends to return to it. Along the first line of observation some distinctions begin to appear: he guides us to the realization that we are situated in the range of visible things. He soon divides that from the invisible part of Nature; the distinction does not signal a dead end for the argument. Continuing, Pascal asks us to use our imaginations, for beyond the visible lies the imaginable; and even *that* does not exhaust everything presented by Nature to our knowing faculties. Incidentally, he has drawn up for us a series of unresolved paradoxes. The visible we see as large at first and then small, then the imaginable likewise as it is overwhelmed by all that lies beyond it. And, of course, Pascal administers exactly the same intellectual shocks, though in inverse order, when he has us look in the other direction: visible-small turns to visible-large when put alongside the imaginable-small, and that he soon dwarfs by invoking the *infini en petitesse*.

Clearly we are heading into the stage of logical opposition, of antithesis, with the term "infinite" serving in its large and small applications to gather up and label all that has preceded. If we compare this situation with the preceding examples, however, I think that something new is going on here, something quite different in the status of things. Pascal conceives his basic paradox and the realities it covers in terms of quantity whereas in treating grace, human nature, and the Bible his reductive drive resulted in contraries or extremes of quality. He places everything in Nature on a single scale where he marks off quantitative divisions as he needs them – though they are no sooner made than their significance pales, in view of the fact that, depending on the direction in which you look for a reference point, all magnitudes become larger or smaller without end.

As for the observer, he will forever go *in medias res* between the two infinities and will mirror in his way the duality of Nature, since with reference to one infinite he amounts to very little but with reference to the other his size is colossal. As a being subject to this paradox he is in fact like everything else; and Pascal traces the implications of his vision out to their conclusion (though he does add one tentative note, in the word "presque").

Quand on est instruit on comprend que la nature ayant gravé son image et celle de son auteur dans toutes choses elles tiennent presque toutes de sa double infinité. (L526c, f199; S128, f230)

He has relativized completely, it seems to me, the antithesis on which he is going to achieve – or not, as will become evident – the dialectical connection. The two infinites do not have the same relation to each other as do pairs like the *grâce suffisante* of the Molinists and the non-regenerative grace of the Lutherans, like the *misère* and *grandeur* of human nature, or like the literal and the spiritual senses of Scripture.

We should note in passing that all of this natural reality stands outside of what Pascal refers to as the *néant*, which is strictly nothing. This means that he affirms a radical distinction at the logical outset of his argument between that *néant* and his quantified *Nature entière*. He never attempts to effect a reconciliation of this antithesis. But he does assert that the *infini en grandeur* and the *infini en petitesse* meet in God:

Ces extrémités se touchent et se réunissent à force de s'être éloignées et se retrouvent en Dieu, et en Dieu seulement. (L527a, f199; S129, f230)

Pascal hurries over this resolution; it takes place without ceremony or amplification, though it does mark a contrast with the situation of man *vis-à-vis* Nature that Pascal develops in the remainder of the fragment.

NATURE AND THE STATUS OF MAN

Here below and apart from God there is no way to bring the infinites together. And it is significant that Pascal now redirects our attention from man as a physical being, as having a paradoxical *masse* at a certain point on the grand scale, to man as a knower, or more exactly, a would-be knower, who tries to grasp the spectacle he has before him.

The effort is doomed to failure, and for a reason related to an essential characteristic of connections in the dialectical mode. In fact, a valuable approach to the characteristic logical pattern consists in examining incomplete procedures and negative results such as the ones that we encounter here. It is clear that human faculties cannot understand or even apprehend the infinitely distant ends of Nature's scale; and the natural impulse will be to shift attention to the middle region, to what one may observe directly. There at least one may take hold of a part of reality and attain some knowledge. But no: we shall be attempting to know the parts without knowledge of the whole; and that is impossible.

In the dialectical mode there can be no separate elements or isolated regions. Pascal is simply coming to grips with that necessity when he refuses to let his human subject think that he can have knowledge that is at one and the same time partial and genuine. Not only is the whole greater than the part; in reality the whole defines the part, assigning nature, function, and intelligibility to it. Or, to come back to the context of the present fragment, for Pascal to accept a reasoning as valid according to his habit of dialectical connections, he must have a sense of some whole into which parts have been fitted. I am tempted to add, fitted with the certainty of *évidence*, although discursive justifications may be needed to bring him (and his reader) to the point of self-evident vision.

Two consequences flow from the preceding. First, Pascal can now advance to the notion of a parallel holding between Nature and man, such that the latter constitutes in his way a subject that reflects, shares the paradox of the former: as a point on the scale he participates in the double infinity. Second, if he has thus, in the fashion of a microcosm, a status in being like that of Nature, then he cannot know himself satisfactorily as a body and on the quantitative spectrum. When he seeks to know, he has the same problem with himself as with Nature. One might say that infinite quantity or magnitude defeats epistemology in the physical world, and, as a creature inserted in that world, man cannot escape the force of the principle.

Having a certain momentum now – achieved in the distinctions and assimilations we have just noted – Pascal moves on to something deeper. His thought continues to be reflexive; he is still concerned with the knowledge that one may have of oneself. However, he leaves the level of bodies, of physical size and begins to think in terms of the "puissances de l'âme."

Notre intelligence tient dans l'ordre des choses intelligibles le même rang que notre corps dans l'étendue de la nature.

Bornés en tout genre, cet état qui tient le milieu entre deux extrêmes se trouve en toutes nos puissances. (L527a, f199; S130, f230)

To our surprise, perhaps, he engages once more in quanti-
fication, in that he assimilates exactly the situation of the soul
and its powers to the situation of Nature. In all of our powers,
feelings, and values we find ourselves in the presence of infinitely
extended extremes: as before, but now in the psychological and
moral sphere, we float uncertainly on a "milieu vaste" that
exceeds us.

Something curious is happening to the basic logical pattern.
One might have expected Pascal to resolve the infinites of
Nature, but he did not (except in the quick and rather
parenthetical reference to the extremes that touch and are
united in God); one might have expected some decision on the
oppositions in man as a corporeal being, but it is not there. Now,
as Pascal pushes forward to a new subject – our minds, our
inner life, our intellectual and moral existence – he uses once
again the theme of the two infinites as the means of depicting a
new situation that has no resolution. He has constructed so far
three stages of an argument, each of which involves a manifold
that he has summarized by two opposed terms, but so far he has
given us no hint of a comprehensive or unifying term. Instead,
he has moved us (1) from the plane of bodies other than
ourselves (2) to another plane, I mean, the plane of ourselves as
bodies, and then (3) from the outside in, as he and we begin to
consider introspectively our "puissances" and their operations:
and in every one of these changes of level he merely restates, he
does not solve, the problem.

This line of thought may remind us of other things said and
implied in the *Pensées*. In an early fragment that forecasts a
possible outline of his total argument Pascal envisages a
discussion in two stages: at the end of the first part the combined
misery and greatness of man would become clear to the apologist
and his interlocutor; and then they would go to consult the
philosophers. We know from other fragments what that would
have given – merely a restatement of the problem in more
abstract language, the two sides or points of view being those of
the optimistic dogmatists and the relaxed skeptics. In other
words, Pascal suggests a movement from the level of common
experience and the contradictions found there to the level of

technical speculation, where a strictly analogous situation is found. In a similar way the fragment on the "Disproportion de l'homme" takes us from a broad view of Nature as bodies to a perception of man as body to a summary of human mental or psychic operations; and at each stage Pascal has us encounter essentially the same impasse.

He has other surprises for us here. He has quantified the definition of "extreme," by including it in his scheme of the two infinites: we noted that above. But a moment arrives when he sees another tack that will be useful in showing the "disproportion of man," which is his overriding aim in these pages. The final paragraphs of the fragment depend on a new opposition, on the fact that the human being consists of two substances, soul and body.

This distinction signals the arrival of still another context in which unresolved contrarieties may be pointed out. Pascal has already made us aware of difficulties the mind has as it tries to grasp the polar infinites and the middle zone between them; he now gives a very different turn to the reasoning, concentrating on matters that seem more metaphysical than epistemological. He wants us to consider a new antithesis, to see whether we can make some kind of unified sense of the two substances in our make-up. First, he spends some time and space stressing the difficulties we have in thinking of body without attributing mental qualities to it and of mind without applying to it terms more appropriate to bodies. Then, something more fundamental: what is mind? And what is body? We cannot really answer either question. It seems safe to say, however, that Pascal is here working along a line of thought guided by notions of quantity and of kinds of being; he has made in earlier passages of the fragment his points in regard to quantity in the natural world. At the close of this complex text Pascal leaves his reader or interlocutor in a quandary: the human creature is a *prodige*, with two incomprehensible sides to his nature, and most incomprehensible of all is the fact that the two have somehow been joined together!

PROPORTION AND DISPROPORTION

When thinking and writing in the dialectical mode Pascal usually works through his connections to the ultimate step, in which he brings contraries together. In the fragment we are analyzing, however, he gives us only one resolution – that of the two infinites of Nature in the mind of God. As for the rest, he composes a set of variations on the theme of unreconciled oppositions. We are not surprised on turning back to the title he put at the beginning of the text: "Disproportion de l'homme." The meaning of the first word is the key to the argument set out in this text: a disproportion is a difference, a dissimilarity, an essential barrier to the making of *rapprochements* and the achievement of unity.

Pascal attributes this barrier to the human nature and condition. In being and in knowing we cannot exceed certain limits or bridge certain gaps. God and his mind are beyond us; that is the first and original disproportion. With Nature, an exact analogy – I mean, an exactly similar frustration – forces itself upon us: we cannot know the physical universe in a complete and therefore true way. Again, with reference to ourselves and our efforts to reach by reflexive means adequate self-knowledge: we repeat in our way what we see in Nature, for in all our actions we can never get out of an obscure middle range of possibilities, with no hope of ever overcoming the pull of the intellectual and moral extremes. In fact the disproportion of man to himself is even more radical: to the preceding we must add the incomprehensible dualism of body and mind or soul in which we are involved. Facing God, Nature, and himself man cannot establish a proportion, a relation that is harmonious or unified. Such is the lesson in humility that Pascal intends for his reader by presenting this complicated string of puzzles.

The notion of proportion – or lack of it – throws much light on the specifically dialectical form taken by what one might call Pascal's epistemology. Knowing starts with two, with two somethings to be brought into a correct relation; and such a relation is precisely that of proportionality. To know means to establish and explore proportions or similarities. For example, we can know something of bodies other than our own because we have a body: our bodily characteristics, being given and known immediately, at least to some degree, enlighten us as to other bodies and their characteristics. On this point he writes at the beginning of the fragment in which he is moving toward the *pari*:

Nous connaissons donc l'existence et la nature du fini parce que nous sommes finis et étendus comme lui. (L550b, f418; S354, f680)

Immediately thereafter he introduces the *infini* and a disproportion:

Nous connaissons l'existence de l'infini et ignorons sa nature, parce qu'il a étendue comme nous, mais non pas des bornes comme nous. (L550c, f418; S354, f680)

Likewise, each of us has a mind, and can therefore enter into proportional relations with other minds and their possibilities. As the scholastic maxim says, "Only like knows like."

In what way, however, is this attitude or approach to knowledge specifically dialectical? It is in this, it seems to me, that Pascal starts with an opposition between the knower and the object to be known, between two antithetical terms; and of course, if anything is to happen, that opposition must be overcome. "Proportion" supplies the third and reconciling term. Knowing can occur after an underlying proportional relationship is posited, and such knowing will consist in a process of explication, in the course of which the knower on his side brings into the open details of the basic analogy that connects him to the object to be known. Two steps are thus involved: first, affirming an original likeness, and then, second, deriving a chain of proportions from that initial assimilation.

Thus what Pascal says in the concluding sentences of "Disproportion de l'homme" becomes, perhaps, clearer than before. If we cannot know what "corps" is, or what "âme" is, if no grasp or analysis of those terms is possible, we have no basis for assuming any sort of basic analogy between a would-be knower and a would-be known. In the absence of a proportion – functioning as a comprehensive and reconciling term – at the outset, the process of forming dialectical connections comes to a halt. It is precisely the intention of Pascal in this fragment, I believe, to leave us at such a way station.

I have proposed four different illustrations of the habitual way in which Pascal approaches questions of morality and religion. Let us review the situation and the kinds of logical connections or sequences that he seeks to create, adding to the general account with which we began those qualifications that his practice has shown to be necessary.

(1) His first impulse is to survey some area of action or discussion, some collection of problematic data. At the outset it has a certain minimal unity; it is not a random *poussière*; it has some relevance to a question already present in his mind. (2) This unity, more potential than actual, soon gives way to tentative divisions that become more definite as the data are further examined and characterized. (3) The preparatory phase of the argument now comes to a close, as Pascal formulates for himself and for us a sharp opposition or contrariety. It may have the form of a pair of terms or two propositions or, more than that, the two positions implied in his vocabulary and statements. (4) To this point Pascal's procedure is the same, whatever the context or problem.

Henceforth, however, variations will appear as he begins to treat the conflict he has posed. (4a) For one thing, he may refuse to go further – at least for the moment – and decide to leave his reader in suspense, in the presence of a clash, which he may make all the more striking (and uncomfortable for the reader) by the resources of his rhetoric. Actually, he associates this option with the Pyrrhonians: on any subject they like to develop contradictions and then assert the impossibility of coming to a decision, so that a skeptical attitude becomes the final norm or refuge. But Pascal is not a skeptic, except in temporary circumstances and in view of something else to come in an argument.

(4b) The next option involves him in an effort of adjustment such that the terms or positions do not tend simply to destroy each other. For they may coexist in a particular relation, one that is not antagonistic, as when Pascal assigns to one a priority over the other. He does not eliminate one of the possibilities in favor of the other; he simply puts it on a lower degree of some scale. The lower term becomes a grounding for the higher term, which can then be seen as throwing light on the lower factor or justifying it. This device of setting priorities may be used in successive episodes so as to create a ladder or hierarchy.

However, it is not the only way out of the problem posed by an antithesis. (4c) Pascal may choose something more radical: the introduction of a relation more complex than that of priority; and I mean that of resemblance or proportionality. The whole line of reasoning found in the fragment on Nature and the two infinites is built on this notion. Of course, what Pascal does in the "Disproportion de l'homme" is to demonstrate that disproportion and put put his reader back in situation (4a) above; but the negative argument serves to clarify in a particularly effective way the functioning of proportions and proportionality in Pascal's theory of knowing, especially as it applies to the subject matters of mathematics and physics.

(4d) Finally, instead of introducing complementary levels of consideration as in (4b) and instead of instituting a proportion as in (4c), Pascal often has recourse to something less mathematical in inspiration than either (4b) or (4c). He chooses to reconcile the two sides of the opposition by means of a third term or view toward which the others may be oriented and into which they are integrated after suitable revision. I think we must emphasize the notion of revision, because of the fact that the realities involved in the argument suddenly become ambiguous. And without that ambiguity the dialectical process would come to a standstill. Pascal must show that each term in the conflict at hand has, after all, something worth saving. Until he does this, each term of the conflict is in status 1, so to speak, and it has a negative coefficient; after he works with it, each term moves to status 2, which is positive and acceptable. As we have seen in several instances, Pascal manages to discern and define positive counterparts of the opposed items; and then he can go on to the phase of reconciling them. (I am describing this inventive use of ambiguity in connection with Pascal's fourth option; in fact, something like it occurs in the two preceding choices, when he is setting priorities or framing a proportion.)

Such is, I think, the inventory and anatomy of the principal kinds of connection established by Pascal in discussing matters of morals, philosophy, and religion. He does not construct chains of statements that lead the mind in an unbroken and linear fashion from principles to consequences. He does not propose a theorem with justifying propositions in its train. He creates something much more like a diagram that sums up a complex situation at a glance. It may remind us of something that fascinated Pascal in physics – an equilibrium of quantities or forces. He does, however, follow a real sequence in the logical process, from confusion to clarification to conflict to ranking or proportion or integration. Although in particular applications the pattern undergoes important refinements and adaptations, it remains nonetheless fundamentally the same.

AN ART OF CONNECTIONS

In order to bring into focus the existence and working of the art of connections one might decide to put the matter in the form indicated by the expression: *question–answer*. There is a sense in which an art consists ultimately in that pair, with some complication added between the two terms. An art originates in a question, and an intellectual art corresponds to a particular type of question, such as, *what* do we wish to know about a subject-matter? In answering that question we discover what our end is; and then a subsidiary question arises regarding means: *how* can we come to know what we want to know? The term "rules" tends to appear at this point, or, in the fuller expression, "rules of the art"; and they designate the means to be used in reaching the objective set up in the question. If the questions – principal and subsidiary – are clear, and if, as a final piece of evidence, a body of results is at hand, we may be sure that an art is present and outside of the sphere of mere possibility. A question, some means of pursuing it, some answers: all of these ingredients are included in Pascal's way of working. What he seeks is a balanced, unified position in a situation defined by a conflict; how he achieves that is by asking and answering questions concerning the opposed terms, opinions, and parties; he actually produces effective syntheses that eliminate contradictions in discussions of grace, human nature, and Scripture (and incidentally, of various other topics).

That is a relatively simple way to look at the problem, and without doubt it makes a beginning. But it emphasizes too much, I feel, the linguistic aspect of the art of connections here. And so I should like to turn to another way, less tied to language – and therefore more adequate, it seems to me. When we observe a complex, integrated, and productive process, that is to say, an ensemble of operations, clearly purposive in character, involving language, thought, and things, and specified as to subject-matter, principles, procedure, and aim: then it is obvious that we have an art. It is my view that the examples we have been analyzing and annotating satisfy the conditions indicated.

Actually, there is a still deeper level of understanding what Pascal does, a level that we reach when we put his procedure into a setting where it is not so disembodied. His results, his solutions, his rankings and reconciliations presuppose certain operations, some of which, at least, we have made explicit here. However, lying behind those maneuvers and guiding them is a subjective inclination, a habitual tendency to act – not mechanical, but clairvoyant and free – and I think it is thanks to this stable disposition, built on and attested by repetition, that we may finally speak of an art, and in this instance, an art of connection and sequence. It takes its place as part of his intellectual equipment, of his second nature – the strength of which is indicated by what he says about *coutume*: "la seconde nature, qui détruit la première" (L514b, f126; S85, f159). There is an analogy between *coutume*, as Pascal understands that term, and an acquired "art of the mind," as I use the expression here.

A LOOK BEHIND AND AHEAD

If we look back at the typical aims and end-results of the arts of interpretation and invention, we may see how the art of connections makes use of what the other two have accomplished in doing their proper work. The first of the three furnishes guidance as Pascal formulates statements of fact and value, of what is the case and of what is to be sought in morals and religion. It helps him in the task of recognizing in particular contexts the dualities of things and their dependence on their Creator. In this first field of reference the emphasis lies on recovering and commenting on facts – affirmations and denials – that Pascal has encountered in his reading and in his experience. The second art, that of invention and discovery, provides guidance in the choice of terms and concepts to be used in inquiry. Pascal makes use of it in looking back over traditional habits of thought and investigation, in identifying inadequacies or errors, and in bringing forward new topics, new points of departure that open up fruitful lines of thought and study. In this field, the emphasis lies on assembling a technical lexicon, a task that has both conceptual and linguistic aspects.

In its turn, the art of connection or presentation supplies guidance in the preparation of sequences, of structures composed of parts that define and imply one another – units such as those examined above. And of course the materials entering into these sequences must be, ultimately, the statements and terms elaborated in the frameworks of the other two arts. But this latest phase, which concentrates on orderings and movements, is *par excellence* the phase of discursive activity, by means of which connections are established, traced, and justified in the data. The emphasis on discourse sets this technique apart from the other two, for they have in each case a narrower scope and focus.

Pascal's use of the dialectical mode as a source of logical patterns poses for us a general question concerning its possible uses on a broader scale. He has applied this way of reasoning in relatively restricted frameworks or contexts, on topics such as the possibility of accomplishing basic Christian precepts, the *double délaissement* involving man and God, the various concepts of grace, the argument of the wager, the disproportion of man, and so on. He can assemble his data, draw up the issue, and settle the differences regarding any one of those matters. And yet, these sectors of activity and thought must appear at last as partial aspects of the total scheme that Pascal takes to be true.

Then, in a sense, he frees dialectic: instead of being a technique of local argument, of giving design to certain features of his position, it becomes an instrument of general integration. In its former use Pascal engages, it seems to me, in micro-dialectic. What will happen when he removes all limits from the scope of the inquiry, when he attempts to achieve a total view, encompassing not only the physical universe and the world of human activity and culture, but also the designs of an infinite and hidden God? It is not easy for him or for us to keep the two roles of dialectic separate. The truth of the matter seems to be that the two are strictly analogous. The dialectical instrument, by its essential tendency, which is to unify multiplicities and to harmonize conflicts, includes something of the whole in every local argument or procedure; and Pascal, as a master of this method of thinking, communicates to his reader, it seems to me, even in details, an inkling of what his final and panoramic solution will be. However, there are interesting large-scale features of the works we have been discussing, and we shall now need to examine what happens as Pascal moves onto higher and higher levels of assimilation and synthesis.

INTEGRATION

THE ORGANIZING TENDENCY

From an early age Pascal seems to have had a particular attitude toward intellectual work. It seeks to balance a grasp of details with the achievement of broad views. Whether in arithmetic or geometry or physics or morality and religion, he gives always the impression of confidence as he approaches the area or situation that he has decided to investigate, standing over it, dominating it. He combines with this attitude something closely related to it, the desire to make any conclusions that he reaches as clear as possible to the kind of reader he is addressing. And in many places he even gives evidence of wanting to refine his practice into a method that can be stated in a small number of rules.

As we turn, in the sphere of dialectical discourse, from the analysis of his art of forming logical connections in the sphere of dialectical discourse, we may imagine him raising his eyes from particular statements and locally significant arguments. Following him from bits of text to blocks of text, we gain altitude and see emerging in his reflections distinct fields – and features in those fields – that were not prominent before. To say more literally what I mean: Pascal draws on a stock of important and often dichotomous distinctions that set up essential boundaries in realities, in ways of thinking, and in vocabularies.

He may turn, in order to sustain his analyses, to familiar pairs like Christian and non-Christian, eternal and temporal, nature and grace, justice and force, knowledge (*science*) and power or authority, *géométrie* and *finesse*, finite and infinite, *raison* and *coeur*. Or he may resort to triadic series like morality, philosophy, and religion or nature, man, and God. Under these clarifying and differentiating ideas, taken as points of departure or reached as points of arrival, moves a procession of subject-matters.

The question for us becomes, which of these or similar terms, sometimes overlapping in sense and application, does he promote to a superior status, to the status of organizing principles whose proper function is to provide a broad view or even a totalizing perspective? Furthermore, what conclusions may we come to as to how Pascal goes about selecting, defining, and using such first principles for his systematizing purposes?

MOMENTS OF INSIGHT

In drawing on the resources of his technical lexicon, he does not have constantly in mind the aim of achieving an inclusive view of his universe with its scientific and moral foundations. But he does arouse in us the feeling that such a thing is possible, and the anticipation that at some point it will be forthcoming. For the recurrent topics and distinctions just mentioned indicate, indeed, preside over – in every case – significant sectors of reality. Pascal sees them not as disembodied, but rather as correlated with subject-matters. Exactly what those subject-matters are may not always be evident; that is, they may not be so yet – in the details of the page lying before us. But when he moves under the impulse to systematize, he naturally considers, it seems to me, details to be less important than the guiding notion of a correlation between ideas and the realities whose boundaries are fixed by those ideas. In other words, the fundamental insight occurs for Pascal (and for us as his readers) when some province of reality comes into view as a possible object of study, and at the same time when he (and we in turn) begin to see how it can be studied so as to situate it as a region in a territory and a part in a whole.

What can we say, then, of Pascal's practice in the selection of first principles, as his art of systematization comes into play? As a first step, I think, he brings intelligibility into his universe by taking up and applying the notion of *ordre* – not, of course, in the sense of "command" or "sequence," but in the sense of "realm," or "domain." An *ordre* is the proper locus of a particular kind of beings.

Two sources of inspiration, with their characteristic connotations, seem to converge here. The first is mathematical: "ordre" occurs frequently in the treatises dealing with problems of arithmetic and geometry. Pascal studies at length the notion of number-series and works out the various but related "ordres" that appear as he constitutes the series according to different rules. Something similar may be seen in geometry, where the division into plane and solid establishes two realms, two areas for exploration, each with its limiting conditions. This understanding of *ordre* and of the fact that there may be a plurality of orders gives us an important clue to Pascal's strategy. But he goes further, of course: already, in mathematics, he shows an inclination to arrange the orders onto levels, with a clear separation of the lower from the higher.

This tendency to seek hierarchical arrangements comes to a focus at once clearer and broader if we consider another set of connotations that surround the leading ideas here. They derive from metaphysical and theological sources – specifically, it seems to me, from the Christianized neo-Platonism of Augustine. His universe includes different sorts of beings, arranged in a hierarchy that comes to a summit in God, who transcends them all as their source and eternal ground. These two semantic streams, one coming out of mathematics and the other from a religious faith that has sought and found understanding in certain philosophical terms have contributed much to Pascal's habit of thought in matters of systematization. They prepare and reinforce the basic impulse that leads him (1) to identify and define *ordres* and then (2) to make of them an inclusive scheme of levels. If we analyze what he does along these two main lines of thought with their correlated data, we can begin to understand how they eventuate in specific operations and bear witness to an art of systematization.

UP THE SCALE

"Dieu doit régner sur tout et tout se rapporter à lui" (L624a, f933; S456, f761). Pascal's thought has a built-in drive toward integration, because of the great *évidence* – supplied by faith – of God as infinite Person, partly hidden and partly revealed, to whom everything must eventually be related, since everything depends on him originally, continuously, and finally. This principle being taken not simply as granted, but from the experience of November 23, 1654 as certified, there is never any need to argue the question of whether his universe tends to unity. Pascal concentrates instead on tracing implications: on listing the possibilities before him, defining the specific forms they take as he moves from context to context, and determining what distinctions will have the deciding role as he situates things in his universe and brings them, at last, into their proper relation to God.

As one means of grasping Pascal's way of mapping reality, one might concentrate on the two opposed notions of *Nature* and *Ecriture* and watch the ways in which they subdivide and ramify.

It would be tempting to take this tack, since it lays out two great fields of investigation, each radically distinct from the other. However, he introduces this pair in the *Pensées* at the outset of his *apologetic* undertaking: he will proceed first, it seems, to establish a decisive proposition ("que la nature est corrompue") on the basis of *Nature*, and then, apropos of a related proposition ("qu'il y a un Rédempteur") he will argue from *Ecriture*. The context is a bit narrow for our purposes here, where we seek a total vision.

For another possible standpoint: from time to time, as we have seen, Pascal's texts show traces of philosophical commonplaces, more or less Aristotelian in origin, regarding categories and levels of being. In the *Pensées* he sets down references to stones, which are mere physical bodies, to plants, which are alive, and then to animals; and at that point he becomes very aware of a kind of life that is guided by instinct alone. He likes to draw the contrast between *instinct* and *raison* as a principles of behavior: the former, because of its fixity, explains the inapplicability of the notion of progress to what animals do, and the latter, as a source of discoveries and sciences, opens up a scene of unending advance for the human race. All this suggests a cumulative scale of beings and perfections, to which is then added the human animal, who is physical, alive, sentient, and rational. And when Pascal says that he who tries to play the angel ends by being the beast, he makes a bow to the category of pure intelligences. But in all this, apart from the *instinct/raison* distinction, we are in the realm of mental associations, which Pascal does not bother to justify in any technical way, rather than of functioning principles.

Perhaps the simplest and most direct way to proceed is to follow Pascal as he identifies the *ordres* one by one and begins to place them on the degrees of a scale. At the bottom he sees body – or bodies – and on this level there is at once a privilege and a lack. Bodies have *étendue*, occupy space, interfere with the movements of other bodies; and therefore they exist: they represent a victory over *le néant*. Moreover, they are marked off by shapes, limits, *bornes*; and, therefore, they have natures. He uses our bodies as he makes the basic points:

Nous connaissons donc l'existence et la nature du fini parce que nous sommes finis et étendus comme lui.

Nous connaissons l'existence de l'infini et ignorons sa nature, parce qu'il a étendue comme nous, mais non pas des bornes comme nous. (L550bc, f418; S354, f680)

It is interesting to note the ease and the assurance with which Pascal uses traditional terms, like *existence* and *nature* – at the same time that he redefines them drastically by means of geometrical notions. In this way he fixes the identity of bodies and lays the groundwork for their location in the hierarchical scheme. If such is the privileged or positive aspect of Pascal's concept of body, what is its negative shadow? What do bodies lack, what absent quality leads us upward from them to a more complete level of being? It is this: bodies have nothing of the soul about them, and so have no essential link with life, or – *a fortiori* – with thought.

De tous les corps ensemble on ne saurait en faire réussir une petite pensée. Cela est impossible et d'un autre ordre. (L540d, f308; S179, f339)

As the next step in his reasoning Pascal takes body and puts it with soul and mind, to form the level or order of human creatures. The combination is strange, even unintelligible, but it exists. Let us note, incidentally, that the progress Pascal makes here comes as a result of an inward direction taken by his reflections; he shifts his attention from external things and the *sciences des choses extérieures* to a complex being that has an inner life and to its special discipline, *la morale*. Of course, he does not stop at this point. Again, something is missing, inaccessible:

De tous les corps et esprits on n'en saurait tirer un mouvement de vraie charité, cela est impossible, et d'un autre ordre surnaturel. (L540d, f308; S179, f339)

The structure formed by the body, the soul, and the mind (which came into the picture with the appearance of the soul) includes at its summit something else very Pascalian: *le coeur*; and it is the seat of the "mouvements de charité."

Curiously enough, it is apropos of this human complex and using it as a point of departure that Pascal expresses in the fullest way his concept of a cosmic set of orders. He gives to the three fundamental aspects of the human being – body, mind, and heart, *corps*, *esprit*, and *cœur* – an extraordinary power of extension: by analogy they become the ways of access to all things and, indeed, the measures of all things. Mind and heart (the latter taken as including the order of charity) stand over all the rest of creation: you cannot, he writes, extract a single thought out of all the physical universe, nor a single movement of charity out of all the activities of the mind. And, as he says with great conviction, there is no possibility of bridging the infinite distance that separates each of the orders from the other two; in a bit of *renchérissement* he adds that the infinity between the mind and the heart is greater than the one between body and mind.

PEOPLE AND THE ORDERS

Here Pascal's thought takes an interesting turn toward some implications. Although the three levels enter into the make-up of every human being, it is possible to take them distributively, so to speak, to use them for sorting people into classes, and to arrive at a sort of characterology. Individuals may live exclusively or mainly by the values associated with one of the orders and let the other two go more or less uncultivated. This way of applying his terms allows Pascal to set up another scale: at the bottom, he puts the *charnels*, who are attached to things, power, and goods of this world; above them are those who live the life of the mind – Archimedes appears as the great example – and work on mathematical and scientific problems; at the top, in the order of *charité* and *sainteté*, which is dominated by the figure of Jesus Christ, Pascal evokes those whose lives embody and exemplify religious values.

The "distance infinie" separating the orders makes it impossible for those on one of the lower levels to understand or appreciate what happens above them. The carnally inclined cannot follow what great intellects do, and neither of these two groups can comprehend the achievements of the saints; the *sagesse de Dieu* found there is invisible to them. Thus does the original distinction of being into three sorts – bodily, mental, and spiritual – give rise to a set of proportions that classify people into three hierarchically arranged groups.

Now Pascal is ready for another extremely significant step. Since, on each level, he imagines people and their activities, he offers a more precise determination of what is going on as those in each group do characteristic things. He begins at the bottom of the scale, locates terms that fit particularly well there, and then extends his vocabulary by analogy so that it will serve in the other parts of his scheme. For the *charnels*, the kings and captains, the rich and powerful, he writes of "grandeurs," "éclat," "lustre." On the next higher level, Pascal resorts to and adds to the same vocabulary, even though we are infinitely far away from the realm of bodies:

Les grands génies ont leur empire, leur éclat, leur grandeur, leur victoire et leur lustre, et n'ont nul besoin des grandeurs charnelles où elles n'ont pas de rapport. Ils sont vus, non des yeux mais des esprits. (L540c, f308; S177, f339)

Great minds have their struggles, their achievements, their great *inventions*, and the glory, the *éclat*, that follows from them. On the third level Pascal develops his ideas once more according to parallels, – *empire, éclat, victoire, lustre* – as when, for example, he calls up the passion, the death, and the victory of Christ.

I should like to add here a reference to Pascal's correspondence. In the nine letters to the Roannez (written in the latter part of 1656) where the context has to do often with moral and spiritual conversion, Pascal expresses himself again in terms of beginnings, struggles, perseverance, movement toward a *couronnement* that includes specific goods and satisfactions. The value of these letters as serving both to exemplify and to clarify his integrative scale of values has not been sufficiently noted, I believe. They are direct, luminous, and intimate.

Similarly, for a quick review of the three orders and the hierarchy that keeps them in their proper relation, one can hardly do better than to reread the letters to Christine of Sweden, to Huyghens, and to Fermat (of 1662, 1659, and 1660;

the first two dates are probable only). Writing to Christine in connection with the presentation to her of a *machine d'arith-métique*, Pascal distinguishes between the two orders of power and of mind: he says that he respects sovereign authority and solid science; and, as it happens, she is doubly entitled to respect, for she combines in a unique way both of those. In the letter to Huyghens, he expresses his gratitude for the "présent," Huyghens had made him of his "dernière production"; and Pascal tells him that he would be glad to furnish his correspondent with as many copies of the treatise on the *roulette* as Huyghens might wish to have; in advance of that, he informs him that he is sending already some "avant-coureurs" of that larger package. It is the sort of exchange that one would expect between two scientists on the level of mind, where *inventions* count for more than anything else. And finally, in his letter to Fermat, Pascal pays tribute to geometry as "le plus haut exercice de l'esprit," and as good for testing our powers; but, in spite of being "le plus beau métier" in the world, it is only that – a "métier." A man who is only a geometrician differs but little from a clever artisan. He thinks that Fermat agrees with him in this judgment; and he adds, shifting to higher ground: "Mais il y a maintenant ceci de plus en moi, que je suis dans des études si éloignées de cet esprit-là, qu'à peine me souviens-je qu'il y en ait" (L282d; MIV923).

THE SYSTEMATIZING OPERATIONS

In the texts of which I have sought to give an account above, what is happening that one may plausibly think of as symptomatic of an art of systematization? Are there recurrent devices and maneuvers in Pascal's procedure that tend to an integrative effect? The first thing that such an art must do is to engage in boundary-fixing, in assignments of subject-matters to disciplines. Interestingly enough, it appears that in the present context Pascal does not work primarily with a notion of particular subject-matters and associated sciences – as he did in the preface to the treatise on the vacuum – but rather with something like a diagram that lays out terrains or problem areas for exploration and possible scientific treatment. He has in mind not an encyclopedia but an encyclopedic outline. He goes about the task of integration by first isolating and defining ranges of being, or more precisely, ranges of beings.

However, he does not simply differentiate: simple juxta-posings or coordinations will not suffice for his purposes. The distinctions are so drastic and involve such enormous "dis-tances" that oppositions result. Then, having set his terms against one another, he can go on to order them along a scale. He will discard nothing; he ranks all the elements of his analysis, including the inferior ones, which are kept firmly in place. In fact, he proceeds through both of the necessary phases of systematization: first, that of definition, which assigns identities to his *ordres*, and second, that of establishing priorities, which involves him in making judgments of relative value on the basis of explicit criteria. (That means, as we shall see, judging the degree of approximation to the top of the scale, and above that, to God.)

A continuous process of dialectical unification is taking place here. It differs in a significant way, I think, from what I described in the preceding section as Pascal's way of making connections in limited cases and local contexts. But the difference is eventually hard to maintain: much of what turned up on the microscopic scale applies here, where he is thinking in macroscopic terms. That is true because of the peculiar genius of dialectic, and its way of growing and flourishing on assimilations. In his logic Pascal brought together under characterizing labels great masses of data and collections of individuals; and, of course, he does something quite similar here in setting up his orders. "Corps" unifies in its range an infinitely large number of physical beings (they may be infinitely large and infinitely small); "esprit" does something similar for minds and for the objects of mental attention; "coeur" and "charité" assemble according to their kind of unity intellectual principles, spiritual impulses, and saints. In Pascal's art of dialectical connections we saw something exactly similar when he was preparing his materials on his way to the reconciliation of antitheses.

Now, however, as he moves from one level to another, Pascal produces an effect suggesting not a movement toward local unifications of opposites under a third term but something else that we have seen before, in the context of certain logical connections: his taste for rankings or hierarchies. One might argue that in any instance of ranking the relation of priority itself, when set up between a lower and a higher term, takes on the function of a third something and serves to bind the opposed levels together. However, I think it useful to keep the technique of logical reconciliations separate from the technique of rankings, the latter being particularly relevant to my immediate concern here, the role and power of dialectic in a systematizing inquiry.

The formula seems to be: to use the outer to get to the inner, and then to use the lower to reach the higher. He leads us from the outside in, from external and purely physical things to beings that have an inside or soul, and then within the soul he takes us from inferior kinds of knowing and desiring to the higher kind that is attained on the level of charity. If we add now to those two pairs and tendencies, a third and concomitant movement from creation and creatures to Creator, from multiplicity to unity, we shall have, I believe, Pascal's final device for clarifying his scheme of orders. This last pair presides over everything he does in the progress from external bodies to internal minds to the high plane of charity. Going up the degrees of Pascal's scale always involves moving away from the particulars and differences visible on each level and getting closer to God, the last unifying principle.

HORIZONTAL INTEGRATION

After proceeding from (1) body to (2) body plus mind, to (3) body plus mind plus heart, Pascal takes the human creature – of which (3) is the formula – as supplying the levels and aspects of a great synoptic view. This triple distinction in (3) allows him to construct and project a scheme of panoramic scope. Each of the dimensions lays out an unlimited terrain for exploration containing, respectively, all that is corporeal, all that is intellectual, and all that is moral or spiritual (or religious). As those subject-matters emerge, they are matched by another and correlated set of terms, since there is a human faculty particularly concerned with knowing in each of the domains: the *sens* for bodies, *esprit* or *raison* for the realm of the mind, and the *coeur* for matters of morals and religion. Incidentally, the functioning of the reason is mainly discursive, while that of the senses and the heart is mainly intuitive; and – to complete the picture – the heart not only knows but also desires and wills.

As Pascal's division of orders unfolds, it functions as a three-dimensional matrix, giving rise to a system of *parallel structures* within which concepts may be defined and statements made about subject-matters. It generates classes of things to be known, and along with them, the outlines, at least, of matching epistemologies. What appears at first to be simply a hierarchy invented for vertical ordering permits Pascal to engage in horizontal movement and integration. The key to all this lies in the force of analogy. We have already seen it at work when Pascal, beginning at the bottom of his scheme, posited classes of people and notions like struggle, victory, and glory first on the level of bodies, and afterward on each of the other two. I should like now to call that vertical analogizing, and then to draw attention to a complementary horizontal movement, which results in a series of tripartite frameworks standing in exact proportion to each other, in such a way as to give great breadth to Pascal's field of view.

Let me explain more fully what Pascal does as a way of extending the orders in the horizontal direction. He conceives first, as I said above, the three constituents of human nature, then correlates with them classes of things, then correlates with them faculties of knowing; and at that point we have the sketch of a broad project. Next comes the characterizations of moral types – the *charnels*, the *génies*, and the *saints* – forming still another lateral extension of the basic outline. And that same outline can, of course, provide the framework for considering individuals as well as character types and classes. It is no doubt interesting to watch Pascal place groups of people on this or that level of his diagram according to what predominates in their style of life. It is even more interesting and a bit paradoxical, in view of the infinite distances that separate the orders, to note that each one of us includes in his make up the three dimensions – the bodily, the intellectual, and the spiritual – and that fact defines for us the context of our personal and moral existence. Each such context, with its choices and commitments, embodies the three *ordres* in a particular way, in a fresh extension by analogy of the original outline.

In fact, when Pascal thinks according to this ethical version of his diagram, which puts all the parts in proper relations to one another, he can represent easily what his and our inner lives should be like. Each of us has a body and associated senses, with what that implies of an inclination to concupiscence and disorder; but that side of our nature becomes acceptable when it is kept under the influence of the mind. In turn the mind will function properly when it is kept under the rule of the heart, which provides not only the first principles of discursive thought for the knower but also the first intuitions of God – and consequently of values – for the moral agent.

Although the schematism has validity when presented in that essentially static fashion, it comes to life and movement in passages where Pascal imagines it as giving the stages of an itinerary that an individual might pass through on the way to a conversion. Suppose, for example, that a *libertin* caught up in a daily round of *divertissements* meets someone who finally causes him to do a bit of reflection; as their talks continue, he develops a sense of the mobility and vanity of his pleasures; to get further insight into his situation, the two decide to consult some moral philosophers; that project fails because the philosophers are busy with their paradoxes, which in any case only repeat what the seeker has already come to realize, namely, that human nature is enigmatic; the guide on this journey then suggests to the interlocutor that there is another step he might take: listen to what God and the Bible have said; and that leads to further advice about the means of bringing the conflicting sides of one's personality – body, mind, and heart – into harmony, so that there will be a chance of hearing the message contained in divine revelation.

This little scenario, which is inspired by the opening chapters of the *Pensées*, should be put alongside the outline of conversion so powerfully described in the pages of *Sur la Conversion du pécheur*. There Pascal draws out the opposition between the order of this world, with its transitory goods, and the order of grace, of religious commitment. The repentant soul, coming to its senses, realizes that it is not enough to say that things are perishable – they are in the very act of perishing and even, in a sense, have already perished. From them it rises to a comprehensive view of creatures, Creation, and Creator; it makes a resolve regarding the rest of its existence in this life, and prays for the means of overcoming its natural weakness. Such changes in inner life are latent in the distinction of the three orders, and need only the proper occasions for Pascal to specify them as indicating the moral habits and decisions open to individuals.

From the original matrix to a framework including the kinds of being in the universe, to a matching epistemological framework, to an analytical view of society, to a plan for individual ethics: such is the path along which Pascal adumbrates, in part by explicit statement, in part by implication, a series of proportions defined by three basic terms, whose meanings vary analogically – but not equivocally – with the shifting contexts. I started with the aim of showing how Pascal invents a scheme of vertical integration. However, we cannot appreciate the systematizing power of the *ordres* simply by concentrating on the upward movement into which Pascal draws us, or on the terrains that open up level by level; we must also notice, as we rise, the fruitfulness of the triple distinction taken as a whole and applied along another axis. Pascal suggests to us a horizontal procession of specific but similar contexts within which questions may be raised, debated, and resolved. In so doing, he gives us hints of the truly encyclopedic range that he has achieved in his thought.

FROM DOCTRINE TO HISTORY AND BACK

There is, in fact, one more very important analogical extension to be observed: Pascal sees in the ethical framework and in the itineraries of individuals that may be based on it the possibility of a collective application. Of course, he had already begun such an application when he identified classes of people living on the various planes, but he did not there put them in a historical perspective. When, however, in the *Ecrits sur la grâce* or in the later chapters of the *Pensées*, or at the beginning of the *Abrégé de la vie de Jésus-Christ*, he looks at the history of the human race, taken in all its stages, he finds himself applying in fact the doctrine of the *ordres* as a principle of explanation. The structure and sequence of that collective history – which sets human events against a background of divine initiatives and interventions: Creation, Eden, the expulsion of Adam and Eve from it, patriarchs and prophets, Moses, the Incarnation, the founding of the Church, Fathers, saints, Popes and Councils, down to seventeenth-century France and the *péripéties* of the struggle between Jesuits and Jansenists – make sense to Pascal in terms derived from the three orders.

Take the example of the Jews: Pascal tends habitually in the *Pensées* to put them on the level of the *charnels*, though he also locates regularly among them some who are genuinely spiritual, for it is they who keep alive the theme of God's redemptive plan – present in *perpétuité* – for humanity. Or, take the collective understanding that occurred when the hidden significance of the Old Testament became clearer than ever, and when the need to interpret it in figurative (spiritual) as well as in literal (material or corporeal) terms became obvious to the early followers of Christ. What Pascal does here in the perspective of history resembles what he does in the *Ecrits sur la grâce* in a context more purely exegetical in nature, though the results in the latter instance are not devoid of historical significance. Having to deal in the *Ecrits* with certain problematic statements concerning grace, taken from the Bible and from the writings of Saint Augustine, he interprets them literally wherever possible and up to the point of a difficulty; then he looks for an ambiguity and a figure; when that is established, he has the option of taking the one of the two meanings that fits into the ensemble of what he has already accepted as true in a literal sense. Or, again, there is the controversy with the Jesuits at the time of the *Provinciales*: the ultimate explanation for Pascal of their words and actions lies in the choice that he thinks they made in favor of power over spirituality.

In applications of the order of charity and grace to the lives of individuals – as in many passages of the *Ecrits* – one is struck by Pascal's emphasis on the precariousness and uncertainty of ethical existence: if one is in a state of grace, fear and trembling are appropriate, since one may be abandoned, *délaissé*; and, vice versa, if one is not in such a state, hope is proper and a change for the better may occur. It seems to me that this same uncertainty, this ever-present possibility of falling from or returning to grace characterizes the fate of groups and nations in the movement of history. It promotes humility, a virtue found especially on the plane of the heart and charity.

With the emergence of sacred history into Pascal's thought and the possibility of integrating that history into his outline of entities and values, we reach a decisive point in the far-reaching dialectical progression being analyzed here. Clearly, much of the time in the works of moral and religious reflection, Pascal intends to place himself on the plane of doctrine – of abstract and generalizing discourse. If we wish, however, to understand how he works out the inner drive toward unity implicit in his dialectical method, it is important to note that at critical moments two streams of reflections flow together – that of doctrinal or apologetic argument and that of historical narrative. Like *logos* and *mythos* in Plato, like Christian doctrine and the story of the terrestrial and celestial cities in Augustine, the *ordres* of Pascal and the stages he believes mankind has gone through are not only compatible; they depend on and reinforce each other. He writes in the light of a doctrine that is embodied in history – both pervading it and issuing from it. His theology of history is actually inseparable from his history of theology.

THE LAST STEPS

Let us recapitulate before concluding. Pascal has two basic integrative operations to perform – first, distinguishing, and then, unifying. These he specifies in the various fragments concerned with the orders (especially L540b, f308 and L624a, f933; S177, f339, and S456, f761). Having distinguished three fundamental levels of analysis, he unifies them, first, by arranging them on a scale of ascending dignity and, second, by suggesting that on each level something similar will be found (it is indicated by the repeated references to battles and victories). But the closer we look at the results achieved by these operations, and at other important texts in the moral and religious works, the more we are struck by the possibilities for lateral expansion inherent in this rather bare schematism. Further distinctions (epistemological, characterological, ethical, historical) suggest terrains for exploration that are different from one another as to subject-matter and emphasis; and yet they are also proportional to one another – it is the unifying impulse at work again: they fit as parts into a complex synthesis. They fill out by sidewise development Pascal's ascending scale of beings, values, and accomplishments, and they prepare the way for further movement upward.

To understand what is involved on the next level of Pascal's synthesis, we must review his conception of the heart and its functions. The seat of feeling, desire, and will, it has in addition a crucial power of knowing. It provides some extremely important intuitions that serve as principles, in the formal sense of that word: starting and ending points of intellectual processes. By its natural light the heart grasps notions such as space, time, number, movement, and it affirms the real existence of what they denote. These acts of the heart are immediate and their objects are self-evident. Assuming the principles and drawing out their consequences, reason – located on the level just below the heart – may explore within itself the subject-matters of mathematical science, or it may turn downward toward bodies, combining mathematics with experiments in a method that yields a science of things and their operations. It moves

discursively rather than intuitively as it assembles its demonstrations and produces its inventions, always with reference to
the small stock of clarifying ideas.

However important all that may be for Pascal – or may have
been for him in his own scientific researches – it pales beside
what the heart does as it directs itself upward rather than
downward and opens itself to the object indicated by the key
phrase: "Dieu sensible au coeur et non à la raison" (L552b,
f424; S359, f680). But the nearness that seems implied here is
deceptive. Actually, another great division in Pascal's universe
appears, the abyss that separates the whole order of finite being
from the infinity of God.

Pascal could go far toward a solution of the problem of
identifying and ordering elements as long as he and they
belonged to essentially the same province of being. Having now
reached the top of his structure, with its vertical and horizontal
developments, how can he proceed? Not, he thinks, by the way
of human initiative. As in the case of the apologetic argument of
the *Pensées*, he comes to a point beyond which there must be a
reaching down from above. One possibility consists in turning
to the Bible and to a famous verse in the *Epistle to the Romans* that
offers a truly panoramic scheme of analogies comes into view.
Pascal (and Jacqueline) write to their sister Gilberte:

… car, comme nous avons dit souvent entre nous, les choses corporelles
ne sont qu'une image des spirituelles, et Dieu a représenté les choses
invisibles dans les visibles (Rom. 1, 20). Cette pensée est si générale et
si utile, qu'on ne doit point laisser passer un espace notable de temps
sans y songer avec attention. (L273a; M11582)

However, I think that Pascal shows us best his understanding of
what he and we must do in certain things that he says about
Jesus Christ.

Non seulement nous ne connaissons Dieu que par Jésus-Christ mais
nous ne nous connaissons nous-mêmes que par J.-C.; nous ne
connaissons la vie, la mort que par Jésus-Christ. Hors de J.-C. nous ne
savons ce que c'est ni que notre vie, ni que notre mort, ni que Dieu, ni
que nous-mêmes.

Ainsi sans l'Ecriture qui n'a que J.-C. pour objet nous ne connaissons rien et ne voyons qu'obscurité et confusion dans la nature de Dieu et dans la propre nature. (L550a, f417; S40, f36)

The Incarnation gives answers to innumerable questions that we may ask in our efforts to understand Nature and our own nature. The mediating connection established by the God-Man brings everything belonging to the finite order into line with what stands above it.

There is still more. In this life, according to Pascal, we ordinarily go no further than the integration that I have just indicated. But in the next life, in the state of beatitude, the final degree of unification is consummated. In the prelude to the argument of the wager Pascal tells his interlocutor that we can know of God's existence by faith, but we shall know of his nature "dans la gloire." When that occurs, Pascal will have no further need for dialectic. Until it occurs, we may in exceptional experiences have a foretaste of beatitude, that single and unique act of knowing and loving. The *Mémorial* gives us a record of one such experience: "Le monde ne t'a pas connu, mais je t'ai connu …" I think the kind of fulfilment that Pascal found in it had, among many other consequences, the effect of certifying the correctness of the whole process of inward and upward movement that we have been retracing.

TWO MOTIVE FORCES

Pascal has in mind a journey of the soul back to God: the ultimate importance of beatitude makes that unmistakable. This journey has its origin in a very special situation, one that came about from the act of Creation, which was at the same time an act of separation. Thus was posed the problem to which the end of the journey gives a solution. I have tended so far to present Pascal's dialectical scale as though it were essentially the way in which he could present the echelons of an encyclopedic order. But speculative completeness interests him less than personal destinies that lead creatures back to their Creator. What are the motive forces that make the journey inevitable, at least for someone willing to enter the universe of Pascal? They are already quite familiar to us, though their parallel dynamism has been seen in less comprehensive and less symmetrical arguments.

The incentives are two in number – the aspiration of the mind toward the acquisition of truths, and that of the heart toward the possession of goods. These two motives – efficient causes, really, to introduce language of which Pascal might not have approved – initiate the motions of every human nature as it undertakes to find what it needs to complete itself and to reach a state of repose. They move the soul up Pascal's ladder, each operating in its way, along two lines of activity, one intellectual and the other moral.

On the level of his first order Pascal locates things; and things function as sources of sensations, taken either simply as elements of common experience or – in a more technical way – as the means whereby hypotheses may be verified. But things, when conceived as offered not to the powers of knowing but to those of desiring, constitute the order of the flesh and of *biens charnels* like pleasure, wealth, and power.

The two aspirations meet something similar in the domain of the second order. As the locus of demonstrative sciences and of intellectual inventions, this plane must provide the mind with the kind of truths that such science and innovation require. As for the faculty of desire: it now finds itself in the realm of satisfactions and joys that arise from victories won over intellectual difficulties.

Pascal assigns new objects and possibilities to the two powers on the third level. On the side of knowing: here intuitive truths are grasped – the principles that reason needs for its discursive work on the preceding level. On the side of desiring: the domain of the heart has *sentiment* or religious intuition, charity, grace, and other spiritual goods, all of them gifts of God.

Of course, Pascal means to convey to us a sense of limits, and to do so in two ways, for just as there is something partial about the truths and satisfactions found in each order considered by itself, there is a similar incompleteness about the tripartite scheme as a whole. Indeed, the finiteness of what is known and what is enjoyed becomes clearer as the whole picture emerges –

and that entails insight into the essential infinity of the objects sought by the basic tendencies of human nature. What they aspire to is not truths but the Truth, and not goods but the Good. The inadequacy perceived in each situation propels the soul upward.

By virtue of the descent of the divine onto the plane of the human heart the two appetites may come to rest, inchoatively in this life, but with the prospect of a complete and final joy in the next world. In the presence of God, the separate faculties tending to the true and the good will be focused on the same object, the divine Person in whom truth and goodness coincide and with whom the seeker is united.

Dialectic has now reached its culmination as an intellectual art that systematizes being, expression, thought and – I must now add – feeling. It is imperative that we do not make the end of this journey seem easy. We must avoid facile triumphalism and try, instead, to grasp the particular sense and some of the emotion that Pascal attaches to the end of *his* ascent. The *Prière pour demander à Dieu le bon usage des maladies* is extraordinarily revealing on this point. There, in a state of poor health, Pascal attempts to characterize and to understand himself as someone here and now on his way to the next life and a meeting with God. He cannot think simply in terms of a happy and ecstatic reunion of a knowing and loving creature with a Creator who is inseparably Truth and Goodness. When Pascal thinks of God, he thinks of the One who is both Alpha and Omega, of course, but also of the Person who is Three-in-One, the Trinity, and again of the loving Judge, in whom absolute mercy and absolute justice are combined.

It is necessary to recognize this complexity of the Being whom Pascal sees at the top of his system. My emphasis, in analyzing his argument in a general way, has been placed on God as beginning and end. In the *Prière* those ideas are certainly present, but the personal attributes come into the foreground. Pascal interprets his illnesses as signs of divine justice already at work in his life: when his health had been good, he had made bad use of it – "un usage tout profane" (L362b; Mɪv998). Now he finds himself appealing to God's mercy; and that

appeal leads, at the end of the *Prière*, to the invocation of the
other two Persons of the Trinity. He prays that he may be filled
with Christ and with the Holy Spirit, that his suffering may be
associated with that of Christ, who suffered before being
glorified (and will continue to suffer in the members of his body,
the Church, until its perfect consummation), and that he may
thus come to participate in Christ's glory.

INVERSIONS AS TYRANNIES

The notion of hierarchy stays in the forefront of Pascal's mind
when he engages in systematization. One consequence of this is
that he and we must take care to observe scrupulously the
relation of lower to higher things, as we go up and down the
scale. It is interesting to see what happens when something
interferes or attempts to interfere with the established ranking,
when values found on one of the higher levels are subordinated
to those of a lower order. Pascal uses the word "tyrannie" to
characterize such reversals.

In the fragment bearing "Tyrannie" as its headword (L507a,
f58; S59, f91) he develops a complex theme of personal merits,
of differences among them, and of the duties called for in the
presence of the differences. He explores a triple distinction, and,
although the term "ordre" does not appear, it is not ex-
travagant, I think, to say that something like the idea of the
three orders stands over his argument. He refers to two of them
plainly, and he certainly hints at the third. *Mérites* as he
conceives of them are *force*, *science*, and *agrément*. These correlate
nicely with the orders of the body, the mind, and the heart –
though, we must add, without all the connotations that we have
seen above. Now, according to Pascal, merits have consequences: where *agrément* is present in someone as a quality, that
person is entitled to affection, *amour*; where *force* is concerned,
one is entitled to fear, *crainte*; and in the case of knowledge or
science, the one who knows may expect belief, *créance*. Falsity and
tyranny begin when one says: "I am handsome (*beau*, the term
being linked with *agrément*), and so I should be feared"; or "I
am strong, and so I should be loved." Pascal does not in this

fragment finish the series; he might have said: "I know, and so I should be loved or I should be feared." Instead, he goes into another series of statements, based on negations. One might say of someone, "He is not strong, so I shall not esteem him," or "He is not knowledgeable (*habile*), and so I shall not fear him" (the implication being that even though he may be ignorant, he may be strong and to be feared). Still other negations are possible, though not worked out in the text. The point is that the absence of a merit in order A (let us say) has no relevance to the duty one has toward someone whose merit lies in order B.

In the *Provinciales* one of Pascal's fundamental convictions regarding the nature of the controversy between the Jansenists and the Jesuits consists in this, that the latter are engaged in an attempt to overthrow truth by force. As he diagnoses the situation, the Jansenists are concerned with the truth about grace, whereas the Jesuits are thinking primarily of the standing and power of their company. They are willing, he believes, to use any means, including falsehoods and slander, to overcome threats to their position, which is basically political rather than doctrinal. In terms of the three orders, one may say that theology uses the mind to develop truths that depend finally on the heart; and in this controversy, the two higher faculties are being subverted by principles and actions characteristic of a lower order.

Or, for another example, take the matter of *divertissement*. To be caught up in distractions means, for Pascal, to succumb to the appeals of things that lie outside of us, to live for them, and to think that they will bring us happiness. The result is that inner goods, goods of the heart, are undervalued and sacrificed. And it is interesting to note that mathematics and physics, as *sciences des choses extérieures*, may function in somewhat the same subversive way, because in our preoccupation with them we may forget that in times of affliction they cannot console us. In painful circumstances, we must put them – with their achievements, prestige, and claims – in their proper place, beneath morality and its principles. Of course, the theme of *divertissement* looms large in the argument of the *Pensées*; but the search for the underlying *raison de l'effet* sends us back to original sin and – in the thought of Pascal – to the *Ecrits sur la grâce*. There he analyzes and expounds the doctrine in detail, laying out the two states of human nature, the first with all goods and desires in the proper order, and the second with the inversion of that order after the choice of Adam.

The *Comparaison des chrétiens des premiers temps avec ceux d'aujourd'hui* unfolds along a line of argument quite similar to the preceding in the values evoked and defended. Pascal draws a contrast between what used to be that was good and what exists now that is bad. The early Christians were not admitted to the Church until they had been given thorough instruction and had made a serious commitment to a Christian style of life. Now, he says, we have a situation in which, as a result of infant baptism, people come into the world and into the Church at almost the same time. They often suffer from the absence of serious later instruction and from the lack of serious later commitment to a life led according to religious belief. What the Christians of the present need is to understand the difference, the opposition, the antagonism between the Church and the world, "l'Eglise" and "le monde." That understanding entails the definite ranking of the former above the latter, and, in a real sense for Pascal, it means leaving the one for the other, moving out of confusion and inversion of values into a clear grasp of the right priorities – and of their consequences for moral behavior.

For Pascal, as we noted above, the sciences may have the character of distractions. In its turn, philosophy may be involved in inappropriate claims to attention and dignity. At a certain stage in the apologetic argument of the *Pensées* Pascal intends, it would seem, to put to the test what the dogmatists and skeptics have to say about the human condition, once it becomes clear to his interlocutor that repeated efforts, attested by the *libertin*'s own experience, to know the truth and to possess the good seem fated to end only in quandary and mystification. Both Stoics and Pyrrhonians profess to have the answers for us in matters of knowledge and morality; but their propositions are strictly on the level of the mind. Their perspectives do not include regulation from the higher order of Christian religion – which explains, incidentally, why they cannot solve the problem posed by their antithetical teachings. For Pascal and his interlocutor to stop at this stage of the inquiry would amount to joining them in a situation where philosophy has priority over religion, and mind over heart.

HIERARCHY AND THE *ORDRE DU COEUR*

In each context Pascal defines or suggests a reversal, an actual or threatened overthrowing of higher by lower values. There is another, and equally fundamental – though opposed – way in which Pascal may approach and revise his scheme of *ordres*. But this time the way followed and the results achieved are positive. Let us go back once more to the formula that sums up the *ordre du coeur*: "Cet ordre consiste principalement à la digression sur chaque point, qui a rapport avec la fin, pour la montrer toujours." The reference to the "fin" and the adverb "toujours" remind us that, in a thorough-going dialectic, like that of Pascal in his moral and religious reflections, the effect of the controlling principle is felt in the universe of things and discourse as a whole and in every one of its parts. Nothing is exempt from its influence, nothing is outside its scope.

Now it is always possible to work out the relation of an object of attention to the final principle by proceeding discursively through a series of intermediate terms or stages. However, in the mind of Pascal, I think that the other possibility is present at every moment also: one may disregard the hierarchy, forego the movement up and down the ladder. When Pascal engages in such a pretermission, the movement of thought ceases to be linear. It radiates, so to speak, from a center, going freely in any direction and stopping on any point or object. Then only two things are involved: the unifying principle or end and the contrasting term that is taken as subordinate to that end. Any development or "digression" on the point where Pascal's thought has stopped is caught up immediately in the subordination that results from the constant presence of the end. Is this not precisely what he means by the order of the heart, of St. Augustine, of Jesus Christ, of the Bible? This option, which substitutes juxtaposition and insight for sequential development, is always open to Pascal as a way of thinking and composing. And I might add, it gives us as readers a valuable way to understand what he is doing: any fragment can be read as a digression on a point related to the comprehensive end. When, in interpreting him, we de-emphasize the hierarchical apparatus, we appreciate more easily than we otherwise might his ability to express much or all of his vision in short passages or, indeed, in short phrases.

AN INTEGRATING ART

All of the preconditions of an art of systematization are visible in Pascal's practice. In the preceding discussion I have attempted to present a sort of map, done in the spirit of Pascal, with comments on what may be seen in the main regions. Now, by way of a summary, I should like to give a sketch at least of a more formal analysis, one that isolates the factors at work and shows their roles. Since an intellectual art defines and guides the process by means of which a problem is solved, Pascal does not need an art until a problem has emerged, but from that point on he finds himself engaged in inventing and refining a technical process. As we have seen before, four elements become explicit: (1) something that initiates discursive movement; (2) something underlying, to which the operations of the art are addressed; (3) some procedures that take hold of the problematic aspects noted in the subject-matter, treating them in an orderly and purposeful manner; and (4) some aim, which may be thought of in two ways: as the end present from the beginning of the process or as the product resulting from it.

In connection with mathematics and physics we have isolated two kinds of problems that fascinate Pascal. But they are not in question here: as we study the situation that prompts him to systematizing activity, we must keep in mind always his overriding aim, which is to unify. In geometric the aim is to construct and/or to verify, and the process takes off from some complexity that has been reduced to its least parts. In the dialectical perspective, however, Pascal confronts a situation characterized by some degree of division: it includes contrasts, oppositions, conflicts; and it requires of him that he apply distinctions to disparate objects of attention. At the outset neither the oppositions of terms nor those of the things signified are clear, though, in the case of the latter, we do have a sense of their importance to us as occasions for knowing and desiring.

In actual fact, it is difficult to separate the terms Pascal uses from the things to which they are applied, since the two illustrate and clarify each other. But if we emphasize both *what* he is talking about and *how* it is divided up, it is not difficult to locate the problematic differences on which Pascal focuses the systematizing impulse of his dialectic.

Three distinctions appear at once in the situation with which Pascal is concerned. (1) Man versus Nature: he sees a first contrast between us and the mute unthinking things surrounding us at close range; and then, as he and we raise our eyes, he evokes a second contrast, this time between us and the whole of Nature as spread out along an unbounded scale of largeness and smallness; this distinction leads to bewilderment at the incongruous traits – insignificance and dignity, knowledge and ignorance – that come to mind as describing the human situation. (2) The constituent realms of being in the universe, occupied by bodies, minds, and hearts: three components so different, so distant from one another that bewilderment comes over us again at the presence of these realities in the universe and at the fact of their co-presence in human beings. (3) God and Creation: what is and what should be the relation between these two? Here any observer must find himself once again in bewilderment and concern; the question is intensely interesting but humanly unanswerable.

These distinctions define, it seems to me, the highly perplexing state of affairs with which Pascal begins; in it he will want first to identify and to characterize more clearly the different degrees of reality it contains; that done, he will undertake to draw them into relations that are no longer puzzling and repellent but intelligible and desirable – in short, relevant to our needs for truth and goodness.

At this point procedures become important. Indeed, art is in a fundamental sense a matter of finding instruments that may be used tactically and strategically for the accomplishment of an aim; and in their present application, they will be put to work on a problem arising from the presence of opposed realities in the situation confronting Pascal. He seems to welcome the challenge. He understands and explains the difficulty by resorting to two kinds of operations that are carried on more or less simultaneously: (1) in a downward (and tactical) movement of the dialectic he differentiates, clarifies, and defines; and (2) in an upward (and strategic) movement of the argument he arranges, assimilates, and unifies. In other words, (1) by acts of specification that serve to lay out and justify briefly the troubling distinctions and (2) by acts of correlation or interrelation that bring the divisions back together, Pascal introduces a single structure into the problem-situation, and makes progress possible toward a systematic view.

In establishing interrelations he may assign priorities to the factors that emerge in his analyses: he does that in showing us the sides of human nature that rise in dignity from body to mind to heart. Or he may think in terms of analogies: he obviously finds comparisons possible in connection with the activities – struggles, solutions, reputations – he observes as he goes from one level to another. Indeed, the scope of analogy may widen without limit, as when he writes to the Roannez: "Toutes choses couvrent quelque mystère; toutes choses sont des voiles qui couvrent Dieu" (L267c; MIII1036–37). Sometimes he sets up proportions: I see this in Pascal's treatment of knowing, where the fact that we occupy space and have limits opens up to us the possibility of grasping those characteristics as they manifest themselves in bodies; or, again, in the encyclopedic trend in his thought, which leads him to make what I have called lateral analogies in the direction of sociology, ethics, and history. Finally, he may opt for reconciliation or mediation: there the eminent example is furnished by Jesus Christ, the divine and personal Mediator, who serves to connect the whole of the created universe with its Creator.

Pascal's dialectic offers him an elaborate hierarchical framework with reference to which topics may be explored; sometimes he must contend, in himself and in others, with inclinations to overturn that proper order and to put in its place tyrannical *dis*order; sometimes – and more frequently – he approaches a topic for reflection from an altitude that allows him already to have in view the end of his inquiry, and then the framework recedes into the background, so as to permit an immediate grasp of a true relation, a relation that ties the particular subject at hand to the end – *pour la montrer toujours.*

He achieves thus a comprehensive outline and a synoptic vision. It makes sense of every one of the original distinctions; it gives them places in a totalizing picture; it substitutes a synergism for their opposed and mutually destructive tensions. The scheme has great theoretical power: it is a theory of everything; it encompasses all realities, but in so doing it also defines principles with enough precision to allow us to see or, at least, to foresee an investigation of details on any one of the levels of being or on lateral extensions of the three taken together. It has, also, extraordinarily important practical consequences: it fixes the outline of a complete moral itinerary, with all the main stages laid out in their proper sequence; it alludes to the graded advantages that will be found as one moves along the way; and it indicates as well the deficiencies of each lower level when it is referred to the one above it – an essential feature, and the source of a dynamic impulse, for Pascal knows that any unfulfilment seen and felt will keep him and us moving on an ascending line.

CHAPTER 4

Ends, means, and rhetoric

COMMUNICATION AND PERSUASION

In this review of Pascal's arts of the mind I have often referred to something in his writing that is never far from the surface: the presence of an addressee, of an interlocutor, even. Quite typically, he thinks and expresses himself in a situation that involves more than one mind; in fact, Pascal was recognized in his own century as a master of what the authors of the Port-Royal *Logique* called "la véritable rhétorique" (in a note added to the second edition of that work). His intentions in this sphere of interpersonal discourse naturally have consequences in the texts, as he conceives and shapes their external forms and as he elaborates their internal traits and sequences. In *De l'esprit géométrique* Pascal uses a familiar formula in naming the discipline relevant here: it is the "art de persuader." In the *Pensées* he speaks of "éloquence," which I take to be a correlative term. But the correspondence is not perfect: Pascal enjoys saying that "la vraie éloquence se moque de l'éloquence" (L576d, f513; S347, f672), so as to put down the pretensions of any technique in these matters that tends to reduce everything to rules, to favor "géométrie" at the expense of "finesse."

We have already seen how this art may be of help in selecting terms and concepts that are to be deployed in the inquiries of geometric and dialectic. From its use in those two fundamental arts, rhetoric appeared to us as a method of invention. But now, if one accepts my hypothesis, to the effect that geometric and dialectic are focused respectively on problems of demonstration and integration – rather than on persuasion – it is possible to

210

discern the presence of rhetoric in another and broader sense than before. In several important situations the other two modes of thought recede in Pascal's mind, making way for problems of communication, controversy, and achievement of assent. This change of emphasis brings with it a new status and an enlarged role for rhetoric, which we must now examine.

As I say, it is a fact that Pascal, when he sits down to write, often has in his mind the image of a reader; and this reader may, as circumstances suggest or require, take on the status of an addressee with quite definite characteristics and opinions; and he may even leave his passive role and begin to engage in exchanges. The situation is in essence rhetorical, serving to focus Pascal's attention on a definite problem area and leading him into recurrent distinctions, projects, and developments. It sets for him, I think, specific conditions for the emergence of a curiously complex ensemble of intellectual procedures.

Here it is well, however, to keep in mind an important distinction. One often notes in Pascal's non-scientific texts the phenomenon of a locally appearing interlocutor and of a resulting passage in dialogue or near-dialogue. This emergent person is usually not characterized; he simply asks a question or poses an objection and disappears soon after. The phenomenon is signaled by grammatical forms in the first and second persons, with the format tending to fall into that of question and answer. This is a subject that deserves serious study; in the *Pensées*, for example, one sees interesting differences in the various uses of "je," "vous," and "nous." "Je" may refer to Pascal himself, or to himself *as* writer, *as* apologist; or, it may refer to someone else – to the interlocutor, or even to God and to Jesus Christ. But the use of this trope, which adds life to passages of exposition and argument – Pascal may have appreciated its effectiveness while reading in the works of Epictetus and Montaigne, who resort to it constantly – will not be what concerns us here. I wish to consider, rather, his approach to the problem of contacts and interrelations with persons holding more or less fully elaborated positions.

Even so, it is worthy of note that at times Pascal writes at or near the degree zero on the scale of communication with other minds. One thinks particularly of the *Pensées*, where we see him often jotting things down that are relevant to his themes or his composition, but with such fragments the exact value, placing, and possible development cannot be recovered. I take him to be, at such moments, much like the person writing a journal for no one except himself to see: it is a place for assembling materials; a more or less orderly file of reminders and *pensées diverses*, to which the writer will return some day and from which he can take pieces of use in a later version of the work at hand.

He moves beyond the simple image or situation of writer and text and on to the next degree, when he assumes an addressee: let us say we are thinking here of Pascal's personal correspondence – as in the letters to members of his own family, or to the Roannez. In each case communication is taking place, information is being passed on, spiritual advice is being given. But he has not yet left the private sphere; he has made no contact with a public.

We reach that place on the scale when Pascal writes a letter that is to be made public though directed to a particular person (who may be fictive). This appears to be the situation imagined in important passages of the *Ecrits sur la grâce*: Pascal seems to be writing to someone, in response to questions posed by this addressee; and from the substance and tone of the *exposé*, which treats doctrinal questions concerning nature and grace, it is reasonable to suppose that Pascal wishes to communicate it to a general public. He is not addressing theologians; he is rather putting himself in the role of *vulgarisateur*. Indeed, I see this as being the framework that is implied in the apologetic perspective of the *Pensées*: I mean that although Pascal writes for someone of a definite moral character and attitude, what he says or might have said was intended for publication. The *libertin* is someone to speak to and write for, but Pascal has in mind a larger and more general audience.

The undertaking of the *Provinciales* brings further complications in the schematism. In the opening letter of the series, the writer produces a text for an imagined correspondent (the *provincial*), but Pascal has in mind, surely, a dual or extended addressee, consisting of the whole class of serious and fair-minded people who need to know the facts of the case in order to reach a proper judgment concerning the issues being debated in the Sorbonne. For Pascal has moved into the arena of controversy, and three parties are involved: the author of the letters, the *provincial*, and those whose ideas and behavior are being represented and, in some cases, ridiculed. I do not think it far-fetched to include among the addressees of the letters those third parties whom Pascal has signified by the assorted *docteurs* and clergymen that he evokes.

Finally, I see Pascal as setting up still another situation – actually, an inversion of the preceding. He does this in the last eight letters of the *Provinciales*, when he turns to confront directly the Jesuit Fathers, taking them first as a group, and then choosing one in particular, Père Annat. The inversion I wish to propose is this: first, let us think of the controversy as having something like the structure of a judicial proceeding; then, whereas in the first ten letters Pascal addresses the *provincial* (and the jury that he represents), pointing out, letter by letter, the reprehensible behavior of the accused; in the last eight letters he confronts the accused in the presence of the jury, that is, the general public, who may follow the prosecution's case as the publication of the letters proceeds.

In taking account of the audience, that inevitable factor in the rhetorical situation, Pascal develops, therefore, a number of distinct possibilities. He may have in mind someone – a member of the family, a friend – who really exists, or a fictive but representative person through whom he can reach his intended readers, or a kind of dual addressee that includes those written about (e.g., the Jesuits) as well as those written to and for (the *provincial* and *les honnêtes gens*), and then, this last allows a reversal in which Pascal turns directly on those who had been his target-figures – written about rather than spoken to – and puts the former addressees into the role of spectators. And we shall not want to forget that sometimes the one or ones addressed may answer back: thus, the rejoinders of Père Noël or the flood of letters and pamphlets provoked by the *Provinciales*, to which Pascal replies in turn. As he moves in and out of these changing frameworks, Pascal's aims vary from simple communication (as often in the private correspondence), to spiritual direction (as in the letters to the Roannez), to moral conversion (as in the *Pensées*), to controversy and refutation (as in the *Provinciales* and in the exchanges with Père Noël).

Actually, more is involved here than simply the emergence into the foreground of concern for the audience, because this change implies for Pascal the adoption of a new framework within which to work. I mean the framework established by the four interrelated elements of audience, author, discourse, and aim. Personalities and particular circumstances do not play an essential role in the modes of thinking and writing characteristic in the mathematical or scientific works. In the régime of geometry – even in that of dialectic broadly conceived – Pascal has the attitude of someone speaking and writing *apud sapientes* about the truths and probabilities discernible in the subject-matter at hand. The criteria and influences that shape the reasoning have to do with the aim of producing adequate representations of what is the case – of reality.

As a consequence of the shift into the four-term matrix just mentioned, Pascal takes his thought out of the vacuum in which it exists as theory, and puts it in a context of personal give and take, of particular situations and attitudes that must be taken into account as he proceeds. To his concern for demonstrative or dialectical logic he must add concern for factors that impinge on intellectual discourse from the outside. This more general context, requiring attention to a situation in which minds come into contact and interact, sets the problem for him as a rhetorician. And he elaborates, it seems to me, a distinctive way of proceeding when he finds himself in this situation.

THE EMERGENT ART

In line with comments made in the first part of *De l'esprit géométrique* on the imprecision and inconclusiveness of many discussions, Pascal comes to formulate the rules of an *art de persuader*. Given the context, it does not surprise us that this art is practically indistinguishable from the method that he has just analyzed as being that of geometry. He has simply changed his vocabulary, putting "persuader" in the place of "démontrer." But in his reflections elsewhere and especially in his practice, it is clear that Pascal went far beyond what he said in those pages on the geometrical mind or mentality, and that he developed at least two quite different ways of dealing with the problematic elements encountered in the rhetorical situations that I have been describing. His crucial insights in this instance do not bear, it seems to me, as much on the need for a rhetorical art as on the need to see the consequences for such an art of certain prior considerations to which he is much attached.

Pascal's commitment to truth is overarching; it transcends the boundaries of any particular problem or inquiry or treatise, I believe. In his thinking, therefore, any theory of assent or persuasion is going necessarily to involve coming to terms with the notion of truth. Were it not for some truth, which has become entangled in error and obscured by it, there would be no rhetorical problem for Pascal. In the circumstances described above, and regardless of whether Pascal is engaged in simple communication or exposition or apologetic or polemic, his aim is invariably to lead the readers or the members of the audience away from confusion and error toward truth. What effect will Pascal's overriding commitment have on the way in which he conceives the art of persuasion?

One answer can be set aside at once. Pascal will not accept the methods of discussion and argument that he associates with the Jesuits in the disagreements about grace, Christian morality, Jansenius, the five propositions, and Port-Royal. Their rhetoric, at least in his analysis, consists in doing whatever will produce the effect desired; it resorts even to calumny and the use of political power. He can only see it as an aberration and a failure to distinguish between the order of power-seeking and the order of truth-seeking.

For another answer to the question, we may look back to what happened (1) in the scientific works and (2) in the writings on moral and religious subjects. There we must recognize, I think, the existence of two species of truth. Pascal starts in effect with the assumption that truth is not really separable from method, from the devices and considerations that justify what he takes to be true. Another way of saying the same thing is: if the intellectual arts or methods are paths to truth, and if the paths can be shown to be essentially distinct, what one reaches at the end of the roads will not be exactly the same. Nuances and distinctions have to be introduced.

In *De l'esprit géométrique* he writes about the geometric method as though it were a completely autonomous technique, to be distinguished from ordinary habits of speech and discourse as the right way to go about treating any and all problems. But he had already, in the preface to the treatise on the vacuum, proposed a distinction between sciences based on the free use of reason and the senses on the one hand and disciplines based on authority on the other. He had thus recognized a restriction on the way in which the scientific – I mean, empirico-geometric – method may be applied.

Of course, in other texts, in those where Pascal uses the dialectical mode of thinking and inquiry, we find ourselves in the presence of another major discipline – clearly different from that of mathematics and mathematical physics – that is perfectly capable of searching out truth and eliminating error, and of doing so without limit on its scope. Indeed, as we have seen, this method even provides at last an inclusive framework within which mathematical and experimental sciences have in the *ordre de l'esprit* their rightful place and their terrain for investigation.

Now, when Pascal takes up rhetoric and the art of persuasion, he is looking for a discipline that is grounded in truth. But, the question is going to be, which truth, since there is a choice: the analytical and deductive kind found in geometry and physics or the reconciling and unifying kind found in moral and theological reflection?

AN AUTONOMOUS RHETORIC?

Does he have a third choice? Is it not possible to define a rhetoric that has its particular kind of truth, correlated with its own principles and procedures, and quite apart from what takes place in geometry or in dialectic? Most certainly, this disci-plinary possibility has been worked out and applied – in fact, it existed in the literary domain in France at the time when Pascal lived and worked – and its long history stretches back to Quintilian and Cicero, and beyond them to Greek rhetoricians and sophists. I think it valuable to consider briefly some of the principles, aims, and devices that rhetoric tends to have when it enjoys the status of an independent discipline. In the light of these points we can better understand what Pascal's choices turned out to be, and, I believe, better interpret his criticisms of the Jesuits in the *Provinciales* and his approach to freethinkers in the *Pensées*.

When it has independent status, rhetoric does not work according to a system of transcendental truths or values, though it does presuppose a general humanistic culture in which many different truths and values are examined and judged. The discourse that it produces is tentative, discerning, context-bound, unreceptive to dogmatism of any kind. In a given situation it seeks to formulate a practicable end and then to discover the means in words and actions for realizing that end. Truth is conceived as what will be effective in a particular human context. (The context may also be natural, where scientific investigation is carried out in a rhetorical – that is to say, operational and pragmatic – perspective.) Conclusions are justified by examples or arguments and not by syllogistic proofs. The presence of variations or contradictions in this kind of thinking is not a sign of unconcern for logic. But the rule here is that logic and truth are functions of situations, circumstances, perspectives. What one says or does appropriately on one occasion may not hold on another occasion and under other conditions.

I have tried, in this sketch, to mention themes commonly found in seventeenth-century discussions of rhetoric. We see some of them specified in the developments of literary theory – in the *Pratique du théâtre* of François d'Aubignac, for example; or in Corneille's three *Discours* on dramatic poetry. Pascal presents one version of them, it seems to me, apropos of Montaigne in the *Entretien avec M. de Saci*, and then a slightly different version, with great emphasis on the skeptical potential of the rhetorical *thématique*, in those pages of the *Pensées* where he describes and treats the Pyrrhonians.

The clash with the principles of geometric is evident. That method begins with problems not contexts, analyzing them into least parts or elements, that are accompanied on the level of language by univocally defined terms. By its insistence on orderly acts of composition it paves the way for Pascal to go from simple beginnings in language and subject-matter to a complex construction or sequence like a strict demonstration concerning a conic section, or even the planning and execution of a complicated thing, like the *machine d'arithmétique*. In this mode truth is a function not of circumstances, but of self-evident intuitions and demonstrative procedure; contradiction being a sign of uncertainty and error, it must be excluded from the outset. From the point of view of geometric, an autonomous rhetoric is, therefore, deficient in several ways: as a method it lacks rigor in analysis and language; it is inconclusive; it accepts opposed and even contradictory judgments; it reduces truth to opinion, for, instead of working exclusively with reliable sources of knowledge in reason and observation, it takes into account and even uses deceitful elements coming from prejudice, imagination, emotion, and habit.

The contrast is no less definite between the principles and practice of an integrative dialectic and the essential tendencies – now pragmatic, now skeptical – that accompany a régime of free and self-determining rhetoric. Dialectic leads Pascal upward from subjects divided against themselves by tensions and conflicts to ever higher levels of consideration where resolutions become possible. In this intellectual mode the truth or falsity of what one says is a function of one's relative position in a developing and comprehensive argument. Contradictions are admitted, even welcomed, as data in the problem to be solved; but Pascal's goal consists finally in reconciliation, in pulling the opposing views into a balanced or graduated position, so designed as to include legitimate elements from all sides and levels of the argument. From the point of view of dialectic, the aims, arguments, and contexts worked out in an independent rhetoric will necessarily be isolated and incomplete until they have been fitted into a synoptic tableau.

The partisans of a universalized rhetoric in Greece, Rome, the Middle Ages, and the Renaissance have shown amply that they can defend their discipline, with its contextual truth and circumstantial reasoning; and they are quite capable of pointing out, over and beyond the general danger of dogmatism in the positions of their critics, the difficulties their opponents will encounter in attempts to apply the mechanical precisions of geometry and the facile resolutions of dialectic to problems of the real world – especially the world of human action. But Pascal will not accept the idea of a method and a procedure that addresses arguments to someone with the aim of producing conviction, apart from a logic of demonstrative sequences: his allegiance to mathematical and experimental science is too strong for that. Nor will he espouse the notion of strictly contextual truths and goods, determined apart from a comprehensive scheme: his taste for reconciliations and balances, and his faith, which tends readily to inclusive Augustinian views, will not permit that.

The upshot of all this is that the art of persuasion for Pascal cannot have the status of a free and self-regulating discipline. It can only be derivative; it will be dependent for its principles on the two other arts to which he has, in effect, assigned special status. Rhetoric becomes for him an extension and application of the one – geometric; and it appears as episodes or particular phases of the other – dialectic. Let us now see how and to what degree this twofold subordination works out in specific instances.

AN ART OF EXCLUSION

Variation 1 : Père Noël

The preceding remarks are abstract; but without a general view, a view in which we try to hold three possibilities simultaneously in mind, it is difficult, I think, to appreciate in particular situations the mental operations, the logical currents, and the systematic force invested in what Pascal does. The controversy with Père Noël involves an almost straightforward application of the method recommended in *De l'esprit géométrique*; and it exemplifies the exclusive attitude, the proneness to controversy – rather than to dialogue – usually associated with this line of thought. Note, however, that we are here dealing with questions of physics, and not of pure mathematics. Inquiries in physics add experimental verifications to the demonstrations of quantitative reasoning.

In the exchange of letters with Noël Pascal argues that any physicist must understand the need, in the first phase of inquiry, to imitate geometrical thinking: one starts with univocal definitions (or terms so clear in designation that attempts to define them turn initial clarity and immediate understanding into obscurity and confusion). Then one combines such terms into judgments that are either axiomatic, that is, to follow closely Pascal's words in his reply to Noël's first letter, appearing so clearly and distinctly in themselves to reason or to sense that the mind has no means of doubting their certainty, or judgments deduced by infallible and necessary consequences from such axioms. Such statements, and where required, the justifications needed to deduce them, are to be articulated into a demonstrative sequence or hypothesis, after which one moves to the stage of experimental testing. Thought and language are not automatically in contact with things; they cannot, without testing and possible adjustments, be accepted as representing accurately what happens in nature.

That said, what is wrong with the explanations given by Père Noël regarding the behavior of the column of mercury in the tube that has been inverted in a bowl also containing mercury? For one thing, he does not understand or apply proper demonstrative procedure regarding terms, axioms, statements, and proofs; and, for another, he does not understand the importance or the technique of rigorous experimentation. He proceeds on the basis of metaphysical authority, or of common sense and ordinary observation, of analogies, of experiments that do not stand up under examination. Worse still, on that last score, he has not really understood the experiments that Pascal has performed. And he contradicts himself: from one passage to another or from one letter to another he modifies his terms and explanations. He bases his positions on notions like the following: Nature's horror of the vacuum, or Nature as a *plenum* occupied by the four ultimate elements (earth, water, air, and fire) and their mixtures, which may occur – when the argument makes it useful for them to do so – in invisible forms as *matière subtile*.

Obviously a philosophical gulf separates Pascal and his opponent, a gulf that divides two totally different ways of defining physics. The seventeenth century saw the rise of quantitative physics, which was to be the wave of the future; Noël clings to the ideal of a qualitative and ontological physics, based on an investigation of things as distributed into classes according to their natures and then set into interaction. Indeed, if he had managed to present his theory in a less degraded form, he would have exemplified the problematic line of thought that was, among the ancients, the route taken by Aristotle, and he would have suggested a genuine alternative to the new physics.

Pascal sees the controversy not as concerning two kinds of physics, experimental and ontological, but as taking place within the bounds of a single scientific discipline, and as involving mathematics and experimentation on one side and confusion on the other. In the act of presenting his own case Pascal lays out all that is needed to discriminate between truth and error. In applications of the geometrical art – taken with its empirical follow-up in experiments – he aims to exclude contradictions, first, among statements within an explanation and, second, between differing explanations. Moreover, really to demonstrate and really to verify one's hypothesis in connection with a problem disposes automatically of rival theories. A problem in rhetoric becomes an occasion for applied science.

Variation 2: the Jesuits

For the dispute with Père Noël Pascal applies, with an experimental addendum, the way of thinking outlined in *De l'esprit géométrique*. The view that I want to present now with regard to the main polemical aspect of the *Provinciales* can be summed up as follows: against the Jesuits, and most especially where doctrinal points are concerned, Pascal both applies and adapts that same method. The result is a rhetoric derived from his conception of science and its model of discourse. And so we shall not be surprised to find here another example of the logical tendency to eschew dialogue and to move into controversy and exclusion.

The framework within which Pascal sees himself as working and the list of subjects that appear for treatment evolves as the letters follow one another. Letters 1 through 4 are addressed to the "provincial"; the writer explains to him what the arguments on both sides are in the Sorbonne debates concerning grace and concerning the position of Arnauld. Letters 5 through 10 present, within the same expository framework, a larger picture, a summary of the "morale des jésuites," in which Pascal analyzes the Jesuit attitude toward grace as part of a generally lax conception of Christian morality. After this point, the rhetorical situation changes in a basic way; he turns directly to the Jesuit Fathers, dealing in Letters 11 through 16 with points raised by Jesuits in their reactions and replies to the preceding ten letters: what they have written sets the context in which Pascal now defends himself, as well as Arnauld and the Port-Royalists. In the last two letters, nos. 17 and 18, which are addressed to Père Annat, an influential Jesuit, he returns to doctrinal matters: questions regarding grace, the five heretical propositions allegedly found in the *Augustinus* of Jansenius, and the position of Augustine.

In the complex pattern of exposition so noticeable in the *Provinciales* we may discern some things already familiar to us. Regulating much that Pascal and the Jansenists say is the great distinction between the *question de droit* or *question de foi* on the one hand, and on the other the *question de fait*. The former concerns *what is said*; and under this heading one may identify two sorts of statements: those that are true and compatible with correct Christian doctrine; those that are false or erroneous with respect to that doctrine. The latter concerns *who said it* or raises the question, *did so and so say it or not?*

Here, according to his usual preference, Pascal starts from

epistemological notions. He correlates the two kinds of questions with cognitive faculties, specifically, reason and sense, to which on occasion he adds faith, calling all of them principles of our knowledge ("trois principes de nos connaissances"). Each of the three provides its kind of certainty, its proper *évidence*: the first is rational, the second empirical or experimental, and the third authoritative (and because of their authority, statements of faith have the status of axioms).

As I say, these considerations concerning faculties of knowing are closely related to the distinction between demonstration and verification; and that distinction correlates in turn with the *questions de droit* and the *questions de fait*. Demonstration and verification were the key terms in the controversy with Père Noël; they reappear in a new guise in the dispute with the Jesuits. Demonstration, which is primarily rational, applies here, I believe, to the process whereby one determines the orthodoxy of a statement, its possibility of becoming an item in the body of doctrine that has come into being through the workings of Scripture and tradition. Verification, which is primarily empirical, refers to the process whereby one determines whether a statement (one of the allegedly heretical propositions, for example) can be actually – visibly – located in the author to whom it is attributed.

The underpinnings of the arguments against the Jesuits thus appear to be the same as those to which Pascal had recourse in his exchanges with Noël, namely, reason and sense, to which he occasionally adds faith. But we get more light on his argument if we take into account certain other parallels. In the art of geometrical or quasi-geometrical thinking, sequence is extremely important, *ordre* must be observed, a term or proposition out of its proper place simply loses its meaning and value. According to Pascal, the normal sequence in geometry runs as follows: from terms to axioms to propositions to demonstrations to series of demonstrations (or a treatise, an articulated body of knowledge). This sequence appears to have supplied him with a set of essential topics in the *Provinciales*, with the points of departure on which his differentiating, discriminating, exclusionary arguments ultimately depend.

The debates turn, first of all, on a small group of terms, such as *pouvoir prochain*, *grâce suffisante*, *grâce efficace*, and on the necessity, if we are to engage in responsible discourse, of defining such terms correctly and univocally. What does Pascal find as he surveys the scene? Sometimes, no definitions; sometimes, opposed definitions; sometimes self-contradicting definitions; at other times, an agreement to use terms without bothering about meanings, since to do that causes dissension. To this confusion, with its errors and uncertainties, Pascal brings what is for him the clear criterion of Augustinian efficacious grace: it has a definite meaning, it has undeniable authority, it sets up a standard by which to judge all innovative notions concerning grace.

The debates turn, in the second place, on axioms, on *évidences* – and, of course, statements made in creeds or by authoritative sources, function as *évidences*; and so in Pascal's reasoning the decisive principle will always appear as a theological statement considered to be axiomatic. From definitions and axioms the *esprit géométrique* moves easily to propositions. In the *Provinciales* Pascal concentrates attention on propositions in two important contexts. First, of course, there is the matter of the five propositions that have been declared heretical. They may become involved in a *question de droit*, in the sense that all parties to the dispute want to know whether these statements fit or do not fit into the body of orthodox Christian doctrine: that is the question of right or of faith. They may become involved in a *question de fait* whenever the discussion bears on determining who made the statements and, if the author is alleged to be Jansenius, where in the *Augustinus* they are to be found.

Now it seems clear that, if we think back to what Pascal says in *De l'esprit géométrique* and in the dispute with Noël, we can discern an important similarity to his procedure as he faces the Jesuit Fathers. Something exactly analogous to demonstration – primarily a kind of rational activity – occurs in the process whereby one determines the orthodoxy of a statement, that is to say, the possibility that it may become an item, take its place, in the body of doctrine already in being on the basis of Scripture and tradition. And something exactly analogous to verification

– an activity primarily empirical and involving the senses –
occurs in the process whereby one determines whether or not a
statement (such as one of the five propositions) can be actually
seen in the works of the author who is supposed to have written
it.

But propositions enter into the logical fabric of the *Provinciales*
in a second way. Pascal wrote a series of letters (nos. 5 through
10) in which he examines critically the "maximes" of Jesuit
morality. Those principles, in the light of which the casuists and
priests resolve moral problems, receive at the hands of Pascal
the sort of review that one would expect from a logician having
a geometrical turn of mind. He wants to know on what they are
based, and he enjoys pointing out that the principles in question
have only the status of "opinions" – already a serious deficiency
– to which the adjective "probables" adds little – in fact, it
leads to further comment. These "maximes" have their origin
in the inventive minds of the casuists; they are not propositions
taken or derived from the coherent doctrinal tradition of the
Church. And that fact – at least it is so for Pascal – suggests a
final point here regarding the logical model that seems to
preside over so much of the *Provinciales*. At the end of the
geometrical line of inquiry Pascal saw typically the emergence
of a treatise setting forth an ensemble of truths with their
justifications; similarly, in the controversy with the Jesuits,
there looms in his mind – and, he assumes in the mind of his
readers – the idea of a body of doctrine, built up in orderly
sequence from Scripture to Apostles to Popes to Councils; any
innovation, unless it is rooted in that sequence and is compatible
with it, has to be set aside.

Rhetorical elements in variations *1* and *2*

In the two cases considered so far we have gone into the
analytical, deductive, and investigative aspects of Pascal's
presentations. There is reason to believe that he thinks those
aspects to be typical features of technical discourse when it is
carried out in a quasi-geometrical, quasi-experimental mode.
But we have not given sufficient attention to the ways in which

he copes with the inevitable rhetorical conditions that bear on what he writes. Two of them are human: the audience and the author, since any situation involving communication or controversy is essentially interpersonal; it cannot be impersonal in the fashion of purely technical discourse. There is no way of avoiding consideration of the dispositions and opinions of the audience, nor of the character, intentions, and qualifications of the author. All of these impinge on the choices that Pascal makes in the process of composition. Two other factors have determining roles, also: the discourse itself, with its patterns and sequences, and the aim sought, which is the first principle of any art. Audience, writer, text, aim make up an ensemble of interrelated components; and as Pascal derives arguments from his mathematical-experimental matrix he subjects them to a process of adaptation based on those four parameters.

The correspondence with Père Noël and others in connection with the *vide* serves as a useful contrast with the letters that make up the *Provinciales*. With Noël Pascal engages rather less in a rhetorical exercise than in a simple refutation of bad science. The case involves one scientist of questionable competence and grasp of the problem and another who is extremely competent, scrupulous as to the definition of the problem, and practiced in the method chosen for solving it. Both content and style of the communications tend to be entirely technical. The aim – for Pascal, at least – is to separate clear principles and demonstrated conclusions from confused and incoherent assertions. Being a public exchange between two authors, the dispute has an interpersonal aspect that includes a small audience. However, the authors as individuals have little relevance to the discourse (though Pascal does point out evasiveness and inconsistencies in Noël's behavior); what counts is the intrinsic scientific quality of what is said. As for the audience, it consists of a small group of interested mathematicians and physicists; and Pascal appeals solely to their competence and makes no effort to connect his reasoning with their dispositions or opinions. He uses, it seems to me, not really an *art de persuader* but an *art de réfuter* applied within the bounds of a discussion based on a scientific inquiry.

Things are vastly different in the *Provinciales*. Pascal wishes to widen the circle of participants in the discussion so as to include an indefinitely large number of people. He imagines them somewhat as follows: they do not know what is going on in the Sorbonne, but their curiosity is aroused; they have heard that the *docteurs* are talking about important matters of doctrine and personal status; they appreciate the opportunity to have a report from a reliable observer. The members of this intended audience have no technical preparation in theology, but Pascal is counting on their common sense, their willingness to judge fairly, and the orthodoxy of their religious beliefs. In accord with his logical principles, Pascal assumes that his readers can separate the workings of reason and sense from those of imagination, passion, custom. If that distinction cannot be taken for granted, geometry and science become impossible, and by the same token, in this new application of Pascal's logic, there will be no hope of clearing up the controversy between the Jesuits and the Jansenists. But of course he conceives of his readers as being quite capable of separating logic from illogic, of recognizing the intrusion of self-interest and various passions into the disagreements, and of noting the way in which the argument is thereby debased. Moreover, as noted above, in the *Provinciales* he first evokes, and then in the later letters addresses, his opponents. He has a characteristic way of conceiving them: they are not in ignorance but in error; their aim is not to discover the truth but to save face and to maintain their position; if it is too much to expect them to accept the truth, perhaps they can be reduced to silence – *confondus*.

Pascal establishes the character of the person writing the letters with no less definiteness. He shares a common background and a fund of common sense with his friend, the *provincial*. He has a conservative approach, not wishing to be taken in by novelty and attention-getting events but wishing to put them in their place. In a dispute he will insist on fairness and justice. In particular, he is someone on the scene, near the middle of the action; he will investigate matters in a methodical way and let all sides have their turn; then one may judge the issues not on grounds unrelated to the truth, but according to logic and the facts. Furthermore, the truth, as this reporter conceives it, has about it something of the rigor of mathematical and experimental thinking. When it appears and is properly justified, ignorance, error, and extraneous considerations will be seen for what they are.

What about the character of the discourse itself? How does Pascal bring about a vital connection between the sort of thinking inspired by mathematical and physical science and the need for a presentation that is effective in this particular set of circumstances? One of his tactics consists in changing the outer form of what he writes, from demonstrations that might be assembled into a treatise to letters forming a much less carefully planned ensemble. As opposed to a treatise, a letter makes a friendly approach to the reader, suggesting that a different degree of effort will be required of him, and avoiding connotations of some kind of prerequisite in the form of technical knowledge. What is at stake is "truth-to-be-communicated"; and it may require an initial – or indeed, a continual – process of obstacle-removing if the communication is to succeed.

Within the limits that result from this change of focus Pascal excites interest by using, especially in the first letters of the series, character-sketches and dialogue. He even achieves some of the appeal of narrative as he creates moments of suspense, followed by discoveries and reversals, both for his *personnages* and for his readers. But he does these things without compromising the aim, which is to get everyone up on a level of responsible, objective, precise, and coherent discourse. He builds on contacts that he establishes between the parts of the argument, which tends always to become technical and restrictive – a matter for priests and theologians – and commonly held convictions, based on common experience and expressed in easily understood language.

The tight and impersonal sequences of geometry give way to lines of thought that are more episodic, that may well depend on topics that arise in the interval between letters, as the controversy develops. A treatise has an economy all its own, based on considerations internal to the problem or problems treated; in the *Provinciales* the form is subject to changes in external circumstances – indeed, one of Pascal's great talents is in understanding those changes and making the most of them in his arguments. In short, as the immediate and extraordinary *fortune littéraire* of the *Provinciales* attests, Pascal found a brilliant solution to his rhetorical problem. It called upon him to find a kind of discourse that would meet the requirements of general accessibility and appeal, that would evolve with circumstances, that would, above all, achieve his aims without simplifying difficult subject-matter or sacrificing high logical standards.

On this subject of ends, one must say, it seems to me, that Pascal manages to develop his case in all three of the registers so often evoked in seventeenth-century critical discourse: *plaire*, *instruire*, *émouvoir*. In fact, I would go so far as to add a fourth aim to that list, one that is implied but no less real for that. The general idea was to accomplish those aims by means of works that were well done according to artistic standards. And so I would add *admirer* to the usual triad, to indicate the desire of the artist to arouse a response of appreciation. The *Provinciales* as an achievement had many admirers in the seventeenth century; and I cannot believe that Pascal was completely uninterested in their reaction, or that, with regard to his ends and means, he did not seek always to excel in his performance.

THE IRENIC *ENTRETIEN AVEC M. DE SACI*

Dialectic as a determining force in Pascal's rhetoric does not come into the foreground until we reach the end of the *Provinciales*. In Letter 18 he finally defines the correct doctrine regarding efficacious grace as lying between the two extreme positions of the semi-Pelagians and the Calvinists/Lutherans. The tone becomes irenic; and Pascal shifts into an inclusive and assimilative style of thinking about the intellectual positions of others. It is a dialogic kind of discourse, a way of saying both *yes* and *no*. He asserts, in effect: "You are partly right and partly wrong; thanks to what is wrong we can see more clearly the right part; and, that discrimination being made, we can put your right part with what is right about someone else's position and arrive at the whole truth."

But the process of assimilation must include at least one preparatory stage. Theologians and their disciples must be gathered together so as to give rise to the two sides; their positions must be summed up and ticketed as being semi-Pelagian or Calvinist/Lutheran. Each of those groupings represents an opening reduction of multiplicity to unity. If we leave them simply facing each other, there is nothing, no logical device, on the board to bring them together. Instead they refute each other; they fall into a back-and-forth movement without end that amounts to mutual destruction. Having finished the preparatory phase of his argument, Pascal can bring onto the scene Augustine, who supplies a balanced teaching: it saves some of the pessimism about human nature on the one hand, and some of the optimism about it on the other, and the *renversement du pour au contre* stops. Both opinions, now corrected into partial truths, are ordered to grace and God. This argument, which Pascal addresses to Père Annat, differs essentially in shape from what he used in the controversy with Père Noël and in the earlier numbers of the *Provinciales*. It states the case in a triangular or triadic fashion – in the style encountered so often in the *Ecrits sur la grâce*. Rather than being linear, and based on sequences like the proofs of geometry or the empirical tests of physics, the logical tendency here has a synoptic and diagrammatic character.

In the *Entretien avec M. de Saci* Pascal has already put his views into a form very much like this. At the start of his conversation with M. de Saci, he first works out a contrast, on the level of moral philosophy, between Epictetus and Montaigne. The views of Epictetus are assembled and pulled into a kind of dogmatic and optimistic unity; and then the views of Montaigne are pushed in the direction of the other extreme and treated in exactly the same way, the result being another provisional unity, this time of a Pyrrhonian sort.

In the logic that he brings to his task Pascal follows the typical dialectical procedure in an almost schematic fashion. He passes through two stages of integration before the steps leading to the final resolution begin. First, he gathers up a number of assertions into a dogmatic and optimistic ensemble designed to summarize the views of Epictetus; then he produces, on the other side, a similar synthesis based on the *Essays* of Montaigne, the resulting position being skeptical and pessimistic. Second, he presents his thinkers as the two greatest defenders of the two most celebrated sects in the world, and the only ones in conformity with reason. In other words, these two individuals, whose doctrines have been thus integrated and put into a sharp opposition, represent in their persons and views indefinitely large numbers of *sectateurs* on each side. Just as Pascal assembles many partial views on each side to produce the two philosophies – a first unification – so he also unites the numerous members of two great schools, respectively, in the persons of his two authors.

The negative phase of the dialectic having been brought to a climax in an *impasse*, the positive reasoning can begin. Pascal makes some distinctions: Epictetus is very strong on duty, *devoir*, though he manages to fall into pride, *orgueil*; while Montaigne is very strong on the weakness of man, *faiblesse*, but he falls into moral laziness, *paresse*. The solution requires us, first, to reject the tendency to extremes in the opposition, while keeping the sense of weakness and the sense of duty, and, then, to combine those two remainders in Christian morality. The whole exercise is conceived according to the pattern of dialogue, of discernment and assimilation rather than of out-and-out refutation (such as might be called for in the geometrical mode).

As is known, we cannot take this document as a precise transcript, a historical record of what was said on the occasion when Pascal and M. de Saci met. Nevertheless, I think it worthwhile to comment on it in analyzing Pascal's approach to the solution of rhetorical problems. Even if we cannot accept this account in every detail, we can still learn something authentic, something that will aid us in analyzing certain aspects of the *Pensées*.

What is the situation? Pascal, the brilliant young mathematician and scientist, recently converted, is at Port-Royal-des-Champs. He has a substantial conversation with M. de Saci, a priest and confessor, who spends his time reading the Bible, Augustine, and the Church Fathers. In the conversation Pascal makes a case for reading two profane – one actually pagan –

authors, Epictetus and Montaigne; his thesis is that, although one might think them irrelevant or pernicious, they can be useful in bringing an interlocutor to an appreciation of Christian truth and morals. Obviously we are not in a controversial situation, but in circumstances where the emphasis is on an exchange of views, or, more precisely, a comparison of views. When all the arguments have been put on the table, M. de Saci and Pascal find themselves in agreement: they have reached the same destination, but by different routes. Pascal aims here not to move someone out of error into truth but to present arguments tending (1) to provide information about the two authors and (2) to remove doubts about the value their works may have as stimuli to moral improvement. He takes for granted the authority of M. de Saci; from the start he is quite disposed to accept the judgments of his interlocutor – though he clearly intends to present his thesis as convincingly as possible.

FROM THE *ENTRETIEN* TO THE *PENSÉES*

When we turn from the *Entretien* to the *Pensées*, we see a very different set of circumstances in which Pascal's rhetorical activity will take place. The cast of characters has changed, of course. In the *Entretien*, Pascal is shown engaged, with great modesty, in apologetic discourse about Christian truth; in the *Pensées*, instead of looking up to an authority, *he* is the authority, speaking from his own experience and knowledge. In the *Entretien*, the addressee is a well-known priest and scholar; in the *Pensées*, he is a *libertin*, with feelings of unconcern or hostility toward religion.

As just suggested, in the *Entretien* the discussion unfolds in an atmosphere marked not by opposition and attempts to persuade, but by mutual respect; it involves two gifted people who, in spite of their quite different specialties, want to engage in a serious dialogue. In the *Pensées* – and here I am thinking of the work insofar as it is an apology – the aim will consist in moving the *libertin* from his original attitude to one of respect for religion, and beyond that to the attitude of a seeker, of someone who wants to learn as much as possible of what religion can tell him and do for him. Which leads us to a very important point: enlightenment alone does not suffice to define Pascal's aim. He intends to produce an argument that will have practical consequences in his reader's life.

As for the discourse itself – there, I think, the similarities rather than the differences are striking. In the *Pensées* Pascal continues the sort of dialectical reasoning that he is represented as using so openly and clearly in the *Entretien*. And we can locate in the *Pensées* a particular block of material – concerning the two sorts of philosophy and their mutual difficulties, which are removed by subsuming the virtues of both under the banner of Christian truth – that we have just encountered in the *Entretien*.

However, Pascal complicates the logical situation in an interesting way. To make sense out of what he does, may we not say that he saw how he might use in the *Pensées* the topical sequence that he had arrived at in the *Entretien*, provided that he extended it at both ends? Let me explain what I mean. For a suitable approach to the *libertin* he needs to back up from the starting point of his argument in the *Entretien*. His interlocutor is not a priest, or a philosopher, or even someone who cares about philosophy. And so Pascal will start on the level of daily and common experience, at a point before moral reflection has reached the issue between Epictetus and Montaigne and their respective philosophies. He chooses to orient the discussion in such a way that his reader will identify in his own experience the paradox of *misère* and *grandeur*. Then it will be possible to consider a visit to the philosophers in order to see what light they may shed on the issue that has been defined on a lower and less technical level of discourse. At that point Pascal can rejoin the topical outline from the *Entretien*.

At the end of the discussion of Epictetus and Montaigne, and in the glow of the triumph of Christian truth and morality, we are told that M. de Saci had arrived at the same destination as Pascal, only by a different route: by the study of the Bible, of the Church Fathers, of Augustine. Such were the foundations of his religious thought and life. I believe that we may with some plausibility say that, once Pascal has reached in the argument of the *Pensées* the point of advising, "Ecoutez Dieu," his tactic consists in adding on something like the position of M. de Saci. One thinks especially of the large number of fragments that set forth proofs of various kinds and in various stages of elaboration, resting on evidence found in the Bible. According to my hypothesis, then, Pascal had in the back of his mind an original sequence, rather technical in nature and having to do with the two philosophers; to that he adds a prefix, which makes it possible for him to make easy contact with his *libertin* interlocutor and to lead him into the more technical zone of the argument. Then, at the other end of the original sequence, Pascal completes the argument with "l'Ecriture et le reste" – with his own treatment of biblical, patristic, and Augustinian themes. When worked out, these themes, on subjects like prophecies, miracles, figures, and Christian moral values would constitute a body of proofs, intended to confirm the truth of the earlier parts of the apology.

As we continue to explore the rhetorical aspects of the *Pensées*, let us recall certain basic notions. Instead of working to achieve a carefully constructed demonstration in geometry or an illuminating reconciliation of opposites in theology, Pascal wants to solve an essentially practical problem. What he needs, first, is a clear idea of the particular end to be realized – not some broad or final end, but a purpose that arises out of specific – even unique – circumstances, as one deals with other people and makes contact with other minds. In the next place, he needs to discover means that are appropriate to that end and to that set of conditions. The essential activities of inventing or discovering those means may be carried out without any reference to a value that transcends the immediate context or situation: that is one possibility. But it may, on the other hand, proceed under the regulation of an outside value considered to be decisive in every context. Of course, Pascal chose the latter possibility.

AN ART OF RECONCILIATION

Variation 1 : man and himself

Throughout the *Provinciales*, in order to defend his Jansenist friends and to separate truth from error, Pascal brings into a discussion of grace and heresy some generalized devices of geometrical inquiry, taking advantage of its ways of providing undeniable rational evidence. He imports also into that discussion – by the systematic inspection and interpretation of texts from the books of casuistry, to cite one tactic among others – the spirit and principles of empirical inquiry, for conclusions based on undeniable visible evidence. He considers seriously those who are being addressed, making assumptions about their moral traits and mental capacities. He realizes that, when the judgments of non-specialized readers become important in a situation, he must turn toward the art of persuasion and away from the method suitable for the strictly scientific treatment of a problem.

It is possible, though, in interpreting the *Pensées* and the apologetic posture taken there by Pascal, to go further and to be more precise. There he analyzes in detail the very mechanism of assent, and in so doing lays the fundamental bases of another – and dialectical – variation in the mode of rhetoric.

In the second part of *De l'esprit géométrique* Pascal's stress falls on persuasion – as opposed to strict demonstration – and his attention comes to an intense focus on the intellectual and moral characteristics of the person to be persuaded. He begins to conceptualize the process of assent and to define the steps that lead to it:

L'art de persuader a un rapport nécessaire à la manière dont les hommes consentent à ce qu'on leur propose, et aux conditions des choses qu'on veut faire croire. (L355a; Mɪɪɪ413)

This introductory remark leads into something absolutely basic in Pascal's rhetoric: the idea of two portals through which opinions, and sometimes truths (both human and divine), enter the soul of the reader or listener. The two entrances are the *entendement* and the *volonté*. Pascal assumes thus two sides in the make-up of the person he will want to persuade, two essential "puissances" or powers, one tending especially toward the truth, *le vrai*, and the other tending especially toward the good, *le bien*. But, and this is a significant departure from classical rhetorical theory, the subject possessing these powers is in a corrupt state, in a state of separation from God; and a rebellious will often takes upon itself active control of the process by which opinions and truths are admitted and accepted, whereas its proper role should be, if not passive, at least receptive. That faulty disposition complicates the task of the persuader, who must try to take into account the play of concupiscence and the variations of taste, of *agrément*.

Ces puissances ont chacune leurs principes et les premiers moteurs de leurs actions. Ceux de l'esprit sont des vérités naturelles et connues à tout le monde, comme que le tout est plus grand que sa partie... Ceux de la volonté sont de certains désirs naturels et communs à tous les hommes, comme le désir d'être heureux... (L355c; Mɪɪɪ415)

And so, if I may try to say this in less succinct language than that of Pascal, suppose that I want to persuade someone of something. What I want to put across has certain qualities; and I must show that those qualities or aspects can be related to the addressee, to some truth toward which his mind tends and to some good toward which his will tends. When the reader or the listener perceives these connections, he will come to the desired conclusion, and the process of persuasion will be – in theory anyway – complete.

How are these theoretical views related to Pascal's project in the *Pensées*? In the last fragment of the chapter entitled "Ordre" and after recalling his headword, he continues:

Ordre.
    Les hommes ont mépris pour la religion. Ils en ont haine et peur qu'elle soit vraie. Pour guérir cela il faut commencer par montrer que la religion n'est point contraire à la raison. Vénérable, en donner respect.
    La rendre ensuite aimable, faire souhaiter aux bons qu'elle fût vraie et puis montrer qu'elle est vraie.
    Vénérable parce qu'elle a bien connu l'homme.
    Aimable parce qu'elle promet le vrai bien. (L502b, f12; S43, f46)

One very useful way of seeing Pascal's whole apologetic plan and the rhetorical strategy underlying it comes through these lines. Reverting to the vocabulary we were just noting in the passage from *De l'esprit géométrique*, we may say that religion, which is what is to be persuaded, has for the reader at the outset qualities that create obstacles for both the mind and the will; it seems to propose to him something not worthy of his attention, something hateful, something frightening.

To change this situation Pascal will, in the first stage of his argument, lead his reader to the point of seeing that his powers of knowing and desiring are in a state of uncertainty, mobility, and unfulfilment; they are not attached by any logical relation to a truth that is really convincing or to a good that is really satisfying. That process of self-examination, concluding in puzzlement and despair, serves as the basis of the rest of the argument.

How can the Christian religion be connected with that? Pascal does it by showing that from the first, from Creation, indeed, the religion in question has known the story and the predicament of mankind; and so, rather than being unworthy of our attention, it has a title to our respect as a source of insight, it is *vénérable*. We do not say at this point that we accept it, but we can say that it is not *contraire à la raison*: reason has no reason to scorn it. All of that constitutes an appeal to that one of our two fundamental aspirations that turns toward truth. Of course, Pascal has not forgotten the other side, that of *la volonté*; he intends next to show that religion is *aimable*, attractive, lovable. And why is it so? He indicates the line of reasoning he will follow: *aimable*, because it promises the true good – and for Pascal the true good is exactly the object toward which the will naturally directs itself.

Religion is not, then, something for reason to look down on; nor is it something for the will to hate or fear. One wishes that one could accept it; but, is it true? Can one get to something more positive than the notion of religion as not being contrary to reason? The third great panel of the argument emerges: "... et puis montrer qu'elle est vraie." It seems clear that what he calls in the *argument du pari* "... l'Ecriture et le reste," the whole complex of proofs turning on topics like perpetuity, prophecy, miracles, morality, Church history, and so on, would be brought to bear on the problem. The result would not constitute a demonstration, but it would offer a collection of convergent proofs sufficient to remove the obstacles, *ôter les obstacles*, which is, after all, to reach the limit of apologetics. As a rhetorical discipline, it cannot do more than put the reader in a receptive state of mind and will. The rest depends on the divine initiative, which Pascal always safeguards: he took care to say, a few lines above those I am now commenting on, that faith is a gift of God, a *don de Dieu*, and not a gift of the apologist.

I should like to make the steps of the process even more explicit, to reduce them to something like a formula. Though lacking in nuance, the result will be useful because, as I hope to show, Pascal works out the sequence (wholly or in part) in more than one context. Let us state the matter in terms of what happens in the intended audience. (1) The reader or interlocutor begins to explore with the apologist an important subject (though its importance may not be at once apparent to him). (2) Then he reaches a point in the argument where further progress seems impossible, the aporia arising from paradoxes, contradictions, contrarieties, opposing views on the same topics. (3) He realizes, with some humility, that finding answers is going to exceed human powers; if solutions are to be had, they must come from a supra-human source, and will be received, not achieved. (4) He learns from the apologist what steps he should take to remove obstacles and to prepare for the possible reception of the answers. (5) After following the line of thought and the course of action proposed, he reaches the last phase of his itinerary, which consists essentially of waiting and hoping for divine inspiration.

Variation 2: man and God (le pari)

Pascal provides a particularly striking example of this scheme in the fragment on the wager. On my view he gives us in these pages one version, in telescoped form, of what his whole apologetic argument extending through his chapters and added *discours* might have been. As in the preceding variation, he works systematically with the two sides of human nature, arranging them finally in a balanced dialectical orientation that makes both dependent on God.

One big difference, however, lies in the source of the aporia. In the argument just summarized, I drew attention to the fact that Pascal leads off with a focus on the self and with an invitation to his reader to engage in self-study. The basis of this *connaissance de soi-même* is sought in a complex of moral and intellectual insights that seem finally to be enigmatic. In the fragment "Infini rien," which, incidentally, we tend to distort and diminish by referring to it simply as "le pari," Pascal sets up an epistemological rather than a moral context, and he leads his reader through a study of the possibilities available to human powers of knowing. This is the initial, exploratory phase of the rhetorical sequence. After finite objects of knowledge, which we can know as existences and as natures, he evokes objects of the infinite kind, first in mathematics, where we can know of their existence though not of their nature, and then, second, in considerations regarding the nature and existence of God. There we reach an impassable limit, for we can know by our natural lights neither whether God exists nor what his nature is: he is completely out of sight. We are now obviously at the moment of aporia in the argument. Through faith, says Pascal, proposing his solution, we can be certain of God's existence; in the next world, in his presence – *dans la gloire* – we shall be placed so as to know his nature.

From this point on in the fragment, Pascal adopts a presentation in the form of a dialogue, during which he takes the interlocutor by the hand through the remaining stages of the five that I have listed above. Since in this life only God's existence is available to us, and that only via faith, Pascal has reached the phase in which he may call for humility and for an appeal to something higher than Nature or human nature. The interlocutor puts up an obstacle of an intellectual sort: he does not have faith, and so it would be better to suspend judgment about God's existence and nature. Pascal goes to work on the obstacle, showing first that the skeptical gambit does not avoid the issue but in fact takes a position on it; then that in any case the wager cannot be avoided – " ... vous êtes embarqué " – and finally that the terms are very favorable for a wager to the effect that God exists. His interlocutor finds himself obliged to recognize the demonstrative character of the argument; and accepting the conclusion according to which orienting oneself toward belief is not contrary to reason, he expresses a desire to know more, to understand what lies behind the game. Pascal proposes study of "l'Ecriture et le reste."

Still, I cannot believe, says the interlocutor. Pascal identifies the remaining obstacle as being moral and as arising from the passions. What the interlocutor needs now is not to hear more arguments but to adopt a line of action. He must go through the motions, conduct himself *as if* he believed, form a new habit of behavior, follow the examples of those who were once like him but have gone on to real commitment. Thus Pascal promotes the use of *la coutume*, of the *preuve par la Machine*, as the way to overcome the ill effects of concupiscence. Finally, with the two sorts of obstacles to progress – due to faulty reasonings and to corrupt acts of will – out of the way, Pascal can usher his interlocutor into the last stage of the journey, wherein the two sides of his nature, now focused on the same goal, are ready and actively waiting to receive the *don de la foi*. What God gives will reconcile and unify them – and, at the same time, validate the steps taken on the path to faith.

Pascal has clearly placed himself on the terrain of rhetoric and is elaborating a personal version of the art of persuading, of obtaining assent. He spends his energy and ingenuity in attending to events taking place in his audience, and specifically, in the mind of one other person, adjusting everything he has to say to the changing attitudes and reactions of his interlocutor. This adaptation is particularly noticeable in the wager argument proper. It is, in fact, inevitable, after the point in the text where Pascal slips into the mode of dialogue. He wants to build his discourse on a series of true propositions *and* the matching acts of assent that they entail; until those acts are obtained, he neither will nor can go forward.

And here a fascinating paradox occurs. It is clear that Pascal is preparing us for a dialectical redirecting of reason and will so that, instead of being aimless or opposed, they will begin to wait upon divine inspiration. However, his effort of invention turns back to mathematics and probability calculations: he undertakes to prove a theorem, namely, that a positive attitude toward religion and belief is not contrary to reason. At the end of the justifications concerning stakes, odds, and rewards that he offers as warranty for that proposition, Pascal adds an unmistakable Q. E. D.: "Cela est démonstratif..." To which his interlocutor adds, under the pressure of the reasoning: "Je le confesse... je l'avoue." And so, within the general outline of a dialectical sequence, Pascal inserts an elaborate episode of geometrical rhetoric, designed to remove the intellectual obstacle and to prepare the reason for the role that it will play alongside the will, as the *chercheur* turns to the moderating of his passions and the lifting of that second stumbling block. When that has occurred, inspiration and grace may bring the final moment of reconciliation with God.

Variation 3: man and Nature

In this variation, which is worked out in the fragment dealing with the "Disproportion de l'homme," Pascal asks us to turn away from things immediately present and to look up into the sky – more specifically the night sky – and then down into the parts of something small, like the mite or *ciron*: the two infinites, *en grandeur* and *en petitesse*, become explicit. These two views or acts of inspection complete the exploratory phase of his argument, and he moves on to formulate the aporia. How can we grasp and know with our finite powers what is at the two ends of the extraordinary scale perceptible in the natural universe? Pascal's answer is that we cannot; nor can we answer the more personal question regarding our place in this paradoxical natural order. In a new context, that of the whole of Nature – rather than that of moral experience or that of the existence and nature of God, as in the first two variations – Pascal is offering us the same lesson in humility as before.

Then he engages in a sort of retracing of his logical path but with slight changes so as to produce not one but a series of aporias and humbling experiences. He reasons that every human being partakes in all his powers of the dual infinity shown to exist in Nature, and so that basic paradox enters intimately into the human constitution. But Pascal does not rest even there: taking an epistemological turn, his thought fixes on the duality of body and soul. He asks how, since we are combinations of those two principles, can we know bodies without confusing them to some degree with minds, and likewise, how can we know "les choses spirituelles" without some contamination from the body? He concludes that there is no way out of this dilemma, which involves the interaction of body and mind. He reaches the crowning aporia when he asserts that we neither know what *corps* nor what *esprit* is, and least of all can we conceive of how the former can be joined to the latter. All of this is summed up in the notion of the baffling *disproportion de l'homme* – a disproportion with reference both to Nature and to his own nature.

This stage in the argument reminds us of the midpoint of the *pari*, the point at which our *lumières naturelles* simply have to admit defeat. But, interestingly enough, Pascal does not here lead us into an active search for supra-human answers to the questions that come to the fore when we contemplate Nature, ourselves in relation to it, and finally ourselves as composite beings. He does say that the overwhelming size of Nature is the greatest "caractère sensible" of God's omnipotence and he does say that the two infinites coincide ultimately in God; but he makes no effort to remove obstacles to further understanding, to get us off the plane of mere human speculations. In sum, although Pascal starts here his familiar apologetic sequence, he does not finish it to anything like the degree found in the pages on the wager.

However, the fragment that precedes immediately the one on the *disproportion* tells us a great deal about how the inquiry might have proceeded. In fact, it even suggests the way in which Pascal might have brought together two lines of thought and argument: the contemplation of Nature undertaken in the following fragment and the analysis of the human condition presented in the first chapters of the *Pensées*. He begins as follows:

En voyant l'aveuglement et la misère de l'homme, en regardant tout l'univers muet et l'homme sans lumière abandonné à lui-même, et comme égaré dans ce recoin de l'univers sans savoir qui l'y a mis, ce qu'il y est venu faire, ce qu'il deviendra en mourant, incapable de toute connaissance, j'entre en effroi comme un homme qu'on aurait porté endormi dans une île déserte et effroyable, et qui s'éveillerait sans connaître et sans moyen d'en sortir. (L525c, f198; S125, f229)

Those lines sum up admirably the first moments we have noted in Pascal's formula: what I have called an exploration, accompanied by an awakening, a new awareness; and then a number of unanswered and apparently unanswerable questions; and then feelings of puzzlement and humility (to which fright is added here). In the present text, the "je" in question looks around at the state in which his fellow men find themselves: it is not different from his, though they have become attached to "quelques objets plaisants." The "je" here in question has not been attracted to such things: and he moves on to the next moment in the familiar sequence, which involves a turn toward a supra-human principle:

… et considérant combien il y a plus d'apparence qu'il y a autre chose que ce que je vois j'ai recherché si ce Dieu n'aurait point laissé quelque marque de soi. (L525d, f198; S125, f229)

Then, unless I am quite mistaken, Pascal launches into the phase of removing obstacles – of an intellectual kind, it would seem – as he tells what he sees on the plane of religion, or rather, of religions.

Je vois plusieurs religions contraires et partant toutes fausses, excepté une. Chacune veut être crue par sa propre autorité et menace les incrédules. Je ne les crois donc pas là-dessus. Chacun peut dire cela. Chacun peut se dire prophète mais je vois la chrétienne et je trouve des prophéties, et c'est ce que chacun ne peut pas faire. (L525d, f198; S125, f229)

This looks very much like the theme of "l'Ecriture et le reste," pointing the way to arguments much more fully developed elsewhere in the *Pensées* on the subject of "Fausseté des autres religions" and on the role of prophecy in establishing the preeminent place of the Christian religion.

As an example of rhetorical reasoning and, more particularly, as a sample outline of the way in which Pascal might develop a comprehensive apologetic argument, the fragment preceding the "Disproportion de l'homme" is extremely revealing. It even indicates and characterizes the two parties who might confront each other: the one who has seen and sought and found, as opposed to the ones still blind, who have not become *chercheurs*, who have let themselves be distracted by goods ultimately vain.

Variation 4: digressions sur chaque point

We still have to consider the fact that the smooth progressions foreseen in *De l'esprit géométrique*, where Pascal said that the art of demonstrating and the art of persuading were identical, are not in any obvious way realized in the *Pensées*. The chapters of the apologetic project do not move in a deductive fashion – as one descends to details from the general level of the fragment on "Ordre" that I have been discussing – through the three-step sequence, from *vénérable* to *aimable* to *vraie*, though I believe there is plenty of evidence to affirm it as giving one valuable outline of Pascal's argument. My suggestion now is that we turn to another fragment that is found in the chapter entitled "Preuves de Jésus-Christ." Curiously enough, this text begins with the same title- or head-word that we saw above: "ordre."

L'ordre. Contre l'objection que l'Ecriture n'a pas d'ordre.

Le coeur a son ordre, l'esprit a le sien qui est par principe et démonstration. Le coeur en a un autre. On ne prouve pas qu'on doit être aimé en exposant d'ordre les causes de l'amour; cela serait ridicule.

J.-C., saint Paul ont l'ordre de la charité, non de l'esprit, car ils voulaient échauffer, non instruire. Saint Augustin de même. Cet ordre consiste principalement à la digression sur chaque point qui a rapport à la fin, pour la montrer toujours. (L539cd, f298; S175, f329)

Where order is concerned, Pascal obviously intends here to place himself in the line of Christ, St. Paul, and St. Augustine.

He saw that his message, which is the message of Scripture, could be presented in the order found in Scripture – an order which is perfectly defensible, if one takes the trouble to get beyond superficial objections. He saw that, instead of proceeding by principle and demonstration, he could follow the three great models whom he mentions specifically, and that a rhetoric of apology, while certainly not giving up on the mind, would place special emphasis on preparing the heart. After all, as he says elsewhere:

C'est le coeur qui sent Dieu et non la raison. Voilà ce que c'est que la foi. Dieu sensible au coeur, non à la raison. (L552b, f424; S359, f680)

Let us reread the last sentence of the fragment on *ordre* that I am discussing, for it is packed with meaning: "This order consists mainly in digressions upon each point that relates to the end, so that this shall be kept always in sight." The end will always be present to one's discourse; one moves away from it on each point without ever forgetting it. This gives us a new way of looking at Pascal's rhetorical invention; it may work not according to the planned stages of an intellectual and moral itinerary but by a kind of dialectical radiation from a center. It is essentially intuitive rather than discursive.

Pascal had already said something similar in the chapter called "Raison des effets": "Il faut avoir une pensée de derrière, et juger de tout par là, en parlant cependant comme le peuple" (L510d, f91; S74, f125). The context seems more specific in the present fragment concerning the order of the heart; it would appear that for the apologist, the origin or center of those digressions on each point, "digressions sur chaque point," will be God. I conclude, therefore, that Pascal's argumentation in the perspective of dialectical rhetoric can be (1) sequential and discursive, as in the preceding variations, or (2) digressive and intuitive – or it may consist in some combination of the two.

RHETORIC INTO DIALECTIC

It is the fate of rhetoric in the dialectical mode to disappear, to have a limited sphere of application, to be introductory but not final. In order to understand what happens we have only to prolong the notion of those *digressions sur chaque point* that are always seen with relation to an overriding end, which is ultimately the formula for a dialectic rather than for a rhetoric. The latter comes to an end when the interlocutor is no longer dependent on the apologist. Having become a seeker on his own account, he will think and act along the lines observed in exemplary figures, like those evoked at the climax of the *pari*.

Vous voulez vous guérir de l'infidélité et vous en demandez les remèdes, apprenez de ceux, etc. qui ont été liés comme vous et qui parient maintenant tout leur bien. Ce sont gens qui savent ce chemin que vous voudriez suivre et guéris d'un mal dont vous voulez guérir; suivez la manière où ils ont commencé. (L551c, f418; S357, f680)

The *art de persuader* is about to be cast off. From this degree of assent to the views of his guide, the reader or interlocutor is about to set out on his own. Pascal sees in store for him a deepening sense of the priorities that are leading him inward from things outside that distract him, and upward from things within that hinder his progress, toward the state and moment at which expectation may be answered by grace.

This personal movement away from rhetoric, inevitable when that art is associated with dialectic, contrasts strikingly with its fate when it takes its principles and spirit from the mathematical mode. That species of rhetoric, as it is exemplified in the *Provinciales*, imports a proven technique into a new and somewhat unexpected context, theological rather than scientific. In its original as well as its second context, where it is specified to a new sort of problem, Pascal uses it to produce conviction, or if not that, if that proves impossible, to confound his opponents and reduce them to silence. Such rhetoric is not preliminary; it is not finally absorbed into another kind of thinking and behavior. On the other hand, in Pascal's apologetic rhetoric one sees not an art borrowing, extending, and applying a scientific logic, but an art that emerges in and has a particular place in an overarching dialectical process of assimilation and integration. It adopts an interpersonal style of argument that undergoes in its final stage a mutation into something more certain and decisive. The change occurs as a consequence of the fact that where religion and morals are concerned, Pascal recognizes only one kind of thought, and it is truly inclusive by nature. He thus prepares the way for his readers to relate the apologetic episode and its rhetorical technique to everything else. He intends to have them engage for a while in a limited enterprise, an excursion; and they are to do that until, having become independent *chercheurs*, they commit themselves freely to the kind of reflection and action that is typically called for in the hierarchical perspective of religion and theology.

CHAPTER 5

Restatement and conclusion

Here are four short texts, each pointing in a different direction, that lead into the hypothesis on which this study of Pascal's works depends.

1. Je veux donc faire entendre ce que c'est que démonstration par l'exemple de celles de géométrie, qui est presque la seule des sciences humaines qui en produise d'infaillibles, parce qu'elle seule observe la véritable méthode, au lieu que toutes les autres sont par une nécessité naturelle dans quelque sorte de confusion que les seuls géomètres savent extrêmement reconnaître. (L349b; Mɪɪɪ392)

2. Tout auteur a un sens auquel tous les passages contraires s'accordent ou il n'a point de sens du tout. On ne peut pas dire cela de l'Ecriture et des prophètes: ils avaient assurément trop de bon sens. Il faut donc en chercher un qui accorde toutes les contrariétés. (L533a, f257; S152, f289)

3. De Paris, ce 23 janvier 1656. Monsieur, Nous étions bien abusés. Je ne suis détrompé que d'hier. Jusque-là j'ai pensé que le sujet des disputes de Sorbonne était bien important, et d'une extrême conséquence pour la religion... Cependant vous serez bien surpris quand vous apprendrez, par ce récit, à quoi se termine un si grand éclat; et c'est ce que je vous dirai en peu de mots, après m'en être parfaitement instruit. (L371d–72a)

4. L'homme n'est ni ange ni bête, et le malheur veut que qui veut faire l'ange fait la bête. (L590a, f678; S288, f557)

Each of those passages bears visible witness to distinct structures and inclinations that are more or less invisible – invisible because they are mental, because they have the character of habitual ways of thinking: in short, because they are intellectual arts. I have taken the term "art" in the technical sense of a kind of productive knowledge that guides the possessor in the treatment of problems and, perhaps even, in finding solutions to them. Of course, an art in this sense *may* be set down in a treatise and published in a book. But my emphasis has consistently been on art as a psychological disposition, as something that exists not in a manual but in a mind. A habit, yes, though not a routine; rather a flexible and rationally controlled tendency to activity and performance. And so I have been proposing reflections on some arts understood in this way as they seem to be detectable in certain major and minor works of Pascal.

As regards the term "mind," I have sought to follow in the main Pascal's usage. He divides the soul or the mind (*l'âme* or *l'esprit*) from the body (*le corps*). The mind or soul is where thinking, broadly conceived, takes place. I doubt that there has been any difficulty in granting me this distinction. But, as must be clear by now, to concentrate on the mind and on thought does not at all limit us to the study of mental phenomena – sensations, ideas, feelings, images. To deal adequately with my subject it has seemed advisable from the first to recognize that meanings and mental activities usually involve expressions in language and references or designations in things; and each of the three factors when specified to the data of a problem has a contribution to make to their mutual intelligibility.

I have just mentioned "things," and with Pascal one does indeed find oneself dealing with realities in the plural. His curiosity ranges over an astonishing spectrum of subjects. In one group: *nombres* (plain numbers with their powers, multiples, orders, and infinites, but also "magical" numbers and beyond that some magically magical numbers – *nombres magiquement magiques*), without forgetting probability calculations and the *machine d'arithmétique*. And then, in geometry: lines both straight and curved, and figures both solid and plane (one of Pascal's favorites is the cone and the sections to which it gives rise), plus a new method of perspective-drawing. Then, moving out into the physical world, he studies liquids, solids, water, mercury, air; and of course the behavior of air and mercury leads him to work on the *vide* or vacuum, which we must take care to distinguish from another subject of interest to him, nothingness or *le néant* (remembering that for him *le vide* or empty space is not the same as *le néant*). Or, again, leaving behind local effects, he invites us to try to take in Nature as a whole, with its four pairs of infinite magnitudes, stretching beyond anything we can see or even imagine. Another turn of his mind finds him considering animals and angels and the human creatures situated between the two. He evokes and judges many sorts and conditions of men, and the way in which they do laws, politics, eloquence, and philosophy. Those subjects lead him to religion, to the two Testaments of the Bible, to Adam, Moses, the prophets, Jesus Christ, St. Paul, to the Church and St. Augustine, to God, grace, and God's ways to humankind. My list is rather arbitrary; and it makes no mention of something else with which Pascal was actively concerned: the historical circumstances and changes – familial, social, political, intellectual, religious – through which he lived in France in the decades from 1623 to 1662.

However, it is my conviction that, although he has a great many things to think about, he favors a relatively small number of ways of thinking about them. And so it has seemed possible to isolate more or less satisfactorily some lines of thought that occur and recur in Pascal's works. I do not claim that my list is exhaustive, though I do think that it gets at some fundamental trends that come into play as he approaches the various subject-matters of interest to him.

I should indicate one other supposition that underlies everything I have attempted to do here. I take it that Pascal starts from a commitment to truth, or to put it more actively and distinctly, he constantly seeks to *discover* the truth, to *demonstrate* or *prove* it, and to *distinguish it from error*. The arts and lines of thought proposed here are among the chief means he uses in order to attain that complex, yet single and sovereign, end.

Geometric

One method discernible in much of Pascal's thinking is that of geometry, suitably generalized or particularized as occasions require. It has two principal phases: it seeks first to find the ultimate constituent parts of the subject being considered; and then, when all the elements are at hand and self-evidently so, it seeks to build up a coherent discourse – or for that matter, a coherent and workable calculating machine – using those clear and distinct materials. In geometry proper one starts with explicit definitions and axioms, and from those beginnings one goes on by combinations that are deductively correct to formulate theorems and groups of theorems that, in their *suite géométrique*, to use Pascal's phrase, make up a larger ensemble or perhaps a treatise.

He offers us many examples in the mathematical and physical treatises of the way in which this constructive method can be applied. There is nothing particularly new about this line of thought; but one thing that makes it remarkable here is that on some important occasions Pascal undertakes to extend the scope of this method, to show that it is *the* way to think and talk regardless of subject-matter. In such passages, which have something of a Cartesian ring to them, he proposes that we adopt the form of geometrical discourse as our general model.

For relatively pure instances of this mode of thinking one naturally looks in the writings on mathematics and on physics. Pascal provides a theoretic discussion of it in the pages of the text we know as *De l'esprit géométrique*. It is necessary to note, however, an important derived form of geometrical discourse, the form that serves in the investigations of physics. Statements made in that science – when we are talking of the vacuum or of the equilibria of liquids – must fit into a deductive framework at the start of the inquiry. There the faculty of reason dominates, but it must give way later to activity regulated by the senses, activity in which empirical observation validated by measurement (for the auspices of mathematics have never really been set aside) determines whether or not the hypothesis corresponds in fact to what happens in the external world. Pascal's "Récit de la grande expérience de l'équilibre des liqueurs," shows just such a progression from rigorous definition to consequential reasoning to quantitative verification.

Dialectic

Pascal may move in a different direction, on another line that is just as important as the preceding, if not more so. Instead of starting with a technique of construction, he may have in mind a process of integration. And here, again, one may see two phases or movements: in connection with his subject he must show at least two – and perhaps more – factors that are opposed or contrary. He finds such *contrariétés* or paradoxes in all the important subjects: *misère et grandeur* in human nature; the two infinites in physical nature; justice and force in society; Old and New Testaments in the Bible; humanity and divinity in Christ; justice and mercy in God, who is hidden yet revealed. Sometimes in this phase of his presentation Pascal contents himself with a brief indication, but at other times he develops, enriches, orchestrates his opposition until the tension between the two sides is almost overwhelming.

Then he begins the second phase, wherein, by introducing a comprehensive or inclusive third term, he reorients the factors in the opposition and brings them into balance or harmony. The geometrical method proceeds from elements to a deductively produced composite, that is, from simplicity to complexity; the method I am presently describing, which is clearly dialectical, proceeds from complexity to simplicity, or more precisely, from multiplicity to unity. To revert to the examples just cited above, Pascal rescues and brings into balance captive truths from each of the opposed extremes in human nature, in Nature, in society, in the Bible, in the persons and roles of Christ and God. The *Ecrits sur la grâce*, the *Pensées*, and the shorter works on moral or religious questions abound in examples of this kind of integrative, synoptic thinking.

Rhetoric

The third direction taken by Pascal in certain circumstances is motivated by yet another aim. Instead of working to achieve a carefully constructed demonstration or an illuminating reconciliation of opposites, he may want to treat an essentially practical problem. Here what he needs, first, is a clear idea of the particular end that he wants to realize – not some broad or final end, but a purpose that arises out of a particular situation, as when he must address and influence people of a given sort. And then, in the next place, he needs to discover means that are appropriate to that end and to that set of circumstances. Practical discovery and invention are the marks of this method; and I think that we may properly call it rhetorical, especially where the problem is to invent discourse. One may call it pragmatic or operational if one decides to use it mainly for the planning of action or the contriving of experiments.

The central activity here, which is invention, may be carried out without any reference to values that transcend the *immediate* context; that would involve the kind of rhetoric that I have called autonomous or independent. It may, however, proceed under the regulation of outside values – I mean principles not established by the discipline itself, but imported into it – considered to be decisive in *every* context. Such a subordinate art, that is, a rhetoric that is called into the service of transcendental values, has a great role in the *Provinciales* and in the *Pensées*; and it turns up also in the shorter works on moral subjects and in the correspondence. One can find evidence for at least five rhetorical situations, according to the addressees Pascal has in mind; and for two lines of argument, one leading to controversy and refutation (as in the *Provinciales*), and the other emphasizing dialogue and leading to assent (as in the *Pensées*).

According to the first line of argument, which borrows its principles from geometric, the texture and shape of demonstrative and persuasive discourse will be the same; the rules regarding definitions, assumptions, inferences, and the like have general force; and Pascal, in his more enthusiastic moments, sees no need to set limits for their application. In the context of persuasion, though – as opposed to that of strict demonstration – there is a new concern with the mental and moral characteristics of the person to be persuaded, along with a new sense of the aspects or steps typically found in the process of assent.

He advances the idea of two portals through which opinions

and, it may be, truths (both human and divine), enter the soul of the reader or interlocutor. The entrances are: the *entendement* and the *volonté*, one tending especially toward the understanding of the truth and the other tending especially toward the possession of the good. The aim of the art of persuading is to establish a link or a series of links between the two tendencies or aspirations on the one hand, and on the other, the qualities of the thing to be persuaded. To evoke the *Pensées* once more: Pascal adjusts the qualities of the Christian religion to the requirements of this scheme. (1) *Vénérable*, because of its insights into human nature, it supplies food for thought, for the understanding; and (2) *aimable*, because of its clear view of what is good and of how it is to be attained, it has an attraction for the will; and (3) *vraie*, because of the mass of convergent evidence that can be brought forward to justify what it asserts, it prolongs and completes the appeal to understanding indicated in (1).

In the definition that I suggested above I stressed its inventive aspect of the rhetorical art, its concern with the discovery of effective means for accomplishing a particular end. Pascal has that concern in the *Pensées*, and the distinction regarding the portals of the soul throws light on how, in the presence of a reader whose mind and will are in disorder because of Adam's fall, he intended to solve his heuristic problem. The determining line of argument here is not inspired by the deductive model of a generalized geometry, however, but by the progressive stages of a dialectical process. Those two powers of the soul – understanding and will – often confused and aimless in their activities, provide just the situation needed for paradoxes and tentative answers, in preparation for the eventual resolution in which the two aspirations come to be related to *the* Truth and to *the* Good, which are one and the same in God.

But there is a significant complication to be brought into the scheme of the two portals, the two gateways into the soul. One of the two may assume special importance. "Le coeur a son ordre," Pascal writes, then adding, "l'esprit a le sien qui est par principe et démonstration" (L539cd, f298; S175, f329). The aim of the former is to move, to warm (*échauffer*), and not to instruct (*instruire*). When Jesus Christ, St. Paul, and St.

Augustine sought to influence their hearers and readers, they chose the way of the heart – which is, one might add, also the way *to* the heart. Surely they have in Pascal an attentive disciple. And how does this order proceed? Not in a linear but in an excursive fashion, *ad hoc*, deriving its unity from the fact that it never loses sight of an overriding end. It works neither through the planned stages of an intellectual and moral itinerary, nor by axioms and their consequences, but by relations that are seen immediately, in light radiating from a central source. We have thus another way of looking at rhetorical argumentation in Pascal; and we must conclude, it seems to me, that his inventions may be discursive, sequential, progressive, or they may be intuitive, discontinuous, digressive. Or, again, a combination of the two.

The problematic art

Let me complete my list by indicating a fourth direction that Pascal takes occasionally. I have not wished to attempt a chapter-long consideration of it, since I find in his works fewer examples of this way of asking and answering questions than of the other three; but they do occur, emerging from the background at interesting points in his demonstrations and proofs. The central aim is not to construct, or to integrate, or to invent, but to identify and in some later phase, to classify what is being talked about; and, moreover, to do that by an analysis of intrinsic characteristics. This methodological tendency may be called investigative or problematic; if allowed to develop freely, it leads to an ensemble of inquiries, separate because of shifts in what is taken as fundamental in subject-matters, but complementary because of analogies noted among things and traits. Here one moves backward from properties and operations to natures or essences.

The vocabulary I am using here is not very Pascalian, because of its origins in scholasticism and the Aristotelian tradition of metaphysics: two things that Pascal had little or no patience with. However, as I say, there seem to be important traces and sometimes more than traces of this reflexive kind of reasoning, at those times when Pascal wants to make inferences concerning the inherent traits or structures of things. Numbers have such natures and properties; so does the arithmetic triangle. In the scientific writings Pascal uses regularly and even dogmatically the classical conception of the powers of the soul, correlating them with characteristic operations and objects. That conception turns up again in the *Provinciales*, as we have seen – and in the *Pensées* as well, though there the stress begins to be laid on the fact that the soul's powers are "trompeuses." Still, he makes there effective use of the distinction between the existence of a being and the nature of that being, a distinction that expresses one of the most powerful insights of classical metaphysics. The passage that I have in mind, which is developed insistently and in some detail, occurs near the beginning of the fragment containing the "wager." The reasoning forms a necessary prelude to Pascal's calculations; it is not rhetorical or dialectical in spirit; and, although Pascal introduces some supporting geometrical vocabulary and imagery, the thrust of the argument is ontological – or, to come back to the term I am using, problematic.

REVIEW

The four recurrent and habitual lines of thought, the four arts of the mind, as I am calling them, are ways by which Pascal undertakes to find and to prove truth. We must keep in mind, however, the risks of ambiguity due to the fact that each of these ways carries with it a specific conception of truth, and a characteristic attitude toward contradiction.

(1) In the mode of geometric, as when Pascal analyzes a conic section or constructs a machine, truth is a function of the demonstrative procedure; and all contradictions must be excluded from the outset. (2) When he follows a dialectical path, typically from lower to higher levels of consideration, truth or falsity is a function of where he is in the developing argument, and of what is to be discarded and what is to be kept at that point; contradictions are admitted, even welcomed, as data in the problem to be solved, even though the preferred

solution consists in a final ranking of views or balance of factors. (3) When Pascal takes a rhetorical path, the particular situation with which he must deal leads him from a grasp of the end sought to activity in which he invents and adapts means to the desired end. Truth is a function of what will be effective for communication in a specific human or technical context. I must qualify that statement, however; I do not mean to turn Pascal into a sophist or a pragmatist. In the background of his rhetorical writing one always sees some principle that keeps him from asserting simply that all knowledge is opinion or that what works is true. The guiding principle may be the scientific ideal of geometrical and empirical reasoning or it may be the ideal of transcendent truth as revealed by God and felt by the heart. When inspired by geometry, his rhetoric eliminates contradictions; when inspired by religious insight, it behaves like dialectic, first accepting paradoxes and then reworking them so as to produce harmony. (4) And, finally, Pascal's path is occasionally problematic: it leads him to inspect his subject – inspect it in the etymological sense of that word, without reference to atomic parts or to all-inclusive *tableaux* – and to try to determine what its intrinsic character and consequent properties are. Truth is a function of classifications, definitions, and statements arrived at reflexively. Here contradictions simply indicate that boundaries of separate inquiries have been crossed and that one is in the presence of complementary statements about different aspects of the subject-matter.

Beyond the concern with the notions of truth and contradiction, I should like to summarize briefly some typical discursive operations associated with the arts and some consequences they have for the subject-matters that Pascal wishes to investigate or discuss. To simplify what is inevitably a complex business, I shall limit what I have to say to the three dominant arts discernible in Pascal's thought.

(1) Proceeding by decomposition and reconstruction, Pascal's geometric starts with *things* – Nature and natural phenomena – moves on to *thought* about abstract quantities, thence to *action* in experiments or applications where appropriate, and concludes typically with a treatise, with an account in *words* of what has

been discovered, proved, and done. (2) Proceeding from multiplicity to unity, from separation to reunion, his dialectic begins with the *words* of Scripture, moves on to *things* – Nature and Creation, apart from the Creator – and thence to *thought*, turning inward from the world outside for an exercise in introspection that serves to justify a line of *action*; and the resulting conversion prepares the way for access to a transcendent plane on which the soul may return to its author and end. (3) Having been assigned a status subordinate to that of the other two disciplines, Pascal's rhetoric borrows analytical and systematizing devices from them; it has its beginning in *things*, in existent situations – including people and attitudes – that need to be changed; it moves on to the two tasks of working out *thoughts* relevant in the particular circumstances and of selecting for their expression *words*, both technical and from the common fund, that may be effective in the circumstances; it ends with a focus on *action* in the process of communication itself and in its consequences.

That said, I must recall and underline an important fact. Any one of the intellectual modes I have described may be present in either of two ways. It may be dominant in a given problem area, and thus tend to be autonomous, independent; or it may find itself imported into a context where it is adjusted to the aims and sequences of one of the others – this is true of all three, and not simply of rhetoric, where the point is quite clear. When an art has this secondary or derived status, it is not in a position to develop freely its principles or to realize all of its possibilities. Geometric does not have the power to lay down its rules for precision and sequential order in every instance; in the fragment where the terms of the wager are set out and in the fragment on the "Disproportion de l'homme" we see episodes of geometrical thinking in a perspective where the controlling method is obviously dialectical. Or, again, dialectic may have to trim its integrative ambitions and be content to throw incidental light on a problem being treated in mathematics, as at the end of the little treatise where Pascal brings the measurement of continuous quantities into an exact relation to the summation of numerical powers, and he is inspired to give credit for this coincidence to Nature, with its love for unity: " … unitatis amatrix natura… " (L94d; Miii272). The phrase is a bit paradoxical: Pascal will not allow Nature to abhor a vacuum, but it – or should we say, she? – may love unity.

Although Pascal arrived at a personal version of these arts of the mind, he did not invent them. They have had a long and ambiguous history since they were invented by the Greeks. They have often been defined and distinguished in ways different from those I have found interesting to use, in my free borrowings from original sources and from the scholarship on the subject. As I see the intellectual environment in France in the seventeenth century, the arts in question were involved in a complex process of reinvention. Here are a few examples that come to mind at once. In the geometric mode: Descartes of course, with his *Discours*, or better, the works to which that was a preface – his *Dioptrique*, his *Météores*, or his *Géométrie*. In the dialectical mode Bossuet's *Discours sur l'histoire universelle* is outstanding; and so is Bayle's *Dictionnaire historique et critique*, though of course he turns the method to skeptical rather than dogmatic uses. In the rhetorical mode, there is an embarrassment of riches – the century has been characterized as an "age of eloquence." The discipline of rhetoric lies behind the characteristic way of thinking found in Corneille's three *Discours* on dramatic poetry, and in the prefaces composed by Molière and Racine for the printed editions of their works; it informs Boileau's *Art poétique*; and it undergoes a revision – not an eclipse, as is sometimes thought – at the time of the *Querelle des anciens et des modernes*, in the innovations of Fontenelle's *Entretiens sur la pluralité des mondes* and Perrault's *Parallèle des anciens et des modernes*. As for the problematic mode: the record here is less clear, but the history or fate of Aristotelianism in seventeenth-century science and philosophy is one place to look; and that suggests, in literature, Theophrastus and La Bruyère.

But, to return to Pascal: he adapts these permanent possibilities – permanent because there is something constant about them in spite of their incessant transformations – to his vision and his needs. His case is remarkable in that he moves with such mastery along more than one of these lines. He is not a person who finds at an early and decisive moment some one intellectual style and then stays with it, differing significantly in that from Descartes. He is more like St. Augustine, who intended and partly realized an encyclopedia of the liberal arts, all of which, it appears, would have sought to show the presence of God in his Creation and, moreover, would have contributed in the exegesis of the Bible to the recovery of God's Word: in all a project certainly akin to that of Pascal.

His sister Gilberte says that their father, in carrying out the plan that he made for the instruction of little Blaise, had as his principal pedagogical maxim that he must " ... tenir cet enfant au-dessus de son travail." Pascal learned that lesson, and he applies it. With all of these possibilities, of these ways to truth in front of him, he chooses the one especially pertinent to the work at hand, but that does not mean that he forgets the others. He uses them all with ease, as though they were the claviers of some extraordinary intellectual instrument; now and then he combines their effects in passages of striking and even stunning counterpoint.

This spontaneity that Pascal found *in* and *above* discipline is, I believe, one of the secrets of his achievement.

Bibliography

Bord, André. *Pascal et Jean de la Croix*. Paris: Beauchesne, 1987.

Broome, J. H. *Pascal*. London: E. Arnold, 1965.

Cahiers de Royaumont (Philosophie; No. 1). *Blaise Pascal: L'Homme et l'œuvre*. Paris: Editions de Minuit, 1956.

Cognet, Louis, ed. *Les Provinciales*. Paris: Garnier, 1965.

Coleman, Francis X. J. *Neither Angel nor Beast: The Life and Work of Blaise Pascal*. London and Boston: Routledge & Kegan Paul, and Methuen, 1986.

Costabel, Pierre, *et al*. *L'Oeuvre scientifique de Pascal*. Paris: Presses universitaires de France, 1964.

Davidson, Hugh M. *Audience, Words, and Art: Studies in Seventeenth-Century French Rhetoric*. Columbus: Ohio State University Press, 1965.

Blaise Pascal. Boston: Twayne Publishers, 1983.

The Origins of Certainty: Means and Meanings in Pascal's "Pensées." University of Chicago Press, 1979.

Duchêne, Roger. *L'Imposture littéraire dans "Les Provinciales" de Pascal*. Aix-en-Provence: Université de Provence, 1984.

Edwards, A. W. F. *Pascal's Arithmetical Triangle*. Oxford University Press, 1987.

Ernst, Pol. *Approches pascaliennes*. Gembloux: Duculot, 1970.

Fanton d'Andon, Jean-Pierre. *L'Horreur du vide*. Paris: Editions du Centre national de recherche scientifique, 1978.

Ferreyrolles, Gerard. *Pascal et la raison du politique*. Paris: Presses universitaires de France, 1985.

Force, Pierre. *Le Problème herméneutique chez Pascal*. Paris: J. Vrin, 1989.

France, Peter. *Racine's Rhetoric*. Oxford: Clarendon Press, 1965.

Rhetoric and Truth in France: Descartes to Diderot. Oxford: Clarendon Press, 1972.

Fumaroli, Marc. *L'Age de l'éloquence: Rhétorique et "res literaria" de la Renaissance au seuil de l'époque classique*. Geneva: Droz, 1980.

Gouhier, Henri. *Cartésianisme et Augustinisme au XVIIe siècle.* Paris: J. Vrin, 1978.
    Blaise Pascal: Commentaires. 3rd edn. Paris: J. Vrin, 1984.
    Blaise Pascal: Conversion et apologétique. Paris: J. Vrin, 1986.
Gounelle, André. *L'Entretien de Pascal avec M. de Sacy: Etude et Commentaire.* Paris: Presses universitaires de France, 1966.
    La Bible selon Pascal. Paris: Presses universitaires de France, 1970.
Goyet, Thérèse, ed. *Méthodes chez Pascal.* Paris: Presses universitaires de France, 1979.
Guenancia, Pierre. *Du Vide à Dieu: Essai sur la physique de Pascal.* Paris: F. Maspero, 1976.
Harrington, Thomas More. *Pascal philosophe: Une étude unitaire de la pensée de Pascal.* Paris: Société d'édition d'enseignement supérieur, 1982.
Humbert, Pierre. *Cet effrayant génie: L'Oeuvre scientifique de Blaise Pascal.* Paris: A. Michel, 1947.
Krailsheimer, Alban J. *Pascal.* Oxford and New York: Oxford University Press, 1980.
Lafuma, Louis, ed. *Pascal: Oeuvres complètes.* Paris: Editions du seuil, 1963.
Le Guern, Michel. *L'Image dans l'œuvre de Pascal.* Paris: A. Colin, 1969.
Le Guern, Michel and Marie-Rose. *Les "Pensées" de Pascal: De l'Anthropologie à la théologie.* Paris: Larousse, 1972.
Mackenzie, Louis A., Jr. *Pascal's "Lettres provinciales": The Motif and Practice of Fragmentation.* Birmingham, Alabama: Summa Publications, 1988.
Maeda, Yoichi. "L'Entretien avec M. de Sacy." In: *Ecrits sur Pascal* (with the collaboration of Annie Barnes). Paris: Editions du Luxembourg, 1959.
Magnard, Pierre. *Nature et histoire dans l'apologétique de Pascal.* Paris: Les belles lettres, 1975.
Marin, Louis. *La Critique du discours: Sur la "Logique" de Port-Royal et les "Pensées" de Pascal.* Paris: Editions de minuit, 1975.
Melzer, Sara E. *Discourses of the Fall: A Study of Pascal's "Pensées".* Berkeley: University of California Press, 1986.
Mesnard, Jean, ed. *Blaise Pascal: Oeuvres complètes.* Vols. 1–4 have appeared. Desclée de Brouwer, 1964–.
    Pascal. Paris: Hatier, 1967.
    Les "Pensées" de Pascal. Paris: Société d'édition d'enseignement supérieur, 1976.
Miel, Jan. *Pascal and Theology.* Baltimore and London: Johns Hopkins Press, 1969.
Morot-Sir, Edouard. *La Métaphysique de Pascal.* Paris: Presses universitaires de France, 1973.

Pascal. Paris: Presses universitaires de France, 1973.

Nelson, Robert J. *Pascal: Adversary and Advocate.* Cambridge, Mass.: Harvard University Press, 1981.

Norman, Buford. *Portraits of Thought: Knowledge, Methods, and Styles in Pascal.* Columbus: Ohio State University Press, 1988.

Parish, Richard. *Pascal's "Lettres provinciales": A Study in Polemic.* Oxford: Clarendon Press, 1989.

Pugh, Anthony R. *The Composition of Pascal's "Apologia."* University of Toronto Press, 1984.

Sellier, Philippe, ed. *Pascal: "Pensées."* Paris: Mercure de France, 1976.

Pascal et la liturgie. Paris: Presses universitaires de France, 1966.

Pascal et saint Augustin. Paris: A. Colin, 1970.

Shiokawa, Tetsuya. *Pascal et les miracles.* Paris: Nizet, 1978.

Shozo, Akagi. "Les Pensées fondamentales de la physique pascalienne et leur originalité." In *Etudes de langue et littérature françaises* (No. 4). Tokyo: Hakusuisha, 1964.

Steinmann, Jean. *Pascal.* Paris: Editions du Cerf, 1954.

Suematsu, Hisashi. *La Dialectique pascalienne, suivi de Réflexions sur une Pensée.* Bulletin No. 12, Institut de Recherches, Université de Seinan-Gakuin. Fukuoka, Japan: 1974.

Topliss, Patricia. *The Rhetoric of Pascal: A Study of His Art of Persuasion in the "Provinciales" and the "Pensées."* Leicester University Press, 1966.

Viallaneix, Paul, *et al. Pascal présent.* Clermont-Ferrand: 1962.

Warner, Martin. *Philosophical Finesse: Studies in the Art of Rational Persuasion.* Oxford: Clarendon Press, 1989.

Wetsel, David. *L'Ecriture et le reste: The "Pensées" of Pascal in the Exegetical Tradition of Port Royal.* Columbus: Ohio State University Press, 1981.

Wetsel, David, ed. *Meaning, Structure and History in the Pensées of Pascal.* Paris, Seattle, Tübingen: Biblio 17 (Papers on French Seventeenth Century Literature), 1990.

Index

Cambridge Studies in French

GENERAL EDITOR
Malcolm Bowie (*All Souls College, Oxford*)

EDITORIAL BOARD
R. Howard Bloch (*University of California, Berkeley*),
Ross Chambers (*University of Michigan*), Antoine Compagnon
(*Columbia University*), Peter France (*University of Edinburgh*),
Toril Moi (*Duke University*), Naomi Schor (*Duke University*)